Intermittent Journals

DANNIE ABSE
Intermittent Journals

seren

Seren is the book imprint of
Poetry Wales Press Ltd
Wyndham Street, Bridgend, Wales

British Library Cataloguing in Publication Data

Abse, Dannie
Intermitent Journals
I. Title
828.914

ISBN 1-85411-108-6 hbk
ISBN 1-85411-109-4 pbk

*The publisher acknowledges the financial support of the
Arts Council of Wales*

Cover Illustration: 'Unititled, 1968' by Roger Hilton
Private collection. By kind permission of Rose Hilton.

Printed in Palatino
By The Cromwell Press, Melksham

Contents

Introduction

Gerald Isaaman, the editor of a highly respected local newspaper in London, the *Hampstead and Highgate Express*, affectionately known as the *Ham and High*, is a great admirer of George Orwell. In December 1983, recalling Orwell's lively column for *Tribune* entitled 'As I Please', he decided that during 1984 he would like a similar series to grace the pages of the *Ham and High*.

George Orwell, alas, was not available. So he cast around for other writers, shortlisting a number of these, no doubt alphabetically, for soon he telephoned me. Perhaps, too, he had read the recently published *A Strong Dose of Myself* (Hutchinson) which included some diary pieces of mine called 'Notes from the Clinic'. I could not mimic Orwell. I could only write my own kind of prose. Gerald Isaaman did not seem to mind and I agreed to offer him a fortnightly autobiographical column for one year only. He was to call my non-Orwellian 'As I Please' Abse's 1984. He proved to be an ideal editor. He only very occasionally made suggestions and never changed my copy.

In March 1985, it was suggested to me by my friend, Anthony Whittome of Hutchinson, that I protract my journals from the ant-heap (Abse's 1984) so that it could be published in book form. I could continue writing them, of course, as I pleased, and, more importantly, as far as I was concerned, when I pleased.

Since the publication of *Journals from the Ant-Heap* as an original paperback in 1986 I have intermittently written additional diary pieces. These are now included in the present volume, having been added to the out-of-print Ant-Heap journals, along with the 1981-82 'Notes from the Clinic'. I cannot pretend that I have not enjoyed conjugating occasional autobiographical items while I have been based in London or in South Wales. And I hope they will amuse like- minded readers. They are not private diary entries but were written, as all journalism is, as a public secret.

January 1994

Part One:
Notes Mainly at the Clinic

Notes Mainly at the Clinic

The routine X-ray showed horizontal, linear condensations adjacent to both hemidiaphragms. I wondered if my patient had ever been exposed to any asbestos dust.

'No, but my father worked at Hebden Mill.'

'In West Yorkshire?'

'Yes.'

'You lived nearby, near the mill?'

'Quite near, as a boy, yes.'

When I questioned him further I learnt that his father, on returning home from the mill, had the habit of brushing down his coat jacket. No doubt, infinitely small fibres of crocidolite (blue asbestos) had, as a result, been sprinkled into the air and the young boy had then innocently breathed them in.

The work at the clinic has always been repetitious; these days it is worse — there are fewer patients, longer gaps of not doing anything during the day. I hardly see any people suffering from pulmonary tuberculosis, which used to be such a common scourge. Sometimes I worry whether I shall be made redundant (an increasing possibility); and sometimes I feel, puritan that I am, a little guilty that I'm not working hard enough. Guilty, I mean, of occasionally doing nothing, guilty of waiting like a prisoner for the clock to turn and turn again, guilty of being almost dead for an hour, guilty of postponements on rainy days, of things not done, things not said. A reprieve would be to pronounce to someone, anyone, positively, 'You are ill,' or 'You are cured. ' That would prove that I was alive....

This morning I had to report on some hundreds of routine chest X-rays. One after one I looked at them. I found no abnormality whatsoever: the lung fields invariably clear, the heart sizes and shapes all within their normal limits. At one point, bored, I began to wish I would see something other than normality — some sarcoid infiltration, an aortic aneurysm, a pneumothorax or, better still, a mysterious shadow, one I had never seen before, one perhaps never reported on ever, illustrated in no textbook. Then, like a stern headmaster, I reproved myself: I didn't want any of these anonymous people whose X-rays I was scrutinizing to be ill, did I? I did not want to summon one pale patient to my room and say, 'I'm sorry but....'

Of course not. I carried the X-rays, along with my report, to the clerk in the outer office and said, 'Rejoice, all these patients are healthy.'

The power, within us, of denial. M.S. six years ago had a lung removed because of a bronchial cancer. He now comes to see me only for a reassuring annual check-up. I do not know if he ever truly has understood the nature of his disease. When I first read his case notes I discovered that, while his relatives had been told the truth, he himself was informed that he had 'a lung abscess with complications'. He had had post-operative radiotherapy and saw me regularly for clinical examination and routine chest X-ray. I never saw any reason to discuss with him the original diagnosis. He never raised the matter himself.

In my experience, such an avoidance of an intolerable diagnostic truth is common. The doctor does not have to tell it out loud and plain, is hardly ever challenged with genuine force to do so. The patient will talk about his old symptoms, his old operation, his old wife, the old football team he supports, but he will rarely say, 'Doctor, that diagnosis of a lung abscess was just a lot of old codswallop. I'm not an idiot to be fobbed off with that patently fictional diagnosis. If it had merely been a lung abscess why did I have radiotherapy, why are you seeing me so regularly, why are you palpating my liver *now* with such care?'

Today, before palpating M.S.'s liver, I happened to glance at his fingers. Two fingers of his right hand were clearly nicotine-stained. Why, he had given up smoking cigarettes when he had had the operation. Now, absurdly, had he started again?

'Look, doctor,' M.S. said. 'I know you've given up smoking yourself. You told me so years ago. But it's easy for you — you're looking at X-rays like mine all the time.'

M. S. had undergone major chest surgery, must have had terrible anxieties, must have secretly wondered, if only at dead of night, about his former disease; but now, here he was, saying to me, 'It's easy for you, doctor.'

On one hand the power of denial, on the other the power of suggestion. A number of my patients need to give up smoking because they have been exposed to blue asbestos — there is a synergistic effect with the inhalation of tobacco smoke and blue asbestos fibres. I mentioned this to one of my colleagues, Dr Margaret MacDonald, who has begun to practise acupuncture with what seems to be total enthusiasm. I thought perhaps acupuncture might help those who had difficulty in kicking the habit, through the power of suggestion.

'That is not how acupuncture works,' Margaret insisted.

The continued existence of acupuncture in a 'modern' state like China has sanctioned doctors like Margaret MacDonald, as well as quacks, to practise this form of treatment in the West. In the last decade or so newspapers and popular periodicals have given acupuncture much free publicity; there have been medical journalists who have tried to give acupuncture a scientific gloss. In Britain, and no doubt elsewhere, there exist acupuncture clinics where men in clinical white coats, resembling the glamorous doctor heroes of television medical romances — though frequently they are not, in fact, qualified doctors — stick needles into hopeful patients. Most of the patients leave the clinic (the decor of one I visited resembled a cross between a lush private nursing home and a Chinese restaurant) with the symptoms they had when they entered. All leave with less money in their wallets or handbags.

It is significant that one acupuncture doctor interviewed in the *Sunday Times* declared that he preferred to treat 'chronic ailments which have defeated Western medicine: for instance, migraines and other types of headaches; duodenal and stomach ulcers; indigestive disorders; lumbago, fibrositis, sciatica, neuralgia; acne and other skin troubles; asthma, hay fever; high blood pressure; depressions and anxiety states' — all symptoms or ailments known to be related to stress or other psychological disturbance. The doctor would probably obtain the same results, providing he believed in the efficacy of it all, by sticking the needles into himself while his patients watched him. However, the acupuncturist could well respond, 'Do orthodox physicians prescribing placebos, tonics and vitamins obtain better results with those patients suffering the same intractable conditions?'

Of course, the power of suggestion can be packaged in a capsule or concentrated at the point of a needle. Or, for that matter, in any object which has for the patient certain potent associations. Some years ago I was asked to give a gas and oxygen anaesthetic for a minor operation — a removal of an infected toenail. My colleague had nearly finished scrubbing up so I placed the mask over my patient's mouth and nose ready to administer the gas and oxygen anaesthetic. 'It will be over soon,' I had reassured the patient — and so it would have been but, at the last moment, the theatre door opened. An intruder's mouth opened and closed noiselessly in oral gesture. Then shufflings, whisperings, eyes meaningful behind masks. I gathered my colleague needed to answer, immediately, outside, an urgent telephone call. He temporarily quit the theatre and so I removed the mask from the patient's face. I was about to explain everything as best I could to the inconvenienced patient, to apologize to him for the delay, but he lay there with eyes closed, his head as still as a statue's. He had had no anaesthetic whatsoever. He had breathed in only ordinary air through the mask yet he had swooned. For a half-minute the mask had been over his face and he presumably thought he was breathing in the gas. Accordingly he had fallen into a profound sleep — as profound as Adam's — and I suspect that in that trance he could have had not only his toenail removed but a rib as well. My patient was roused only by strenuous shouting and shaking!

So much for the reports concerning operations undertaken in China with patients 'anaesthetized' by acupuncture needles.

On Friday I hoped to leave the clinic early. I intended to spend the weekend in Wales with my aged mother. Alas, that day, we had a relief radiographer and he proved to be slow and incompetent. Many of the X-rays turned out to be underdeveloped or overdeveloped, under-penetrated or over-penetrated, fogged or partially fogged. Patient after patient had to be returned to the X-ray Department for a repeat X-ray.

At last, it seemed there were no more X-rays to be read and I prepared to catch the later train from Paddington. I was at the door when the telephone rang. 'One more X-ray,' the inept radiographer announced. 'Dr Wicks would like a report as soon as possible. The X-ray'll be ready in a jiffy.'

I settled myself in the chair again to study the current *British Medical Journal*. I waited. And I waited such a long time that I guessed the radiographer had messed up the X-ray once more. I read another article in the BMJ . I looked at my watch. If the X-ray was not ready soon I would miss yet another train from Paddington. Somewhat irritably I hastened to the X-ray Department where I at once encountered the radiographer. 'It's ready, doctor,' he announced cheerfully before I could utter a scolding word.

On the screen, in the dark room, hung the long overdue X-ray. I hoped it would not be fogged or in any other way spoilt, would not need to be repeated. The radiographer touched the switch and the screen lit up brilliantly. Astonished I saw that the patient's chest was tilted at an absurd angle of forty-five degrees — left shoulder up, right shoulder down. What a genius of a radiographer, I thought. However, I could read the X-ray and there was nothing wrong with the man's chest. I could pass it as normal despite it being utterly skewwhiff. I have never seen anything like it.

'I have to congratulate you,' I said to the radiographer with heavy sarcasm, 'that this X-ray . . .'

'The patient's behind you, doctor,' the radiographer interrupted me.

I turned towards the open darkroom door where I could see, beyond, a man sitting in the adjoining X-ray room. At once I approached him, followed by the radiographer.

'Your X-ray is normal,' I reassured the patient, 'though the radiographer here has somehow contrived to tilt your X-ray in such a way that it makes you look as if you're a cripple.'

The patient stared at me uncomprehendingly. No doubt the radiographer, ticked off indirectly in this way, smouldered morosely behind me.

'Can I go?' asked the patient.

'Of course,' I said, smiling.

The man rose from the chair most awkwardly. To my horror I discovered he had only one leg. I observed him limping pronouncedly over the brown linoleum towards the corridor outside the

X-ray Department. I turned towards the radiographer who leaned against the wall, his face a study of sweet, sickly triumph.

The lady wished to interview me for a woman's magazine, *Good Housekeeping*. She was a novelist, Carolyn Scott. So one lunch hour last year, I walked from the clinic to Soho Square to meet her near the statue of King Charles II. Later, over lunch, she conducted the interview, which progressed predictably until she suddenly asked, 'What moves you to tears, Dr Abse?' It was a very bare question. I thought of my very aged mother in South Wales whose powers were failing alarmingly so that now she did not know what day of the week it was. However, I did not speak of my mother. I did not know Carolyn Scott so I spoke rather in general terms — as I can now see for the interview has been finally published. I remarked, 'I am moved by the inevitability of certain things, how people we know and love grow senile, how certain diseases cannot be cured — by the fact that Antigone is condemned, must die, and nothing can change that. There are people, perhaps more mature than me, who are resigned to these things, but inwardly, deep down, I don't think I can be resigned.'

Carolyn Scott's response to this disarrayed me. 'Perhaps I shouldn't tell you,' she confessed softly, 'but I have an incurable disease. Its progress is...inevitable.' Of course, that confession was not published in *Good Housekeeping* nor did Carolyn Scott report our dialogue that followed it. For my part I noticed for the first time how thin she was, cachetic, and how there was an unhealthy, translucent pallor to her skin. I guessed she had a cancer, was taking anti-mitotic drugs. I had to say something and I am no Spinoza. Clumsily, hesitantly, I talked about how some managed to confront a seemingly fatal illness and, in so doing, I leaned on the truthful crutch of a medical cliché: 'There is never such a thing as "never" in medicine.' I know and she knew that 1 in 10,000 cancers do recover spontaneously. Alas, I read in *Good Housekeeping* that Carolyn Scott died before the interview was published.

Early next year, 1 February 1982, I am to be made redundant. As part of a quarter-of-a-million-pound saving there has to be 'contraction and rationalization'. So, as they say in the football world, I am for an early bath.

It will be strange to vacate this consulting room. I have been lucky, until now, in my medical career. I originally took up chest work because of a sweet accident. When I was conscripted into the RAF for National Service and was sent, with a number of other young doctors, to Moreton-in-Marsh for one month's induction (square-bashing) in May 1951, I resented being separated from Joan Mercer (my future wife) who lived (with me) in Belsize Square, London. So when, one evening in the mess bar, I heard that the RAF Mass Radiography Section was based in Cleveland Street, *in London*, I became very interested, suddenly, in mass radiography. After all, Cleveland Street was near Goodge Street station, a short tube ride on the Northern Line. Moreover it was halfway between the BBC and my publisher, Hutchinson!

Towards the end of our induction period a form was circulated to us all in which we were invited to put down our geographical and professional preferences regarding future postings. Though it was rumoured that little attention was paid to our responses, on the form I firmly entered 'HOME COUNTIES' and 'VERY KEEN ON MASS RADIOGRAPHY'. The idea of mass radiography had never crossed my mind until that bar conversation but I figured that while my colleagues would ask for 'GENERAL PRACTICE' or 'SURGERY' or 'DERMATOLOGY' or some other speciality they had some engagement with because of this or that house job, not one of them, no one at all, would elect for 'MASS RADIOGRA-PHY'. Probably, in the whole history of the RAF medical services, no neophyte ever had.

I was posted to HQ Mass Radiography, Cleveland Street, in London for a further month's training. Then, to my horror, I was to join the mobile X-ray unit in Northern Ireland! However, soon after, I was returned to HQ to become an assistant to the squadron leader in charge of all radiography units. The squadron leader had a PC, i.e. a permanent commission. I liked him; he was an easy-going fellow who frequently absented himself from his office without explanation. Too easygoing, the RAF thought, for a year later, because of certain incidents about which I am still not clear, he was court-martialled and I found myself promoted to Squadron Leader in charge of five doctors, five units, the central chest clinic, etc. So began my chest experience.

And when I left the RAF I was offered the job here, a job limited to office hours and of a diagnostic nature only, a repetitious job, one frequently boring, but one that has given me time to write and to pursue a more general academic interest in medicine. Besides, as a doctor practising within the strict confines of my own small speciality, I have been quite good! I do not want an early bath.

My patient, G., was ostentatiously polite. I had the feeling that he would hurry to open a door for me; but now it was time for him to quit, to open the door for himself. Instead he hesitated, then said, 'I wonder if I might ask you a personal question, Dr Abse?'

'Of course.'

'Have you a son called Albert?'

'No,' I said. 'My son's called Jesse David.'

He then mysteriously withdrew a piece of paper from a pocket of his suit.

'This poem of yours is very very meaningful to me and my wife, Dr Abse,' he said.

Surprised, I glanced at the paper, at an early poem of mine, one that I had written when a medical student. It was called 'Albert' — I still liked it well enough though I would hardly expect that particular poem to be very special for anyone:

> Albert loved dogs mostly though this was absurd
> for they always slouched away when he touched their fur,
> but once, perching on his shoulder, alighted a bird,
>
> a bird alive as fire and magical as that day
> when clear-eyed Héloïse met Peter Abelard.
> Though cats followed him the bird never flew away.
>
> And dogs pursued the cats which hunted the bird.
> Albert loved dogs deeply but was jealously hurt
> that they pursued him merely because of the bird,
>
> the bird alive as fire and magical as that day.
> So one morning he rose and murdered the bird.
> But then the cats vanished and the dogs went away.
>
> Albert hated dogs after — though this was absurd.

I handed the paper back to G. 'It's the only poem I've ever written derived from a dream,' I said. 'I dreamed years ago of someone with a bird on his shoulder followed by cats, followed by dogs....' G. nodded. He rose from his chair. 'You see,' he said at last, 'I have a son called Albert. He's six now. A year ago he murdered our canary.'

Despite Albert's father, few of my patients are aware that I write poetry. I am always surprised when they do know — as I was last week when one of them brought in my new book, *Way Out in the Centre*, to be signed. He had read a review of it in one of the Sunday newspapers and, as I signed it, asked me how I felt about reviewers and reviews. It so happened the notice he had read had been a generous one so I was able to respond benignly, though I added Conrad's dictum about how an author should go to a book review only with a ruler.

In truth, it takes some five years to put a book of poems together so it is almost as irritating to be praised in a few lines as it is to be dismissed curtly. Of course, what every poet wants is a huge space devoted to him alone by a reviewer he can respect who writes knowledgeably and sensibly, i.e. enthusiastically, about his new book. It was either a poet, or God himself, who wrote that graffito on a wall near Belsize Road in Swiss Cottage: 'LOVE ONLY ME'.

In fact there are some journals where poets unaccountably, or accountably, may be ignored completely — I mean in publications accustomed to notice new poetry books — in my case, for some reasons that I, wholesomely paranoid after midnight, think I understand, in two literary magazines, *Stand* and *Agenda*. On the whole, though, I am with Chekhov when he declared (to Gorky):

> Critics are like gadflies which stop a horse ploughing. The horse strains, muscles tensed like double-bass strings. Meanwhile there's a wretched gadfly tickling and buzzing on his crupper, so he has to twitch his skin and flick his tail. But what's all the buzzing about? The gadfly hardly knows. It just feels restless and wants to proclaim its existence while asserting its ability to buzz away on any subject in the world. For twenty-five years I've been reading criticisms of my stories. But I don't remember one helpful hint; nor have I heard one word of good advice. The only critic

to impress me was Skabichevsky who once wrote that I'd die in a ditch, drunk.

Most medical authorities may acknowledge a multifactorial cause of cancer. Nor would they necessarily mock W. H. Auden's poem 'Miss Gee'.

> Nobody knows what the cause is
> Though some pretend they do;
> It's like some hidden assassin
> waiting to strike at you.
>
> Childless women get it,
> And men when they retire;
> It's as if there had to be some outlet
> For their foiled creative fire.

Even the occasional surgeon postulates a mysterious relationship between tumour formation and loss of emotional equilibrium. Thus D. Lang Stevenson in his paper, 'Evolution and the Neurobiogenesis of Neoplasia' writes:

> There is evidence to suggest that brain states signifying profound alarm and despondency, particularly in a medium of ageing hormones, are connected with tumour formation and that this indeed may be one of the common causes of human cancer. The time measurement between the event, bereavement of a close contemporary for instance, and the appearance of the tumour has been found constant enough to be statistically significant.

The radiotherapist Professor G. B. Mitchell has also testified on the relationship between bereavement and cancer:

> Not infrequently, one observes the recurrence of a malignant tumour which has been healed for many years, perhaps ten years, sometimes much longer, after surgery or radiotherapy or both.... It appears as if tumour cells had lain dormant and then, after many years, started to grow. Such a recurrence often seems to have been precipitated by an emotional upheaval such as follows the death of a husband, wife, or child.

But perhaps the most startling theory about the aetiology of cancer comes from the Department of Psychiatry at Jefferson

Medical College in Philadelphia. Psychiatrists there suggest that a patient may suffer cancer as an alternative to going mad.

In the Manchester hospital they had arranged a concert for patients and staff. Peter Senior asked me to read some poems of mine that touched on medical themes. I declined. I did not think it wise to read a poem, say, about a brain operation to patients who may be worrying about such surgery! Alas, most of the medically coloured poems that I have written tend to be somewhat grim.

'The Smile Was', insisted Peter Senior. 'That poem celebrates childbirth. It's a very affirmative poem.'

'Yes, but it's quite long,' I said.

Years ago, when a student, I had attended a hundred births. What had struck me then was how the mother invariably smiled when she heard the newborn baby cry out. Not an ordinary smile but one secretive, gentle, ineffable. I became accustomed to wait for that smile and I was never disappointed. Whether the baby had been longed for or not, was legitimate or not, that strange unambiguous smile would appear to transform the mother's recently struggling face into one calm, momentarily beautiful. In the wards I had been taken aback by the ambivalence of patients' responses but the smile of the new mother, it seemed to me then, when she heard her baby crying for the first time, was utterly pure, unadulterated.

In the mid-sixties I wrote a poem about that particular smile and Peter Senior now prevailed upon me to read it. Before I had finished the first section I became aware of gasps, whisperings and sighings to the left of me. As I glanced wonderingly to the audience on the left I read on:

> That agreeable radiant smile
> no man can smile it
> no man can paint it
> as it develops without fail
> after the gross, physical, knotted,
> granular, bloody endeavour.
>   Such a pure spirituality from all that!
> It occupies the face
> and commands it

21

I became aware of dozens of women intensely glowering at me. Why? I was halfway through the poem when it occurred to me that those sitting in rows of chairs to my left were women — only women. Christ, I thought, they're all probably from the gynaeco-logical wards, all probably have had, or are about to have, their pregnancies terminated. And here I was, here I had to continue celebrating the benediction and mystery of childbirth, the mother's pure smile:

> Never,
> not for one single death
> can I forget we die with the dead
> and the world dies with us;
> yet
> in one, lonely,
> small child's birth
> all the tall dead rise
> to break the crust of the imperative earth.

The youthful often indulge in rescue fantasies. In their daydreams, the beautiful, the good, the helpless, are frequently saved from harm by an heroic protagonist who remarkably resembles the dreamer. Walter Mitty owns many faces — not a few of them are sixteen years old. When I was a schoolboy in Cardiff I came out of the Olympia Cinema one late Saturday afternoon having seen a film about the great Paul Ehrlich, the father of modern chemotherapy. I felt uplifted by the film, which featured Paul Muni, glad that one day I would be a doctor. Such a noble profession!

It was half past five and my eyes did not blink as I crossed St Mary's Street, an imaginary stethoscope in my pocket. Before the traffic lights changed their coloured signals, I had saved an old lady from asphyxiating, administered first aid to the mayor shot by Tiger Bay gangsters, and operated on Adolf Hitler — without success.

It has been suggested that rescue fantasies merely represent, symbolically, unconscious desires to save our own mothers from the cruel embraces of the men they married. So that old lady I had

saved in my youthful daydream had been none other than my
mother in disguise! Now, older by far, once again in Cardiff, but
not in daydream, I had to attend, hesitatingly, the old lady who
was my mother. My rescue attempts, as son and doctor, were
hopelessly ineffectual. Her new bridegroom would not be denied.

My mother taught me my name, my father taught me the time.

EXIT

As my colleague prepares the syringe
(the drip flees its hour glass)
I feel the depression of Saul,
my mother's right hand grasping still,
her left hand suspiciously still,
and think — Shadow on the wall,
Nothing on the floor — of your
random, katabolic ways:

merciful sometimes, precise, but often
wild as delirium, or like a surgeon
with cataracts grievously unkind
as you are now, as you visit
this old lady — one beloved by me —
as you blunder and exit, moth-blind,
mistaking even the light
on mirrors for open windows;

and as my colleague prepares the syringe
I remember another butchering —
a botched suicide in a circumspect
bedsitting room, a barely
discernible fake of a girl-corpse,
a marmoreal stillness perfect
except for the closed
plum-skin eyelids trembling;

and as my colleague prepares the syringe
I picture also a victim of war
near a road, a peasant left for dead,
conscious, black-tongued, long-agonized,
able to lift, as my mother can now,
at intervals her troubled head.

And as my colleague drives the needle in
I want to know the meaning of this:

why the dark thalamus finally
can't be shut down when we sleep
with swift economy? Of that king
and his queen— David and Bathsheba —
the old parable is plain:
out of so much suffering
came forth the other child,
the wise child, the Solomon;

but what will spring from this
unredeemed, needless degradation,
this concentration camp for one?
My colleague forces the plunger down,
squeezes the temgesic out,
the fluid that will numb and stun.
'Shadow on the wall...' I call, 'Nothing
on the floor...Patron of the Arts!'

And as my colleague extracts the needle
from her vein, the temgesic acts
till the bruised exit's negotiated.
Then how victoriously
you hold the left passive hand
of the dummy in the bed
while I continue uselessly
to hold the other.

What a patient declares as an afterthought, just before leaving the
consulting room, often turns out to be most important. J.S. was at
the door when he hesitated. 'I know you're a chest man,' he said,
'so I suppose there's no point in raising the problem of my feet with
you. ' I waited. Sheepishly, he explained, 'I've hellishly itchy feet,
doctor. Especially at night, I have to scratch them like hell.' Could
I help him perhaps? Refer him to a skin specialist?

Our interview extended. Soon I learnt how much J.S. was
troubled because of his domestic situation. His wife, he maintained, was getting at him ceaselessly, his son was a delinquent,
and he confessed there was another lady abroad who much occupied his thoughts.

'No wonder you're getting itchy feet,' I said.

J.S. seemed baffled by my comment. *He* could not see the relationship between his almost acknowledged desire to get away from home and the state of his feet which he scratched so ferociously each night.

'Calamine lotion can be very soothing,' I said, 'but if I were you I'd ponder on the connection between your itchy feet and your domestic plight.'

He left pondering! And I sat down wondering whether my amateur psychiatrics had done him and his marriage harm or good.

I remarked on the wireless that I felt myself to be 'a dilettante doctor and a professional poet'. Not a very wise remark, certainly not one that would impress patients. Joke though it may have been, and lightly spoken, yet I thought it had truth in it. For medicine has been for me, in some respects, a hobby that has been well paid, whereas poetry has been a central activity paid poorly. I have worn a white coat so many hours a week and then, with relief, I have discarded it so that on enchanted or/and precarious occasions I could don a purple one. Or so it used to be. But over the years the white coat has gathered to itself a purple glint in some lights and the purple has assumed some white patches.

I used to like Chekhov's response when he was advised 'not to hunt after two hares'. He wrote in a letter:

> I feel more confident and more satisfied with myself when I reflect that I have two professions and not one. Medicine is my lawful wife and literature is my mistress. When I get tired of one I spend the night with the other. Though it's disorderly, it's not dull, and besides, neither of them loses anything from my infidelity.

I could assent to that reflection and savour it because, like those who write poetry seriously, whose ambition it is to write the next poem and the one after, I did not feel that I was a poet except for a few hours, say six times a year, when I had completed a poem to my own satisfaction. Yes, I could persuade myself, I'm no more a poet between poems than I am a doctor when not at this clinic.

But now that I think about it more deeply I am not convinced of its truth. At one time, when I sat behind my desk listening to some soft-spoken individual saying 'It worries me, doctor,' perhaps I did play, in some measure, a given role, a part in a play even though if the blood flowed it would be real; but with the years a man becomes the part he has been cast in until he can hardly be anything else.

'Look! There goes Dr Amazing. See how he leaves the clinic no longer a doctor.' That's not true, someone has fallen down in the street and where a crowd gathers he has to step forward; he arrives home and one of his daughters has a high fever so he must write a prescription; the telephone clamours in the hall and afterwards he has to travel 160 miles to urge other doctors to do this, to do that, because his aged mother is dying. It is no use: though the white coat seems discarded he laughs the laugh of a doctor, he cries the tears of a doctor, he dreams, at night, the dreams of a doctor. Or the dreams of a poet. Or both simultaneously. As a matter of fact, he always wears that purple coat, too — though it only becomes visible some six times a year.

Because of the pre-Christmas snow blizzard last night only one of seven expected patients turned up. I look out of the window. Snow is falling; it seems to fall in slow motion over north Soho; it must be falling all over Britain. My patients are unlikely to come now, not even C. who has always been so keen to continue with his annual chest surveillance.

Five years ago he sat in that chair there, facing me, the X-ray screen behind my head blazing, his X-rays visible on them. I had to tell him that he had a small shadow on the left lung which could well prove to be active tuberculosis. I had half turned to the screens, to his X-rays which showed the soft shadow, the non-homogeneous loss of translucency in the left upper zone and apex. 'Nothing essentially to be anxious about,' I had tried to reassure him, 'but further investigations are needed in hospital.'

The drama of his face and then his voice fatalistic, saying, 'I see,' so that once again I affirmed that if, indeed, it did prove to be active tuberculosis then that condition, nowadays, was most amenable to treatment.

'There are drugs,' I had said, 'even more modern than streptomycin which are very effective against tubercle bacilli.'

Most patients when told there is something wrong with their X-rays — even those without any symptoms, without any possible premonition of such a verdict — remain acutely calm. They do not tend to show too much of their emotional map to me, a mere sympathetic stranger. To be sure there are, have been exceptions: men and women who will not read the lines allotted to them in that well-shaped, well-mannered play written by an Englishman called Anonymous. Some of these exceptional patients have confronted me aggressively as if the disease I had discovered in their lungs was all my fault. Then I have felt like the messenger of ancient days who carried bad news to a king. Others have gently opened themselves to me: in such moments of anxiety, apertures have appeared in their personalities so that their profound selves have been briefly revealed. Why not? Though it makes it more difficult for the doctor — he has to write a fresh script, he has to give something more of himself, and this all takes time — everything profound abhors a mask.

Over Christmas I have been rereading the *Collected Poems* of Sylvia Plath which have recently been published. The notion that poets must suffer in order to write well, be deranged as Sylvia Plath was, has a long tradition. There are those who continue to see in the Philoctetes legend of the wound and the bow the predicament of the poet who, while owning special gifts (the magic bow), is alienated from his fellow men by his suffering psyche (the stinking wound).

The lives and writings of a number of modern American poets, in particular, have been illustrative of the Philoctetes predicament. It has been pointed out how even that apparently impersonal major poem of the twentieth century, 'The Waste Land', was written while T.S. Eliot recovered in Switzerland from a nervous breakdown. In a lecture at Harvard University many years after the poem was published, T.S. Eliot, afflicted with modesty, admitted to a half-truth:

> Various critics have done me the honour to interpret the poem
> ['The Waste Land'] in terms of criticism of the contemporary

world, have considered it, indeed, as an important bit of social criticism. To me it was only the relief of a personal and wholly insignificant grouse against life; it is just a piece of rhythmical grumbling.

Of course 'The Waste Land' is much more than that. In any event, some more recent prominent American poets — Robert Lowell, Anne Sexton, Sylvia Plath — have been altogether less reticent than T.S. Eliot about their personal mental suffering. On occasions, they have boasted of their breakdowns and suicide attempts as warriors might of their war wounds; and these very boastings, it must be said, helped to crank the machinery of a fame-making mythology.

This same machinery continued to be active in Sylvia Plath's case after her death, after her 'successful' suicide in 1963.

Yet, leaving all the sentimentality and all the theatrical hooha aside, it is translucently evident that her talent was extraordinary, that her work, though limited by neurotic elements in her nature, was vibrant and arresting partly because of those same elements.

Al Alvarez was probably right when he maintained, 'The real poems began in 1960 after the birth of her daughter Frieda. It is as though the child were a proof of her identity, as though it liberated her into her real self. I think this guess is borne out by the fact that her most creative period followed the birth of her son two years later.' There are intimations in Sylvia Plath's work that her sense of her own identity was far from secure. Perhaps she felt most herself when she was at work on a poem. In that early, fine poem 'Black Rook in Rainy Weather', she talks of the 'rare random descent' of the inspirational angel who allows her to 'patch together a content of sorts', to gain — and this is the point I'm trying to make here — 'a brief respite from fear/of total neutrality'.

There is no doubt that she felt herself, on one level, to be possessed by the malevolent ghost of her once beloved father. 'I am,' she wrote in 'The Bee Meeting', 'the magician's girl who does not flinch.' She conceived herself to be a passive victim manipulated by a magician's power or a Hiroshima victim or a kind of Jew who survived a concentration camp. As a 'victim' she made her own inward devastation a mirror of recent history.

Many of her late poems have an oneiric quality. It is not surprising that they should be so, given the time of night when they were written. 'These new poems of mine have one thing in common,' she wrote. 'They were all written at about four in the morning — that still blue, almost eternal hour before cockcrow, before the baby's cry.' They were also written apparently when she felt herself to be, once more, a victim — lonely, separated from her husband and, because of her mental make-up, clearly desperate. She was a prey to over-whelming separation anxieties. She had been separated from her father when she was a small girl — by dying he had abandoned her, an act she had not felt as being inadvertent.

In *The Savage God* A. Alvarez wrote:

> As the months went by her poetry became progressively more extreme...the last weeks each trivial event became the occasion for poetry: a cut finger, a fever, a bruise.

But to go a little deeper, it is obvious that these 'trivial' events had enormous significance for her. They represented her deepest feelings and her most central resentment. She wrote a poem called 'Contusion'. She felt bruised spiritually. She wrote a poem about a cut finger called 'Cut' — and that's how she felt herself to be, her whole being, cut. Cut and bruised and wounded.

Besides, the cutting of her thumb ('the top quite gone', she wrote, 'except for a sort of hinge of skin') no doubt nourished her feelings of separation. The separation of a bit of her own body was resonant with her long-held, submerged separation anxiety. Of course, all this may be a wild guess and there will be some who will think it not proper to hazard guesses of this kind. Nevertheless, the nature of her late poems is such that one is tempted to look at her poetry as medical evidence of a state of mind. For her desperation is so clearly touching and so painful even when encapsulated in genuinely wrought poems which do more than express a private terror.

Dr H. often sends his patients for a chest X-ray. Any patient complaining of pain in the chest, any aching muscle, any cough, any tickle or soreness in the trachea, any pimple on the skin of the chest and he rushes that patient to our X-ray Department as if it were an emergency. I happened to be in the X-ray Department when a tall healthy-looking lock forward, if ever I saw one, presented himself. The radiographer handed me the form signed by Dr H. asking for a chest X-ray because...I read it again astonished...because of *impotence*. I cannot imagine what Dr H. thought might be discovered by X-raying this patient's chest.

I'm not quite sure how I feel about Dr H. He is a man ill at ease with himself. I sense that sometimes he is disgusted by his own ineptitude, that though aware of his own ignorance about medical matters he does nothing to remedy the ignorance — rather like the doctor in Chekhov's *Three Sisters*, Chebutykin. It is Dr H.'s acute awareness of his ignorance, surely, that makes him so cautious, why he sends so many of his patients for a second opinion, or for special investigations, however inappropriate. I suppose, sometimes, this or that specialist does discover some abnormality. Then Dr H. feels justified, and will be able, without qualm, to refer his next thousand patients for X-ray or barium meal or electrocardiograph or electroencephalogram.

I should like to meet Dr H. when he's offguard, out of the armour of his white coat, when he's drunk perhaps, without disguise. I suspect then he would resemble Chebutykin even more: 'Damn them all...the lot of them! They think I can treat any illness because I'm a doctor, but I know nothing, absolutely nothing. I've forgotten everything I used to know. I remember nothing, positively nothing.... The devil take them! Last Wednesday I attended a woman at Zasyp. She died and it was my fault. Yes.... I used to know a thing or two twenty-five years ago but now I don't remember anything. Not a thing!'

How frightening to consider those hordes of doctors practising who happen to be ignorant, incompetent — or eyes glinting like scalpels dangerously because of their own personality problems. Yet so many doctors bumble through even if their patients don't.

I wonder if Bill M. is still legally treating people? When I was a student he was the prize duffer of the medical school. Though he studied assiduously and seemed to have no other compelling interests to distract him, he failed his finals, in season, a dozen times. Soon after my twenty-first birthday I had my only operation, a tonsillectomy. I remember being wheeled, euphoric with omnipon, into the operating theatre. I looked up, two-eyed, objectively, in the spirit of science, to see who of my colleagues would be giving me the intravenous injection of pentothal that would turn the switch off from the current of the sun, knock me out. Among those standing there I, perturbed, saw Bill M. masked, gowned, gloved, and ready. That awesome vision sobered me. Gone, suddenly, the unreasonable complacency of omnipon. I managed to cry out despairingly, famously, 'Not... you... Bill.' Then darkness and silence of snow descended.

The administrative people are making arrangements for another doctor to use my consulting room next month when I shall be 'unemployed'. Some official — from the Ministry of Works, I think — came in to look at my desk, my carpet, my curtains. At least, I have felt that they were mine since I have inhabited this office so long. The man was polite enough but when he quit I felt I had been burgled.

There are many people, I am one such, who are basically rooted, who experience much anomie when their life situation changes or even when there are actual journeys to be undertaken and lived through. When I sojourned elsewhere, as I did in 1973-4 in the USA, I felt that real life only continued in London or South Wales! Well, part of me is me because of the introsumption of familiar land-scapes, seascapes, objects, possessions, books, records and, yes, even the curtains, carpet and desk of my office. When things are removed, or I am removed from them, there is a small, a very small assault on whoever it is that I am. Of course, I am not so insecure that I cannot endure it, but I do sense the holes in the air, I do see the patchy oblongs on the walls where the paintings have come down and I do feel, then, temporarily diminished because of such absences.

To be sure it is absurd to feel diminished by such things. More serious is it when those whose lives are so entangled with our own disappear forever from this earth. No man is an Island, entire of itselfe. How just, those walking, emaciated statues of Giacometti becoming thinner and thinner as they walk towards FIN. Did he not sculpture the metaphor, any man's death diminishes me?

*

Once more the uncertain light: snow, ice and freezing fog, as before

Christmas, but in addition a rail strike so again most of my patients cancelled their appointments at the clinic. Having little to do, I chatted for some time with a colleague, Dr B. (who is Polish) about the merciless, created events in that place on the map called Poland where all the successive traffic signals in the cities are at amber. Somewhere else, a closed, official car hurtling through slush; empty streets.

Later, at midday, I walked over to the local library to pick up some books, returning through unpopulated Soho Square: the wooden park benches abandoned, the paths mostly obliterated by the snow and, absolute over the grass, a huge white fitted carpet. The pigeons, baffled, wheeled on a roundabout as if a fair-rifle had cracked. The statue of King Charles II did not cough; he was clear of snow except for his feet. Snow on King Charles's feet. Cold feet. And up there — meaningless, damp, a sky the colour of meths through which I could see its grey lining. Winter entered my mind like a memory and with it, momentarily, despite their absence, the compromising misery of the down-and-outs who usually dangle their shadows listlessly in this square.

A voice in my head, not mine, whispered, 'Be grateful, be grateful.'

Last day — and yet not last day; and no great farewells either because I have now been offered occasional sessional work here later in the year. Anyway it was the last day in this consulting room which I have now occupied for over a score of years. How many times have I looked through the south windows, over the patched rooftops of London, towards Centre Point? Or through the north windows with their view of the Post Office Tower? There are so many unlikely things one can become sentimental about!

I thought the day at the clinic would end on a cheerful note, a rousing finale, for the last patient proved to be completely healthy. Four years ago he had had a nasty-looking X-ray: bilateral extensive mottling in both lungs, a sarcoidosis which could have left some crippling residual scarring. So he had been prescribed steroids, which acted magically; the mottling vanished and when the steroids were stopped did not reappear. Nor did he suffer any side effects from the steroid treatment. His present X-ray showed again the lung fields to be clear with no hilar lymphadenopathy or any other sarcoid manifestation. He left my office smiling. And, after writing up his notes, I was about to follow him but the radiographer requested me to read one more chest X-ray, a routine one.

It belonged to an officer in the RAF who had reached the age of fifty and who, therefore, was required to have a medical check-up, including a chest X-ray. Because his X-ray showed a small opacity in the left mid-zone I had it repeated. It was no artifact. The opacity was clearly there; nor was it present on an earlier X-ray of his taken in January 1977. I wondered: was it a tumour? If so, malignant or benign?

'I don't think it is tuberculosis,' I told the radiographer. 'Could you ask the officer to come up from the X-ray department to see me?'

He would need to be investigated in hospital. He might well have to undergo a thoracotomy — having his chest opened — before the diagnosis became certain.

I did not tell him this. I stated facts not guesses: that the shadow in the left lung could be old or new, could be almost five years old and thus a scar of little significance, or else it could be something of more recent origin. 'That we must find out,' I said.

'Can you tell me what it isn't?'

'No, I can't even do that,' I said truthfully, and then, blessed be all clichés, 'It's like looking at a black cat in a dark room. A light needs to be shone on it before it can be properly identified. That's why I want you to be investigated further.'

We talked some more. I learnt several other facts which could be relevant — that he did not smoke and, then, something that made me pause. It seemed, a few years back, he had suffered an epididymo-orchitis. After a slow, cautious, clinical examination I telephoned the doctor at the hospital chest unit and arranged for him to be admitted after this weekend was over. I tried to reassure my patient within limits and leaned again on the crutch of a cliché: 'Everything in medicine is guilty until proved innocent. So we have to make sure.' The flight lieutenant did not seem unduly perturbed. He shook hands with me and left for his RAF station.

Afterwards I wrote up my report and gathered a few personal papers from my desk before putting on my overcoat. When I put out the lights, I noticed more vividly the lit, peaceful oblongs in the

Middlesex Hospital building across the street. I stood for a moment in the almost darkness, as I have done so many times before, listening to the distant traffic noise of London — a huge, harsh needle scratching continuously on a worn, a very worn record that turned clockwise and turned again.

I have spoken so much lately
of death and of treachery;
better to have sung the forgotten
other song of Solomon.
Forgive me. I do not believe
the rainbow was invisible
till Noah saw it;
nor was I refreshed
by strange bread in the desert,
spring water in the desert.

The two drab tablets of stone
were two drab tablets of stone,
yet, beloved, this is my heritage;
also music of Solomon's song
on psaltery and dulcimer,
that which is lost but not lost—
like the beautiful rod of Aaron,
the beautiful rod of Aaron
first with its blossom
then with its ripe almonds.

Part Two: Journals from the Ant-Heap

January 1984

Shouts from Joan half-way up the stairs. Wild shouts. Caitlin has brought a mouse into our house again.

Joan calls: 'The bloody thing's alive like last time.' Last time I had to kill the mouse. I loathed that.

Caitlin has taken her victim into the living room. Reluctantly, slow as a policeman, I investigate, hoping the cat will kill the mouse before I arrive. Caitlin is crouched threateningly and, whoops, the mouse suddenly flies a yard into the air.

It's not a mouse at all. It's a bird, an ordinary, London, Golders Green, NW11, sparrow. A commotion and the bird has flopped behind a bookcase. 'It's a bird,' I yell. Joan, in no way afraid of birds, enters the living room.

She is more comfortable with birds than I am. I could not kill a bird. We ambush Caitlin, banish her, shut the door into the hall so that the cat cannot come in, open the door into the garden so that the bird, if not damaged, can go out.

The bird is very still behind the bookcase. Has it a broken wing or leg? The packed bookcase proves too heavy to shift. Slowly, trying not to frighten the sparrow, we move the books. The bird does not move. At last we can edge the bookcase gently away from the wall. The bird is exposed.

Go, go, go, bird. There is the door, there is the cold January garden. There is freedom of a sort.

It is a long time before the bird stirs. Then it hops. Its legs are OK. It flies! It flies, it flies through the door, away! We have saved the bird. Joan is a heroine, I am a hero. We are pleased with each other, with ourselves. But all over the carpet there are feathers, here, there, so many feathers.

1984 has begun this way, like an omen.

On January 1, shouldn't those seers with hangovers — poets? — put on their purple magicians' cloaks, stare into their perspex balls and translate silence? King Hussain will be assassinated before the year's out. Someone will mount Arafat. Reagan will suffer from bowel cancer. Heseltine will make a huge fool of himself...again.

Albania will have a new leader.

It seems, though, that when I make prophetic assertions like that I am invariably wrong.

For instance, I recall D.M. Thomas who had just been made redundant from Hereford College of Further Education, telling me gloomily: 'I'll have to write a novel, make cash that way.' I shook my head, tried to dissuade him. 'You're wasting your time, you'll never make money writing a serious novel.' I was absolutely sure I was right.

Then there was that occasion when I was a member of a local charity brains trust. The panel included the M.P. for Finchley, a certain Margaret Thatcher, a mere back-bencher.

Most of the affluent audience, elegant ladies most of them, beamed at the blonde Conservative politician on the platform while scowling at the rest of us. Or they did so at first.

But Margaret the Mouth — as she would be called in Wales — sounded off at a hell of a rate. When a question about architecture was read out by the chairman, the famous architect on the panel seemed set to reply. He had not bargained for Margaret the Mouth.

Ten minutes later a question was posed about the poetry of W. H. Auden. It was evidently designed for me. I was too slow. The dominant voice began: 'When I was at Oxford, W. H. Auden. . .' The audience by this time had turned off their beam.

Arriving home I told my wife Joan: 'Today I met a politician with so little sense of audience she'll never get anywhere though she seems ambitious.' Again I was sure I was right.

Because of my own inability to prophesy correctly I have not much time for magicians. The only one I truly admire has been dead these many years. He was Tyridales, the King of Armenia, who, asked to prophesy for Nero, travelled all the way by land because he believed it sinful to spit into the sea or otherwise discharge into it 'that which might pollute and defile that Element'.

A magician such as he should be made director of British Nuclear Fuels.

'Convictions are prisons.' So they may be and it's odd that the word 'convict' should resemble the word 'conviction'. I have been reading how Trotsky, in 1929, looking back, confessed that 'the feeling of the supremacy of the general over the particular, of law over fact, of theory over personal experience, took root in my mind at an early age and gained increasing strength as the years advanced'.

How repugnant that is. Don't most of us feel the contrary? Don't we feel the supremacy of the particular over the general, of fact over law, of personal experience over theory?

I took the record off— a Beethoven piano sonata — and I sat in the armchair thinking of nothing in particular. I did not even notice the silence after music. I sat there contentedly until the door opened. 'What's the matter?' she asked. I did not reply. 'You're depressed,' she said. I did not contradict her though I wanted to smile at her presumption.

I should have told her that my face misleadingly assumes, in repose, a melancholy aspect. Instead I stared at her without expression.

At once she spoke with such sympathy, such sweetness, such softness, that gradually I began to feel sorrowful. 'What have you got to be so sad about?' she asked. 'You're lucky. You've got so many things going for you. You should thank God...' I interrupted her. I felt that I should have a reason or two for my face, in repose, registering that fake despondency.

'It's 1984,' I remarked, implying that Old Age, like the Post Office, was just around the corner. 'And the leaders of all the nations are so reactionary, near the night borders of insanity as a matter of fact, that it's frightening. Why, if one of those psychopaths punched the button....'

She ceased frowning. She wanted to cheer me up, I could see that. She picked up the record I had not put away — the Beethoven sonata. 'This is so beautiful,' she said. 'Listen to this. It will raise your spirits.'

I sat there hearing Brendel playing again and soon I was restored, felt contented as before. Then I noticed, half way through the largo e mesto, how sad and serious her face had become.

*

Each morning, somewhere in York, a certain Mr and Mrs Brown eagerly turn to an inside page of *The Times*. They are intent upon listing the names of children whose birth or adoption has been announced in those august columns. Each January they complete a League Table of the most popular names given, obviously by the Right People, to boys and girls the previous year.

This January, 1984, they tell us *James* has won again. He's been top of the Boys' League now for twenty years. *Elizabeth* has also, during 1983, scored the most in the Girls' League. She's only been champion for a mere eight years. Royal rather than Hollywood names dominate these Leagues. There are no Carys or Craigs or Mias.

In a recently published book of his *Selected Prose* (Poetry Wales Press) the Welsh Nationalist poet, R.S. Thomas, proudly announces that his son's name is *Gwydion*. No common or garden James or Charles for R.S. Thomas. As a result, though, of his choosing a name so fancy and so Welsh, people continually ask, 'What does the name mean?' Not unfairly, the Rev. R.S. Thomas complains, 'They'd never ask me what William or Margaret meant.'

He goes on to say, 'Our ancestors tended religiously to avoid giving pagan names to their children for fear they might exert an evil influence upon them. As a result, our nation is overloaded with names like John and Mary. It puts a strain on one's belief in the immortality of the individual to cast an eye over the old church registers and see the number of John Jones' and Mary Roberts' who have passed over the faces of Wales like the shadow of a cloud.' Welsh or not, we all have a 'thing' about names. Primitive man knew that his name was an integral part of his personality, a fraction of his soul. So do we, in a less defined way. Rationally I may know that a rose is a rose and would smell as sweet had it any other name. Deep down, though, I don't believe it.

On the contrary, I know, within the depths of myself, that if all roses were called, say, gwydions, these flowers would then tell a different story, their perfume would be quite other, they would smell like nothing else that has ever been.

Do our names not contribute to our destinies? Is it an accident, for instance, that the Director of Waterworks and Sewage in Glamorgan — I'm not making this up — should own the surname of Lillycrap? And that the noted author of *The Psychoanalysis of Culture* and other such Freudian analytical works should be no other than a Dr Badcock?

My Uncle Max, now aged eighty-nine, grumbled because of his arthritis. He then quite seriously proclaimed, 'You know, Dan, it's a pity we can't suffer our illnesses when we're young and healthy.'

At a party, the other evening, I heard another 'Sam Goldwynism'. A *Sunday Express* journalist was talking about the loyalty of his editor, Sir John Junor, to his staff. One journalist, though, apparently received the boot. Sir John complained, 'Sometimes your copy is brilliant, other times it's awful. What I want is consistent mediocrity.'

One actual Sam Goldwyn anecdote I have long relished concerns Billy Wilder who wanted to make a film about Nijinsky. He went to Sam Goldwyn and related how the dancer ended up in a Swiss mental home believing himself to be a horse. Sam Goldwyn was far from impressed. He said, 'You're crazy. That's too downbeat. Who would want to see a movie about a man who thought he was a horse?'

Billy Wilder shrugged his shoulders. 'It could have a happy ending,' he declared. 'We could show that horse winning the Derby.'

I have been unable to finish *Schindler's Ark* , the Booker prize 'novel' of 1982 which is now in paperback. I found it too painful. Oddly, last month, I was able to sit through the television programme about Schindler despite those too true, horrific shots where corpses who seemed to have risen from the Post-Mortem slab walked towards the camera with huge eyes.

Schindler was a strange kind of seedy hero. When the programme concluded I turned to my bookcase to reread an essay by Schopenhauer where he talks about the motives of so-called good actions. According to that pessimistic philosopher, disinterested, noble kindness exists but rarely. If the individual carrying out the good brave deed does not do so blindly because of the moral codes imposed upon him by Society then his actions are generally performed in the unformulated or concrete hope of some reward — if not in this world, then in the next.

Yet Schopenhauer is not entirely cynical. For instance, he finds precious a common engraving illustrating a true scene. It is of a soldier kneeling in front of a firing squad. The soldier is waving a cloth to frighten away his dog that wishes to come to him. Sentimental? Engravings of many selfless common acts in our hospitals would seem as much.

In Brussels, the interpreters locked in their glass-windowed cages were busy, mouth and hand, while poets from the EEC each day, in turn, pontificated on the present trends of poetry in Germany, France, Italy, Greece, Belgium, Luxembourg, Britain and Ireland. (For some reason the Dutch poet didn't turn up. Drunk possibly?) After each lecture a discussion followed. The lectures were unremarkable, the interpreters fantastic, the large audience as patient as fishermen.

The second morning, my stint over, I sat with headphones on, listening to the Flemish poet, Eddy Van Vliet. Afterwards, a hand was raised by an elderly man who looked benign — rather like a plump, rosy-cheeked Father Christmas without a beard. His speech, however, was blunt. 'Your survey of modern Flemish poetry was no good,' he said. 'Hopeless. For instance, you left me out.'

Poets, I decided, were the same the world over. All, whatever their nationality, felt neglected. So that was why I was smiling at the Flemish Father Christmas poet. 'It's not as simple as that,' Eddy Van Vliet whispered to me later. 'You see, that fellow was once head of the SS in Belgium. He was imprisoned for war crimes.There are political undertones to his objections.' I found myself staring at the interpreters busy behind the glass. I did not have my headphones on. I could not hear what they were saying.

One cannot eat in peace in a Brussels restaurant. You sit at a table reading the mouth-watering menu — at least it would be mouth-watering if you could understand it. Before the waiter returns to take your order a loud-clothed gentleman appears. He looks like George Melly. He is not George Melly. He has a basket of orchids and he is offering one to your companion. 'For the beautiful lady,' he says in three languages. He waits smiling. You do not wish to be stingy. Your right hand is furtive, searching for money. The lady is smiling, the George Melly man is smiling, you show your teeth.

The waiter arrives. You order Potage du Jour not only because it is the cheapest item on the menu but also because you can actually pronounce it reasonably. Your companion is suddenly seized with a Hamlet-sized doubt. The Moules Marinière or the Coquilles Saint-Jacques à la Parisienne? She dithers for a whole act. First it's this, then it's that, then it's this, last it's that.

The waiter quits with a dazed look. Never mind, several big laughs later we actually begin our meal when, good heavens, who should enter but The Charming Young Artist flogging his prints. Horribly, the lady seems to take an interest in (a) Movement without Force and (b) Untitled. 'Which do you prefer?' she asks. Your teeth ache, exposed to so much unaccustomed oxygen.

Before coffee you are solicited by a Salvation Army lady, a Lottery ticket seller and, inexplicably, by a comedian trying to sell you—I swear to God—a packet of nuts. He will not go away. He is making the joke with the beautiful lady. You are already wishing you were back home visiting The Great Nepalese Restaurant (recommended, of course, by Fay Maschler) having a quiet tête à tête with your beloved, enjoying the onion bhaji, the chicken tikka, the mutton dopiaza, the shahi kharma. 'We'll be home tomorrow,' you say to the beautiful lady. And you are smiling.

At the football match one unsmiling spectator near me kept on obsessively swearing for the full ninety minutes plus extra time. He swore at his own team, at the visiting players, at the linesmen and, most of all, at the referee. *Discriminate* swearing is one thing, but this was too much. I wanted to shout out, 'Shut your bloody mouth.'

I do not believe that my objection to *obsessive* swearing is because of a prissy upbringing. True, when I was a boy in South Wales, our house remained reasonably oath-free. My mother never shouted in anger anything less refined than 'damn it' or 'Helen of Troy' or 'that dirty dog'; and my father also refused to allow himself, at home anyway, the vivid, improper consolations of a barrack-room vocabulary. Still, my elder brothers let fly now and then.

Who was the first man to swear, I wonder? Adam, probably. I imagine him amiably naming the animals, becoming rather bored by it and adding a robust, forbidden adjective here, an expletive there, to describe, if not the sheep and the goats, at least the stinking vulture and the noxious snake. After all, what word could the fellow utter when his head was excreted on by the fowls of heaven?

I cannot remember which reliable source reported that one sunlit, bell-ringing, car-washing, Sunday morning, the gods came down from the mountains, walked into our towns under the leafy pavement-trees, and entered the cool darkness of our churches. There they stood up when the congregation stood up, kneeled when the congregation kneeled. The service over, they quit these churches as men.

It seems that nowadays some ex-gods are called ex-Prime Ministers. They are shunned somewhat by present Members of Parliament. It is as if their clothes still reek of the pungent smoke of ancient sacrificial fires. We, mere mortals, cannot endure the smell.

For instance, when Harold Wilson resigned his godhood, after attending one of these church services, I am told that fellow MPs in the lobbies, treated him like an untreated leper. He became a lonely, even a pathetic figure. Obviously it takes a long time for sacerdotal, stale odours to wear away and for a god to become wholly human. Being a compassionate chap, I cannot help but be sorry for their families.

Is Mary Wilson, for instance, happier for being married to one descended from on high? I bet the capricious public no longer buy her books of verse in such quantities as once they did. Still I find it hard to cry about that. I recall clearly Sir Robert Lusty, then the Managing Director of Hutchinson, moaning, 'Your *Collected Poems* are not selling as well as Mary Wilson's.' I had to reply, 'I would have to marry Ted Heath to do as well as she does.' In those days Ted Heath still had angels' wings beating the air about him. He was not yet a fully qualified mortal. That was why, surely, my remark made Sir Robert Lusty look so bereft of leaves. Things are different now, to be sure, Mr Heath is, at last, on the way to achieving a reverse apotheosis. Look how he is treated by the newspapers. The other day, as he ate his egg, he must have read the headline in *The Times*: HEATH'S COLLEAGUES ACCUSE HIM OF DISLOYALTY IN VOTE. Apparently, these colleagues are all called Anon. 'Mr Heath's decision,' wrote *The Times*' political reporter, Philip Webster 'to vote against the Government over its rate-capping has upset some of his closest parliamentary colleagues....'

Who? '...most notably Cabinet ministers who served under him when he was Prime Minister....'

Who? 'Ministers who remain sympathetic to Mr Heath's economic views are privately critical of him....'

Who? 'One Cabinet Minister who has always been closer to Mr Heath than to Margaret Thatcher.'

Who? Mr Webster names no names. It seems that anonymous, mephitic figures, men who have never been christened have whispered into his hairy ear.

The trouble is that Ted Heath forgets he is an ex-god. Now and then he proclaims holy things about the way the present government continues to dismantle our Welfare State. He remarks from the mountain, 'We can afford to care. We have never been able to afford not to.' Disgraceful fellow, what?

I have received in the post a communication from a Mr John Sumsion, the Registrar of Public Lending Rights. I now know how much I have earned between July '82 and July '83 as a result of my books being borrowed from the free libraries of Great Britain.

I can't help but wonder if I have done better than Mary Wilson.

Apparently, of the 16 sample libraries monitored one was the Hendon Central Library. I console myself I would have done better had one or another Hampstead Library been selected. After all, I have no friends or relatives living in Hendon. The Uncle who once did so — my Uncle Isaac Shepherd — has for some years borrowed his books from the stacks of Eternity.

Had Uncle still been alive he undoubtedly would have made regular visits to Hendon Central Library to take out my books for my sake. As a matter of fact he was the only person I know who seemed delighted when, twenty or so years ago, we moved nearer to Hendon from our cramped flat in Belsize Park to our house in Golders Green. Then, with the innocence of extreme narcissism, he remarked, 'That's better, Dannie. Now you're more central.'

But the death of my Uncle Isaac is not the only reason why I did not scoop the PLR jackpot. I feel sure it is because of my surname. There is no gainsaying that if you happen to be an author it is a disadvantage to own a name beginning with A. If you are among the L's — Larkin, Lessing, Laurie Lee, Levi-Strauss — you can't miss, you are at supermarket eye level. But the As are way up high, out of sight, out of reach. You have to be a giant to read Abse. On the other hand you have to be a dwarf to read Wilson.

When my Uncle Isaac expressed his approval of my move from NW3 to NW11, I did not know the Talmudic story of that disputatious rabbi, Joshua ben Hanania and the Greek philosophers — otherwise I would have told it to him. I imagine Rabbi Joshua as a small man with a long beard that almost touched his feet. The Athenians, no doubt, with whom he was arguing, were taller and bald. 'Where,' demanded one of that bald number, 'where, Rabbi, is the centre of the earth? In Jerusalem? In Corinth? Syracuse? Damascus? Carthage? Memphis? Antioch? Tyre? Thebes?'

Rabbi Joshua, unadvised by Uncle Isaac, did not know he should have replied, 'Hendon.' (Why else, by the way, is the Tube station called Hendon Central?) Instead, smiley-sweet, Rabbi Joshua pointed at the greenish stony ground beneath him. 'If you doubt me,' he said to those scowling bald philosophers, 'bring your apparatus, bring long rods, bring rope, bring all the string of Athens and measure it for yourselves.'

I am not alone in believing my local park, Golders Hill Park, with its peacocks, llamas and emus etc., to be one of the most pleasant in London. Yet the park remains relatively unknown. One who enjoyed it earlier this century was W.H. Hudson (1841-1922). He often strolled this way with such a literary Hampstead friend as

Ernest Rhys, the editor of the Everyman Library.

Yesterday afternoon the park spread out cold and moody and empty. I walked up its green slopes past the stark black trees towards the abandoned bandstand and the little pond near the walled flower garden. Arriving at that pond I read the red board with its white painted admonition: DANGER, THIN ICE. And standing, asleep, one-legged on the ice, their heads beneath wings, stood the four flamingoes that I had come to visit.

Each winter I observe this odd, dream-like scene enacted. On each occasion, W.H. Hudson's description of a flamingo killing in Patagonia comes to mind. He wrote how he, carrying a gun and accompanied by his dog, encountered a small flock of flamingoes in a lagoon. He wrote, 'I crept up to the rushes in a fever of excitement; not that flamingoes are not common in this district, but because I had noticed that one of the birds before me was the largest and loveliest flamingo I had ever set eyes on... I think my hand trembled a great deal; nevertheless the bird dropped when I fired.'

How dare Hudson have killed such a benign creature? If he had not admired it that flamingo would have lived out its blameless natural life. Nowadays, each winter, I turn angrily from the frozen pond to look for the phantom of W.H. Hudson. Yesterday afternoon I surely heard in the distance, his ghost screech thin with grief. Else it was the startled cry of a peacock.

February 1984

This morning, at the chest clinic, where I now work only part-time — sessional work, Mondays, Tuesdays — my first patient was under surveillance because some years ago he had been exposed to crocidolite dust (blue asbestos). He had no chest symptoms and the X-rays continued to show the lung fields to be clear. I stood before the blazing X-ray screens and turned to tell him the happy news.

He was not surprised. He had no problems with his chest. His concern was with his legs and feet. 'They're getting worse, doctor,' he explained. He told me in detail the nature of his symptoms, when they came on, their intensity and duration, and I told him that his symptoms had nothing to do with his exposure to asbestos.

After I had examined him I half-wondered whether he suffered from what was once called Buerger's Disease. In 1908, a certain Dr Buerger described this rather rare condition and suggested that it was a disease confined to Polish Jews. Forty years later that was what I was taught, it being current medical dogma so many text-books ago, when I was a medical student at Westminster Hospital.

Then, remarkably, King George VI was diagnosed as suffering from the disease.

At once, those medical text-books had to be rewritten, Stalinised as it were. No longer was Buerger's Disease one that attacked Polish Jews particularly. Statements suggesting it did so were erased from the page. The very term, 'Buerger's Disease', became unfashionable. Rather, its scientific name, Thrombo-Angiitis Obliterans came into favour. The fame of poor old Dr Buerger, in Britain anyway, began to fade. Posthumously he was in the dog-house.

What about my patient? There is such a thing as medical confidentiality. I'll tell you this though: my patient was circumcised.

Whenever I observe Margaret Thatcher on TV I have the uneasy feeling she is wearing a mask. Images of politicians are not simply invented by media hacks and by PR hirelings as some seem to believe. The making of a politician's image, his or her mask, is a strange communal enterprise in which we, the public, participate and in which the principal actively takes part.

And it is not only the images of politicians that are delivered into being this way. So it is for all public figures, be they kings and queens, bastards or bards. No wonder our sense of historical reality is so fragile and that the more we investigate the past the more we discover it to be mythological. But then, all of us wear some disguise — except those who are crying.

Margaret Thatcher, for some years now, has been cast as the Iron Lady. She accepts that image and helps to perpetuate it. 'I have an iron determination,' she recently declared in Hungary. If nothing else, she is determined to be determined and many are those who admire her, like her that way. I suspect that Mrs Thatcher's habitual impersonation of herself has become her true nature. The mask has become her face.

But has she not also allowed herself another role in which she extols Victorian values? There is no contradiction. It was a Victorian, Oscar Wilde, who averred that the first duty in life is to be as artificial as possible. Oscar Wilde continued, 'What the second is no one has yet discovered.'

A confession. On weekday afternoons, if I do not engage myself in dutiful or honourable activities such as working, or at least serious reading, then I experience a sense of unease. The ghost in the mirror points his finger at me. I used to suffer those same feelings on the occasions when, as a wayward medical student, I deliberately missed a lecture or a ward round, to spend instead a guilty afternoon at the Swiss Cottage Odeon.

By Wednesday lunchtime, though, I yearned for a wicked game of chess. So I telephoned my friend, the pipe-smoking LSE philosopher, John Watkins, who lives in Erskine Hill, Hampstead Garden Suburb.

'OK,' Professor Watkins agreed philosophically, 'if you come over here.'

The sky was high and February blue, the sun low, the light peculiarly bright and liquid as if reflected from cutlery. I walked down Finchley Road to turn up Hoop Lane, conscious that it was a lovely day. I felt curiously cheerful. Then, as I approached the railings of the cemetery, I observed in front of me the first black hearse with its flower-covered coffin, parked opposite the Crematorium gate.

Behind the hearse, another stationary, black limousine waited by the kerb. Three people sat bolt upright in the back, unsmiling, motionless, not talking to each other. They owned the melacholy faces of sleepers, except their eyes were open, their mouths shut. I walked on towards the roundabout.

Then came, silent as a conspiracy, a second funeral cortège. First the long car with the fresh coffin, followed by another shining, black automobile, chauffeur-driven. And in the back seat, again, three mourners sat upright, neither looking to the right nor to the left. They had similar despondent faces. I looked over my shoulder and saw behind me the parked, mourning car with its first three occupants and suddenly a possible line for a poem came into my head: 'Some talk in their sleep very few sing.'

Some talk in their sleep, very few sing. I thought about that and a few more matching lines occurred to me so that as I walked on I struggled to get the sound of the meaning right. The funerals had set me ticking — as Sylvia Plath said in a different context — 'set me ticking like a fat gold watch'. Why not? The theme of Death is to Poetry what Mistaken Identity is to Drama.

But then those nascent lines in my head became derailed, as if I had been button-holed by a man from Porlock. For on the other side of the roundabout a third hearse with coffin approached. From poetic trance I was jolted into the ordinary, beautiful, common air of a particular Wednesday afternoon and was astonished.

For it was as if, from diverse corners of London, funeral cars were converging to this focal point in Golders Green and each hearse, in its turn, with its chauffeur of Death, had to wait, had to idle the minutes away, rather like an aeroplane circling and circling, not given clearance to land at some crowded airport.

However, behind the third, so-controlled cortège came, at last, another car — one not so sleek, one as a matter of fact battered, shabby, and driven neither by a ceremonial chauffeur, nor carrying three exhausted occupants in the back. The driver was young and the window next to him wound down so that, out of it, came the raucous noise of Radio One. The young driver had evidently turned the knob of his radio on to half past six because the volume of this so-called music was startlingly loud, spectacularly loud.

I was not offended. I welcomed this pollution of silence. For that blaring noise celebrated, there and then, informality, youth, vivid life. For some reason I could not understand, as I progressed into Hampstead Garden suburb, I felt confident that that afternoon I was going to win my game of chess.

Great activity in the house. My son, David, is framing his prints and drawings for his first exhibition which he is to share later this month with the gifted young painter, Sue Morris, at the Leigh

Gallery in Bloomsbury.

Over our bread and cheese lunch we talked, my wife, myself, and David, about the expertise of Art Critics. My wife declared she had a high regard for some critics, among them Edward Lucie Smith and John Russell Taylor. My son seemed more sceptical. He related to us the story of one, Soderini, who, while praising the colossal statue of David, complained to Michelangelo that the nose was too thick.

'So Michelangelo,' my son continued, 'took a chisel in one hand, a scoop of marble dust in the other. Then he climbed the scaffolding around the statue. Reaching the top he pretended to chip away at the criticised nose and, while doing so, allowed marble dust to filter from his hand. On climbing down again, he asked Soderini what he thought now. 'So much better,' the critic said: 'so much better, you've given it life.'

My son stood up and asked me if I wished to look at 'the stuff' he was putting into the exhibition. I nodded. I was going to be very very careful about making any critical remarks whatsoever about *my* David.

Why do young people slam the front door with such passionate intensity? You can tell the age of an individual not by inspecting their teeth but rather by how loudly they slam the front door shut. The youngest in our family had just stepped out of the front porch, leaving our house shaking as if it were in Beirut. No matter, I dusted the ceiling flakes from my shoulders and, in the returning silence, worked away happily.

Then our cat, Caitlin, suddenly exploded. She alighted on my desk — a prodigious leap — scattering my papers. She made it plain that she wished to be fed. Since my wife would not be home for hours yet, since everyone else, one by one, had quit the house with loud ostentation, there was only me around to provide, damn it.

When I reached the kitchen, intent on opening a tin of cat meat, the hall turned nasty. Or rather its sole occupant did — the telephone. 'All right, all *right*,' I yelled, 'I'm coming.'

Eleven paces later, I picked up the receiver and a voice in it peremptorily demanded, 'Is that Dannie Abse?'

'Yes,' I admitted.

'The great poet, Dannie Abse.'

Oh heck, I thought. This was no relative.

'Hunter Davies,' the voice continued, 'this is Hunter Davies. I think your column in the *Ham and High* is fan*tastic* .'

I hesitated. I had met Hunter Davies once. He had seemed pleasant enough, he hadn't gone over the top then. Was this *the* Hunter Davies?

'We're not being recorded,' he said confidentially. What did he mean we weren't being recorded?

'What do you mean "we're not being recorded?"' I asked this Bulgarian spy, Hunter Davies.

He explained. He was doing a programme called *Bookshelf* for Radio 4 and he was telephoning different authors to record their reactions to the Public Lending Right results, those who had become enriched by thousands of pounds and those, apparently, such as myself who could now buy an extra tin of cat meat.

'I just want you to repeat the things you said in your *Ham and High* column, OK?' he ordered.

I tried to recall what I had written for the *Ham and High* some weeks back. The cat, meanwhile, had come into the hall and was looking at me reproachfully with both her eyes.

'OK, is it?' said Hunter Davies louder.

'OK,' I said to the cat who was still salivating away and looking as despondent as coitus interruptus.

Then the phone went dead. I waited. Nothing happened. Hunter Davies, I thought, why when he had just now given me all those verbal medals, I should have responded in kind. 'Not *the* Hunter Davies,' I should have babbled. 'Not the author of that simply magic book that I so admired and liked and cherished, *The Glory Game* ?'

Ignoring the cat who was now rubbing herself against my left leg, I crooned down the telephone-receiver that had gone dead, 'My God, that Wordsworth book you wrote, Hunter Davies, was OUT OF THIS WORLD. And your book, *The Joy of Stamps*, was a masterpiece.'

'Sorry to keep you, Dr Abse,' a woman's voice said on the suddenly alive phone. 'This is the producer. We'll be ready to record shortly.' I nodded. I don't think she heard me nod.

Then, to my dismay, the front door bell rang. Since the phone was silent again I dashed to the door and opened it. 'I've come to service the gas-boiler,' said the man standing and staring there.

'Come in,' I said. ' I won't be a moment, I'm on the phone.'

He stood in the hall. The cat stood in the hall. I stood in the hall, holding the telephone receiver. I was about to ask the man from the North Thames Gas Board if he would mind feeding the cat when the woman producer said, making me jump, 'We're ready now, Dr Abse.'

Some profoundly shocking experiments are being performed at The Chemical Warfare Centre at Porton Down in Wiltshire. The victims of these experiments are monkeys, rabbits, sheep, pigs, rats, mice, as well as, possibly, dogs and cats.

The Junior Defence Minister, John Lee, recently admitted that each year, (repeat, each year) in Britain, 10,000 animal experiments are conducted by the Ministry of Defence. Sheep, for instance, have been shot in wounding tests — the Government being interested, so we are told, in the wounding efficacy of ammunition.

No doubt many would think me absurd when I confess that such facts remind me of the medical atrocity experiments of the Nazis in 1942 at the Ravensbruck Concentration Camp for women.

The subjects there, they would needlessly remind me, were human.

Karl Gebhardt, head physician of the Hohenlychen Orthopaedic Clinic and President of the German Red Cross would not have assented to that judgement. He believed his victims to be sub-human, to be animals.

Dr Gebhardt, along with his assistant, Dr Fritz Fischer, inflicted deep surgical wounds on healthy young women before introducing into the wounds a mixed infection containing septic gas-gangrene organisms and earth.

Pure sadism. Is shooting sheep not sadism?

The scientists at Porton Down would not accept that their experiments are sadistic. They would argue that their results will help in the treatment of wounded soldiers should there be a war.

Nor would Gebhardt and Fischer have accepted the verdict of sadism. By subsequently giving their female 'animals' the then new sulphonamide drugs they felt they would discover the value of such therapy before prescribing it for noble German soldiers wounded on the Eastern Front.

The fact is all victims are described as worthless, as a form of vermin, by their persecutors — if the victims be human then they are perceived as being sub-human; if animals, then they are considered as creatures with little or no intelligence.

When I was a second year medical student studying physiology I liked and admired our professor — Professor MacDowell. I enjoyed his sardonic humour. He once remarked that Life consisted of three instincts, the three Fs: Fear, Food and Reproduction. His office was on the fifth floor where he would occasionally carry out tests on heart patients. Frequently, in those days, the lift broke down and those patients had to climb the steep stairs to his office. He never examined them when they arrived. 'If they're not dead when they reach me,' he used to say, 'their hearts are OK.'

Yes, I was amused by Professor MacDowell. But one day, for the benefit of the second year medical students, he carried out experiments on an anaesthetised, dissected cat. When some of us objected our professor assured us that cats had no intelligence worth talking about. 'They are worthless creatures,' he taught the nineteen year old medical students. For years I believed him, I believed that cats were truly stupid. (Sorry, Caitlin.)

No doubt scientists at Porton Down have found it necessary to have a similar contempt for sheep. What I feel sure of is that Gebhardt and Fischer would have felt very comfortable working at that secret green and pleasant spot in bird-trilling Wiltshire, England, 1984.

They were streaming out of Dunstan Road synagogue in Golders Green as I happened to be passing by. I overheard one bearded man say to another, 'One thing I wanted to say about the soul...' I slowed my pace in order to follow their theological speculations '...is that it does tend to come away from the uppers.'

March 1984

On my way home I read the newspaper placard: TITO GOBBI DIES IN ROME. Immediately I thought of my Uncle Joe — my favourite among the many brothers of my mother. Joe had told me how, one evening while on holiday in Italy, he had wandered into the hotel bar. In no time at all he found himself in conversation with an Italian gentleman.

'No, no, I was born in Bassano del Grappo in the Veneto region,' said the stranger. 'But I like this part of Italy.'

'I was born in Ystalyfera in South Wales,' offered my gregarious uncle.

Soon they were exchanging views about politics, about the relative qualities of Rome and London, about Napoleon Bonaparte, icthyology, the internal combustion engine, Shakespeare, celestial photography and one or two other ordinary conversational topics.

After another drink my uncle, curious about his new-found friend, remarked, 'I'm a doctor, you know. I have a practice in Hampstead Garden suburb in London. What, sir, do you do for a living?'

The Italian replied, smiling, 'I'm Tito Gobbi.' My uncle extended his hand. 'My name is Joe Shepherd. But, as I said, what do you do for a living?'

'I'm Tito Gobbi,' Tito Gobbi repeated, his smile retreating. My uncle decided that the stranger's English was, after all, somewhat deficient. 'Signor Gobbi,' my uncle now deliberated very slowly and clearly, enunciating each word so that he could be understood, 'What...do...you...do...for...a...living?

Joe Shepherd went on to tell me how the fellow unaccountably bolted for the exit.

My uncle, a first-class general physician, a most capable diagnostician, could identify patients' diseases with precision. But he wasn't so hot at identifying the names of the patients themselves.

There was that time when we were in a theatre foyer and James Mason hovered nearby. Because Mr Mason looked familiar to my uncle he assumed the film star was a patient of his.

'Feeling better?' he asked James Mason.

The actor stopped in his tracks. 'Thank you,' he said. My uncle nodded. 'You look better since you've had the treatment,' he added. James Mason looked over his shoulder rather wildly, I thought, as he ascended the staircase.

One summer afternoon, when I was nineteen, I entered a tobacconist's in Swiss Cottage and asked as usual for a packet of Players. The proprietor of this small shop obviously had no commercial sense for he replied, 'You shouldn't smoke. It stops you from growing. You could grow as tall as Romeo.'

That was how I knew Romeo was a tall guy. I was only 5' 8", not much bigger than my Uncle Joe. Years later, when I was also a doctor, I wished I had taken the tobacconist's advice. Not because I wanted to be like Romeo but because I observed too many pulmonary cripples who had become such as a result of the chronic irritation of tobacco smoke. There I sat at my desk in the chest clinic, hurriedly putting out my cigarette, as I recommended patients to give up smoking completely.

I had tried to stop smoking a number of times. My own father had been killed by tobacco's lethal effects. I had looked at his chest X-ray that day in 1964 and seen above the left hemi-diaphragm a shadow that should not have been there, that was, I knew, a malignant growth, a cancer.

For years after that, whenever I looked at an X-ray on a bright, lit screen, my eyes would be drawn to a particular location above the left hemi-diaphragm.

Then during Christmas time, 1968, a wonderful thing happened. I suffered a severe influenza. For days I did not want to smoke and when I began to recover I managed to kick the habit. I'm glad I did so. Multitudes have been killed by cigarettes since then. It has been estimated that over the last quarter of a century a million people in Britain alone have died because of tobacco-induced diseases — cancer, heart disease, contraceptive pill complications, etc.

Now, at last, the British people are catching on. February 29th was Stop Smoking Day. And now Nigel Lawson has done his Budget bit — though he could have done more. In any case, the British are giving up smoking in their thousands, in their tens of thousands, in their hundreds of thousands. The statistics reveal this.

Even inconsequential surveys such as those carried out by the Dateline Computer Agency show that most women on their books desire not only a medium-built young male between 5'9" and 6' but one who is also a non-smoker. That tobacconist was right, Romeo was tall and had no smoker's cough.

However, though as a nation we are giving up the habit of smoking, the tobacco companies based here and in the USA are clawing back their profits. They are exporting their little packets of delayed death to the Third World.

The *Lancet* has reported how some brands, along with those manufactured under licence overseas, 'have a much higher tar and nicotine content than those smoked at home'.

Six years ago a World Health Organisation document advised that, 'In the absence of strong and resolute government action, we face the serious probability that the smoking epidemic will have affected the developing world within a decade.' Already there is a rising and alarming casualty list in India, Pakistan, the Philippines, China, Hong Kong and Cuba. It is sad to see snap-shots of children in these countries smoking and smiling so innocently.

I should not have mocked Joe Shepherd's occasional inability to recognise people. I have just come back to London after finishing a BBC-TV *Return Journey* film in Cardiff. At one point I was required to walk into a house in Whitchurch Road where I was born.

As I waited outside for John Geraint, the director, to give me the signal to start walking to the front door, a bespectacled stranger came towards me smiling warmly. His face seemed familiar. Some old schoolmate, perhaps?

Ignoring the TV crew, he said, 'Hello, hello, how are you? You do recognise me, Dan?'

A sudden illumination. 'Of course, Stanley,' I said triumphantly. 'You haven't changed.'

He hesitated. 'Colin,' he said.

How strange to enter the bedroom where one was born. I tried to imagine my mother lying in the bed, the midwife announcing, 'It's a boy,' and the baby who was me crying like billy-o.

I have been told that when I was born my eldest brother, Wilfred, aged eight, went out and bought me a *Comic Cuts* to read. My other brother, Leo, six years old, not to be outdone, superiorly announced, 'I'll buy him *The Children's Newspaper* .' I can reveal now there is no truth in the report that I pushed the *Comic Cuts* away, shouting 'Rubbish' or that I immediately rejected *The Children's Newspaper* as being inaccurate.

Afterwards, I went downstairs into the kitchen. I shut my eyes and tried to remember something, anything — the noise of peas being shelled, peas falling into a resonant zinc bucket; or of gas hissing until the sound of a paper bag exploded over a stove. But I heard nothing. I opened my eyes and saw only what was there....

Later that day the TV crew followed me past my old elementary school and I recalled how it used to be. There was a war going on in Spain; one of Leo's friends, Sid Hamm, had been killed out there, fighting for the International Brigade; Mussolini was puffed out and ranting in Italy; Hitler, dangerously maniacal in Germany. There was sloth and unemployment in the Welsh valleys and the Prince of Wales had said poshly, uselessly, 'Something must be done'. But nothing was done.

At school we sang, 'Let the prayer re-echo, God Bless the Prince of Wales,' though I mistakenly believed that patriotic lyric to be, 'Let the prairie echo, God Bless the Prince of Wales,' and wondered vaguely where the devil were those grass-waving prairies in mountainous Wales.

Of course, it's all different now, in 1984; there is no unemployment in South Wales, there are no dictators or wars anywhere in the world, the Prince of Wales has a different face, God's in his heaven, all's right with the world.

The lady from Hampstead CND told me that on April 7th at 2 p.m. there would be a march past buildings named in the 'Camden War Plan'. The march would culminate in a 'die-in' at the Whitestone Pond. So, at the Pond, would I read that poem I had once written about the possibility of a nuclear holocaust?

Indeed, I had written such a poem. I had written it in the 1950s at the height of the then Cold War. But what did she mean by a

'die-in'? She informed me how everybody would lie down signi-
fying that the Heath was planned as Hampstead's Mass Grave.

It would be easy to mock such symbolic measures. One could,
though, just as well pour scorn on the wreath-laying ceremony at
the Whitehall Cenotaph on November 11th. After all, one ritual is
a public lament for war casualties of the past while the other is for
possible casualties of a catastrophic future.

On the other hand, like so many of the silent majority, I dislike
participating in public protests, especially if one is asked to be
ostentatious in them. I wish I did not feel that way, but I do. I wish
that I was not so hesitant about signing petitions, joining protest
marches, however just. No doubt, part of my reluctance is the
result of my bourgeois upbringing with its concern for What Will
the Neighbours Think? I hope it's more than that. I do have the
sense that a poet's importance, such as it minimally is, lies in his
or her poetry, and gesturing on public platforms is too often a mere
theatrical, hollow enterprise.

'So will you read your poem?' requested the lady from CND.
'Yes,' I said, wishing she had not asked me in the first place.

A thousand years ago the bard sat at the right hand of his Welsh
prince and spoke for the prince; now, princes such as they are,
disguised with other names, have no use for bards, at least not in
our part of the world. And elsewhere, in certain countries in South
America, or in Eastern Europe for instance, the bard is more likely,
being subversive by nature, to be thrown into a dungeon or a
mental hospital by those who have the power of princes, than to
sit honoured at their polished tables.

Camus wrote, 'The writer's role is not free of difficult duties. By
definition he cannot put himself today in the service of those who
make history; he is at the service of those who suffer it.' Even
Camus' remark is an exaggerated statement. The writer, after all,
is not separate from those who suffer the active decisions of the
princes. He suffers them himself and so whatever he does publicly
is self-serving.

What a bother, you may think, simply because you've been
asked to read a poem at the Whitestone Pond. Quite right. If
someone had asked me to read out the same poem in Moscow I
would have said, 'No.' I would have been too scared.

*

One of my two daughters, Susanna, has been travelling around the world with a friend since last August. Letters arrive from strange places — Thailand, India, Japan. She seems to be enjoying her adventure and will surely be enriched by it, but selfishly I'm beginning to miss her. There simply aren't enough people around this house for me to tell off or to ask, 'Who's the Best Driver in the World?'

So I wish Susanna, now that April is coming, would have some Home Thoughts from Abroad. How can I induce enough nostalgia in her to make a return journey imperative and soon? I shall send her a postcard naming names. I shall speak of the daffodils in Golders Hill Park; the fair at Hampstead Heath; the unexpected bit of canal at Camden Lock; the elegance of Ken Wood; the delightful curve downhill of Fitzjohn's Avenue; the cherry blossom that will soon arrive on the trees of Golders Green like so many bits of the *Financial Times*.

How can she resist the power of nostalgia? Peter Vansittart told me a story I can never forget. It concerned a Chinese general who once — defending a city beseiged by the Mongols and with no food left, no hope remaining — climbed on to the battlements of the city one moonlit night.

The Mongols were all encamped around. The general could see them from the high walls. There was silence; there were the sleepers in the tents; there were the stars flung high above, and the general played on his pipe, played the most lonely, the most desolate melodies of the Steppes.

Soon after dawn, the enemy, now all utterly homesick, departed. Remembering this I too play on my pipe for my daughter: Spaniard's Inn, Jack Straw's Castle, The Flask, The Everyman, The Screen on the Hill, Louis' Teashop, the Whitestone Pond and the donkeys, the *Ham and High*.

Another new, non-steroid, anti-inflammatory drug has been withdrawn as a result of the Committee on the Safety of Medicines turning their thumbs down. Three others over the last two years have met a similar fate.

This family of drugs is taken by hundreds of thousands of people in Britain. They have been prescribed widely in the main for arthritic pains of all varieties. One of them, Osmosin, as a matter of fact, was prescribed for my father-in-law by a hospital doctor in Lancashire.

Fortunately he suffered no ill effects. Others, less luckily, have experienced adverse reactions — some of them dire. There have been medical disasters such as gastro-intestinal perforations and blood dyscrasias. There have been mortalities.

Who is to blame? The greedy pharmaceutical companies or the gullible incautious, prescribing doctors? Both. There's no question that sometimes certain pharmaceutical firms, even in those advertisements they place in such prestigious periodicals as the *British Medical Journal*, make excessive claims for their drugs and print in the smallest type available the serious possible side-effects of these same drugs. Doctors read their advertisements and are influenced by them.

The *Lancet*, another journal which I read regularly with interest, quite justly has castigated doctors for often 'ignoring the hazards of a particular drug'. They further accuse doctors of being 'incapable of making a reasoned judgement' concerning the risks and benefits of this or that medicament.

The *Lancet* is right. Doctors have not the pharmacological expertise to make such judgements and that is why they so often have to accept the information doled out to them by so-called reputable drug companies.

Of course, many new drugs are wonderfully effective but not every physician remembers Alexander Pope's advice, 'Be not the first by whom the new are tried, Nor yet the last to lay the old aside.'

Doctors have always done harm as well as good. My favourite story of one who caused medical mayhem is told by the American doctor, Lewis Thomas, in his autobiography, *The Youngest Science*. He relates how a certain old-time physician, during the early years of this century, became extremely successful in New York, noted for his skill in making early diagnoses — especially of typhoid fever which was then a common disease in New York.

This great diagnostician, wrote Lewis Thomas, placed particular reliance on examining the tongue. 'He believed that he could detect significant differences by palpating that organ. The ward rounds conducted by this man were, essentially, tongue rounds; each patient would stick out his tongue while the eminence took it between thumb and forefinger, feeling its texture and irregularities, then moving from bed to bed, diagnosing typhoid in its earliest stages over and over again, and turning out a week or so later to have been right, to everyone's amazement.'

What we then learn from Lewis Thomas is that the old-time great diagnostician was, in fact, a typhoid carrier!

Driving home I heard on the radio that there is currently an epidemic of hip fractures in older people, especially in post-menopausal women. Such fractures, of course, are serious and it seems doctors are puzzled why, in recent years, there has been such a devastating increase in their incidence. 'You should see the orthopaedic wards of Nottingham hospitals. They are crowded with patients who have broken their hip bones. I'm not exaggerating.'

I listened to the experts offering hypotheses on why there is such an epidemic. Not enough Vitamin D in the diet, not enough calcium, failure of protein metabolism, etc., etc. Much talk of oestrogens and of bone conditions, osteomalacia and osteoporosis. Concern, too, of the cost to the National Health Service.

I have news for these doctors. I recommend they turn their eyes from X-rays to look at the condition of our neglected towns. Let them get out of their cars and walk. Then they may observe the uneven state of the pavement stones here, there, everywhere, in the cities of run-down Britain.

April 1984

We all discover that certain 'facts' we learnt when young turn out to be no more than sweet myths or sour imaginings, born of pedagogic or parental pride and prejudice. Dai Smith, in his television programmes on BBC 2 and in his recently published book *Wales! Wales?* (Allen and Unwin) hatchets away at phoney national historiography.

I was taught at school, in Cardiff, about the particular, invented tradition of Wales, 'the Wales of symbols and gestures' of which Dai Smith speaks with love and astringency. As a result I still find it hard to separate Welsh myth from Welsh history, to erase the country in my mind that has been stencilled there by romantic didacticity and to replace it with the real Wales. I still feel, for instance, beyond reason and knowledge, that St David had two religions, one of these being rugby, and that somehow he, himself, was a useful scrum-half.

Even more bizarre notions have been passed on to me and have proved tenacious. Thus I believed my mother when she declared with passion that 'only common women wear green'. She was looking out of the front room window at a neighbour passing by. That must have been in 1937. I believed her then and I believed her a few years later, that time when Mair Jones lay down on the green grass in her green dress and said, 'Hello, you!'

I believed in my mother's colour prejudice in an undefined way until the mid 1960s when I happened to be passing Heals in Tottenham Court Road. Then, suddenly, a huge car purred to a standstill at the kerb near me. A chauffeur opened one of its doors and out stepped, not the Welsh rugby pack, but a lady dressed in green. She was Queen Elizabeth.

Next time I visited my mother in Cardiff I mentioned my so brief, royal, non-encounter. 'Yes,' my mother said, 'the Queen often wears green.' She nodded as if she were in the know. 'But you have views about women wearing green,' I said, surprised. It was my mother's turn to look surprised. 'How do you mean, son?' she asked.

While the Government is wasting one million pounds *a day* on the Falklands, Messrs Rees-Mogg and Luke Rittner who have been affectionately described by Bernard Levin as 'Butchers and Poulterers to the Gentry' have cut the Arts Council's already parsimonious *annual* Literature grant to £450,000. This particular exercise in butchery has hardly been commented on. Rather it has been the minor shifting of funds from London to the provinces that so far has drawn media attention. One could almost fancy this devolution of funds to be a tactic in order to disguise the real issues: lack of money for the Arts in general and for Literature in particular.

The Literature Panel of the Arts Council was strategically neutralised weeks before the Literature grant announcement. For it was leaked to Arts correspondents of certain newspapers that the Literature Panel was to be abolished. Now that it has been spared (temporarily?) its members are in disarray. Some like David Harsent and Catherine Freeman have resigned in despair. Others, such as Anne Stevenson and Tim Rix soldier on, illusorily hoping to fight some kind of last-ditch battle.

What power have the Arts Council's advisory panels? My own experience of sitting for three years on a past Literature Panel leads me to say, 'Damn all.' Minor suggestions were allowed and acted on but the real decisions were taken elsewhere. Then, as presumably now, one could in committee argue for this or that, against this or that, but often the debate was a masquerade. There is a Talmudic proverb that says it all: the stone fell on the pitcher? Woe to the pitcher. The pitcher fell on the stone? Woe to the pitcher.

Since my day on the Panel it seems the Arts Council's masters have become yet more active in creating an autocracy. Rees-Mogg really does appear to believe that, as in long centuries past, writers should have a private income. I do not know whether he and Luke Rittner are sensitive to the opinions of those in the field, I mean the writers themselves. Do the two gentlemen realise how much enmity they have engendered? At least the authors that I know, and with whom I have exchanged views, intemperately advocate sending them both to the bloody abattoir, and not as employees.

At a conference at the Royal College of Physicians, Dr Jack Dominian, consultant psychiatrist and Director of the Marriage Research Centre at the Central Middlesex Hospital, has produced statistics to prove that divorce increases the risk of mental and physical illness. He asserted that separated and divorced men and women suffer more minor psychiatric illness as well as being more prone to heart disease, road accidents and cirrhosis of the liver caused by drinking too much, than couples who adhere to married 'bliss and take'.

Surely Dr Dominian is wearing his trousers back to front? It seems more likely, does it not, that minor psychiatric illness leads to divorce rather than the other way around; that drinking too much leads to separation rather than being caused by it?

Perhaps Dr Dominian has statistics and arguments to prove the contrary; or has he been misreported in *The Times*? If not he should heed the story of the experimental biologist who placed a grasshopper on his research bench. The biologist shouted, 'Jump! Jump!' and measured the height that the insect reached. He repeated the exercise several times before he cut off the legs of the grasshopper.

After that amputation he again shouted, 'Jump! Jump!' Of course the grasshopper failed to respond to his commands. The biologist then concluded that when a grasshopper has its legs removed the insect loses its hearing.

Woe to the pitcher... Michael Hamburger, I'm sure, would like that proverb because he, himself, has always affected a deep pessimism, as if all the apples on offer were made of wax, all the flowers on display made of paper. When we were both young and easy and hanging around Swiss Cottage I remember him saying that he did not expect to live long in this world. He shook his head mournfully as if he had just taken his own pulse.

On another occasion, at a small dinner party in our rather threadbare first floor flat in Eton Avenue, one of the guests, aged at least 24, remarked, 'I'm already losing hair here,' and he pointed to his growing widow's peak. 'So am I, man,' declared another guest, the American poet Theodore Roethke who, indeed, suffered from a somewhat profounder baldness. He looked across the table, ignoring the ladies. 'So am I,' I added.

Everybody now turned to Michael Hamburger who hesitated, then in a plaintive voice complained, 'I'm not. I wonder what's wrong with me?'

Now Michael Hamburger has recently celebrated his 60th birthday and he is being justly praised in the *Guardian* and elsewhere for his translations from the German and for his own considerable contribution to English Literature. But I expect he is still loudly moaning and groaning. 'Sixty,' I hear him languidly sigh, 'sixty, doctor, and none of my hair is falling out yet.'

After the Clinical Meeting we all sat for lunch, I myself next to a general practitioner. I have specialised in chest work and it is many years since I undertook a general practice locum in my home-town, Cardiff.

I still recall vividly my first morning surgery, my feelings of inadequacy. And later that afternoon when I went on my rounds, I had to hide my lack of confidence. My father insisted on being my chauffeur as I called on patients in Ruby Street or Stacey Road. He waited behind the wheel as I carried my little black bag into the patients' houses. When I returned to the waiting car he wanted to know in detail what the patient complained of and how I, his son, the doctor, had dealt with him or her. I had taken a helluva time to qualify so perhaps my father wanted to get his money's worth.

General practice has changed much since then. The GP next to me at lunch remarked how in his suburb, he now rarely makes house-calls. 'These days,' he reminded me, 'all the patients have cars. Besides there's the telephone.' I flinched. I recalled how the American doctor-essayist Lewis Thomas has justly pointed out that sick people usually need to be touched, that part of the problem of being ill is lack of human contact. Even family and friends tend to stay away from the profoundly ill. Moreover, medicine's technological advances have increased the distance between doctor and patient. After all, there was a time, before the discovery of the stethoscope, when physicians placed their ears on the patients' chests. Such a friendly gesture, such an 'intimate signal of personal concern and affection,' asserts Lewis Thomas.

My GP colleague picked at his salad. 'Yes,' he said, 'there have been some losses as well as immense gains.'

If the reviewers are to be believed the art of biography has reached dizzying heights. The nineteenth century critics were less kind. Thomas Carlyle remarked, 'A well-written Life is almost as rare as a well spent one.'

Nowadays, in the Sunday papers, one can regularly read rave reviews of X's *Life of Y*. For instance, the other Sunday, John Carey wrote that Ann Thwaite's biography of Edmund Gosse is 'one of the finest literary biographies of our time'. On my desk I have two other thick Lives to read: Richard Ellman's *James Joyce* which Anthony Burgess called 'the greatest literary biography of the century' — which may sound a bit MGM but I wouldn't mind such a review myself: and *Dostoevsky* by the remarkable Joseph Frank of which Bernard Levin writes, no doubt justly, that 'it's one of the outstanding biographical artistic works of modern times' (Warner Brothers?).

I cannot imagine myself writing a biography. Think of all the research that has to be done, slowly, painstakingly! I haven't the scholar's patience of my wife, for instance, who a few years ago published a biography of John Ruskin, *The Passionate Moralist*, that also, incidentally, received MGM and Warner Bros reviews. Besides, I would have to silence, too drastically, the clamour that my own senses make, to annihilate self too much for too long a time. It is enough for me to lose myself constantly in my job as a doctor. For a doctor has to be inwardly quiet enough to hear the voice of his patient. He has to lose his own sense of self in order to make sense of a stranger.

Still, if I had to write a biography, if condemned to do so, whom would I choose? Thomas Hood, perhaps, — not only because I enjoy his work, his outrageous puns, but because, at least, I would know how to conclude the book. For Hood's last words to his wife were, punning to the end, 'My dear, I fear you're losing your livelihood.'

My eldest daughter Keren, went with some other women to Greenham Common last week. They were travelling down the M4 in a packed car which had the CND emblem on the back. One of the girls joked, 'Perhaps the police will stop us — like they're stopping the miners.'

Half a mile later, the driver saw in the mirror a posse of policemen on motorbikes overtaking her. They resembled the ominous extras in Cocteau's film *Orphée*. The driver moved to the middle lane. Then, to all the women's consternation, they observed that the police were signalling them to move further over to the left.

Reluctantly, the car slowed to a stop on the hard shoulder. The police riding their motorbikes roared on. Then appeared several Rolls Royces tearing along in the same direction. In one was a visiting Arab potentate, the Amir of the State of Bahrein, who, presumably, had left Windsor Castle and was now on his way to visit the stables of the Queen at Highclere which is quite close to Greenham Common.

May 1984

I went for a morning walk on the beach at Ogmore-by-Sea. The post-Easter blue skies still persisted and sunlight threw down its mercury-backed mirror dazzle on the sea. The beach was empty. I looked towards the barely-outlined coast of Somerset across the Bristol Channel and walked on, half-listening to the erratic rhythm of the sea.

Then, ahead of me, I saw a man, alone, sitting on the pebbles, his trousers tucked into his socks. Nearby lay a white stick. The man looked out, seemingly towards Somerset but, of course, he was blind. And I, walking on sand, and hence silently, suddenly felt myself to be a voyeur, watching him watch nothing.

I noticed how he was feeling the pebbles around him one by one. He picked them up, weighed them, felt, perhaps, the sun's faint warmth in them before replacing them, each one deliberately. He looked my way and seemed to smile so that I wondered, what parable is this? From behind a rock a woman now appeared, obviously his companion, and I strolled on listening once more to the sea and to the sorrowing of some seagulls.

That Saturday afternoon I went, for the last time this season, into Cardiff to watch The Bluebirds play at Ninian Park. Quitting the ground, I moved as quickly as possible back to my car. There was no crowd trouble on this occasion and I did not feel menaced as I have done earlier this year — because of running feet, because of a sudden stampede of rival supporters, because of raw shouts, over-alert policemen and police dogs barking.

These days, even approaching Saturday-afternoon football grounds has its suggestions of hazard. Not such a long time ago I used to enjoy the preliminaries to a football game. It began from the moment you locked the door of your car and some small boy would extend his hand saying, 'Mind it for sixpence, sir.' Afterwards you would join a stream of people, a benign stream that, in turn, would join another to form a river of supporters all flowing in the one imperative direction towards the mouth of the tall Stands.

Waiting there, and somehow contributing to the small excitements, would be the vendors wearing their white laboratory coats, selling rosettes, shiny programmes, ghastly onion-smothered sausages. And, in the ground itself, the dramatic crowds would be good-natured. Never would you hear, as I did at the Millwall ground recently, even before the game began, a whole mass of razor-headed young men shouting in unison, 'Kick their fuckin' 'eads in, kick their fuckin' 'eads in.' And brandishing their right fists rhythmically to this threatening cry, with routine malevolence.

Perhaps it is better that these lynch parties gather at football matches rather than elsewhere. To be sure these ranting, lead-irritable, broken-homed, frustrated, violent youths are a symptom of our unhealthy and increasingly uncaring society. But can football managerial staff attempt to undertake some palliative measures?

I was told by a Rumanian how they solved a crowd problem in Bucharest. Apparently the citizens of Bucharest are not given to queueing up. They have no discipline, the East Germans say. So, in their splendid football stands they would not sit in the seats numbered on the tickets that they had bought. Simply, they acted on the principle of first come, best seat. Then the faceless ones decided that at important games when the Stands were full a car would be given away to one particular occupant of a certain numbered seat. A kind of raffle. However if that occupant did not have the ticket with the right seat number the car was kept in the kitty, as it were, until the next big game. Soon the citizens of Bucharest became as obedient as East Germans.

Meanwhile, lethal crowds or not, I still enjoy watching Cardiff

City, the Bluebirds, play. I'm involved. I almost sing to myself.
'Roll along Cardiff City, roll along, to the top of the League where
you belong....' Some years back a friend lent me his season ticket
to watch Spurs play. At White Hart Lane I had the pleasure of
encountering Hans Keller or Professor Ayer. Refined company.
Alas, that kind of bonus did not make up for not watching my
home team. Despite the classy company, despite the classier football, I could not feel pure enthusiasm. I even felt the referee was
fair!

Besides, the man who sat behind me had the habit of eating
boiled sweets. Each time Spurs scored, one would be launched on
the back of my head — a sticky orange, or raspberry, or lemon
sweet would have to be pulled from my hair. I could tell how many
goals Spurs had scored, including those disallowed, by the number
of sweets I had to remove from the back of my neck. There are no
such mad season ticket holders undergoing oral orgasms at Ninian
Park. But then City don't score too many goals.

'I have writer's block,' the young man asserted, depressed. I knew
the acute feeling of inertia he complained of. Most creative people
have tasted the taste of nothing on the tongue. When writers feel
this sense of deadness usually they are propelled to write something in order to prove to themselves that they are alive. Dylan
Thomas, in his later thirties, suffered from writer's block. Each day
arriving would feel to him to be purposeless and blank. So he
would buy himself a Mars Bar to keep for the morrow so that then
he would have something to do, something to look forward to.

'How sad,' the young man said.

Sad, yes, but I cannot feel too sad these days for writers who
experience this depressing inertia. There are too many unemployed. There are millions unable to face the new day creatively.
How many of them feel as blank as a turned off TV screen? How
many of them walk to the corner shop to buy a Mars Bar? And how
many attend a football game to run riot?

I did not say all this to my young friend. He did not need a lecture
from me. I even resisted telling him the specific statistics that I
learnt last weekend about 'unemployment-depression' in South
Wales. In South and Mid-Glamorgan the number of suic- ides has

increased over the last year by twenty-two per cent. More than half of those in Wales who attempt to kill themselves are unemployed. And those out of work for more than a year are nineteen times more likely to commit suicide than those with jobs.

'When I do manage to write a poem,' the young man said, 'may I show it to you?'

'I'd rather you didn't,' I said.

In our back garden in Golders Green, a host of golden dandelions! Or such was the case a couple of weeks ago. Now, though, the cherry blossom in wedding splendour floats its white petal confetti down to the rough grass and everywhere there are bluebells, bluebells, bluebells. I cannot help being reminded of Manley Hopkins who once remarked, 'I do not think I have ever seen anything more beautiful than the bluebell... I know the beauty of our Lord by it.'

One May, years ago, I had a visit from a Polish writer, Jerzy Sito, who has translated Shakespeare and Donne, as well as some modern British poets, into his native language. Like Hopkins, he was enchanted by bluebells and told me — it still seems improbable — that there were no bluebells in Poland. He asked if he could take some to plant in his garden. Some years later he wrote that there were now active bluebells in Poland and all of them had come from our garden in Golders Green. I stick out my chest, swanky.

My father-in-law, Jack Mercer, who is still a vigorous 94 year old, offered us his new painting. He has been painting, as a hobby, since he retired and over the years he has given many of his pictures away to friends and relatives. Yet one Jack painted, over a decade ago, he keeps on the wall of his front room. It is a self-portrait, an idealised self-portrait. There he is, younger by far, looking somewhat like a blue-eyed film star. My father-in-law is and was a good looking fellow, but this self-portrait glamorizes him, erases the very defects which I think make his face more interesting.

If we could all paint self-portraits as competently as he, would we, too, artfully attempt to make ourselves somewhat more beautiful? After all, when it comes to photographs, the ones that flatter us a little, while remaining recognizably us, are the ones we like best! Mind you, all photographs, if we wait long enough, flatter us. Still, if I could paint adequately I don't think I would want a self-portrait on my wall. I would rather have hanging there some Maja on the balcony, some Virgin of the Rocks. Then with Ezra Pound perhaps I could whisper:

> The eyes of this dead lady speak to me.
> For here was love, was not to be drowned out.
> And here desire, not to be kissed away.

How much do portraits reveal a man's or a woman's character? Hazlitt believed that a man's life may be a lie to himself and to others but 'a picture of him painted by a great artist would probably stamp his true character on the canvas and betray the secret to posterity'.

I hope Hazlitt was wrong. Some years back Josef Herman painted a powerful portrait of me. He sold it to the gallery of the Welsh National Museum and when my mother went to have a look at it there — she was then in her eighties — she made an embarrassing fuss. 'That's not my son,' she apparently said to everybody within megaphone distance, 'that looks like the devil.' They finally had to call the curator. Meanwhile she stared at the nearby idealised painting of Dylan Thomas by Augustus John, all curly hair, all soulful eyes. My mother seethed. No wonder, soon after, Josef Herman's portrait was removed to the darkness of the Museum's store room. As my mother said, 'Now, if Jack had painted you, you would have looked as nice as Dylan Thomas.'

Robert Edwards and Patrick Steptoe, the 'test-tube baby' pion-eers, based at Bourn Hall, Cambridge, have stressed the obstet- rical and social risks involved in promoting multiple pregnancies and have criticised the Hammersmith Hospital team under Mr Robert Winston, who implanted six embryos in the uterus of a certain Mrs Janice Smale with the result that this lady gave birth to quads. (The other two fertilized eggs did not develop.) Robert Winston has responded angrily, 'We do not carry out research on embryos or freeze them for later use as they do at Bourn Hall.'

Bob Edwards is the most audacious scientist I have ever met and one who, since a boy, has been almost obsessively interested in pregnancy, animal and human. I recall with what enthusiasm he once told me how the beginnings of life have never failed to fascinate him. He was thrilled when he first observed the human embryos he had incubated divide into two cells, into four cells, into eight cells, each cell with its own nucleus. It was the beauty of the embryo's growth, the way it became magnificently organ- ised, how it switched on its own biochemistry, and increased its size and prepared itself for implantation in the womb that excited him.

More than that: how the embryo's organs form, the cells gradu- ally becoming capable of developing into heart and lung, brain and eye. 'What a unique and wonderful process it is,' he said, 'as the increasing number of cells diverge and specialize in a delicate, integrated and coordinated manner. One day all the secrets of this early development may be known and those same secrets may help us to repair the ravages and defects in the tissues of sick and ageing men and women.'

Bob Edwards is a man with a bold vision. And Patrick Steptoe, too, is no slouch when it comes to responsible medical advent- uring. So when these two men grumble about others going too far, I feel instinctively we should be alerted. But Mr Robert Winston, too, in his reponses, has made statements to which we should pay close attention. He has written in the *Observer* that the standards of infertility treatment in this country are scandalously poor. He makes the shocking accusation that 'Women are given drugs to ovulate when they ovulate already; much tubal surgery is per- formed with instruments more suitable for sharpening pencils....' Such serious charges should be considered seriously and the pub- lic not diverted into wondering instead about the ethical dimen- sions of freezing embryos.

Not that the practice of freezing embryos is one to be ignored. Already there is a tiny baby in Australia who less than a year ago was but a frozen embryo. In the same Melbourne Hospital where that baby was born there are, it seems, hundreds of other embryos in suspended animation.

Already, in the eighteenth century, the remarkable Dr John Hunter imagined that, 'it might be possible to prolong life to any period by freezing a person in the frigid zone as I thought all action and waste would cease until the body thawed. I thought that if a man could give up the last years of his life to this kind of alternative oblivion and action, it might be prolonged to a thousand years; and by getting himself thawed every hundred years he might learn what had happened during his frozen condition....'

Hunter took two living carp and froze them in river water. When he eventually thawed them out the fish were dead, dead as fish fingers! The embryological researches carried out at Bourn Hall and all over our 1984 world are likely to be much more successful. No wonder scientists and doctors such as Bob Edwards and Robert Winston await guidance from the Warlock Committee who report to the Government in June about the legal, ethical and social implications of 'test-tube' fertilization and embryo research.

I put on an old sports jacket I had not worn for years. In one of its pockets I found an envelope on the back of which I had written: 'I'm never at home in a garden; I'm always a visitor.' I quite like that, but did I make it up myself or did I copy it from some book I had read? I don't remember.

I am a sucker for aphoristic sayings. I love wisdom stories, parables, proverbs. Many seem to stick in my head. When I was a student I stayed in a boarding house which had a card on the wall. It read: 'If you have two pennies to spend, spend one penny on bread that you may live; spend the other on a flower that you may have a reason for living.' This was purported to be an Old Chinese saying and is, I realize now, rather twee. But I liked it at the time and it has stayed with me.

Then there's the old Zen saying I came across and which I'm still not ashamed to know and quote: 'To a man who knows nothing, mountains are mountains, waters are waters and trees are trees. But when he has studied and knows a little, mountains are no longer mountains, waters no longer waters and trees no longer trees. But when he has thoroughly understood, mountains are once again mountains, waters are waters and trees are trees.'

Some 'wise' sayings stay with me from the days when I was a medical student. For instance, there's Pliny's complaint that the Greek physician was the 'only person who could kill another with sovereign impunity' or the dictum of a certain twentieth century

London consultant that 'the anus is the sentinel of social security.'

Parables? Here's one I learned from Martin Buber of the Baal-Shem that particularly appeals to me: 'Once some musicians stood and played, and a great group moved in dance in accordance with the voice of the music. Then a deaf man came there who knew nothing of music and dancing and thought in his heart, "How foolish these men are: some beat with their fingers on all kinds of implements and others turn themselves this way and that".'

I wish somebody would edit an Oxford Book of Parables and Wisdom Sayings. I would be the first to buy a copy. I hope such an editor would sensibly include in it wry Yiddish jokes for some, in fact, are very close to being proverbs. Take, for example, that modern definition of a psychiatrist: 'A Jewish doctor who hates the sight of blood.' Or better still that older one: 'If the rich could hire other people to die for them the poor would make a wonderful living.' I wonder what shadowy, bearded figure dressed in ridiculous black, walking somewhere in Latvia or Lithuania, Poland or Russia, suddenly pulled out his pencil and, inspired and feelingly, wrote that down on the back of an envelope.

June 1984

I was asked to participate some years ago in a pilot programme for a projected TV series entitled *Friends of John Betjeman*. I hardly knew Sir John so was surprised by the invitation. However, I enjoyed his poems and looked forward to spending a day with him at the London Weekend Studios.

Over a lively lunch John Betjeman told me he would begin the programme with Thomas Hood's poem, 'I remember, I remember, the house where I was born.' He continued, 'Some may think it sentimental but it isn't, it isn't, and I don't care if it is.' After Hood's poem, the Poet Laureate then intended to air his enthusiasm for other poets including Edward Thomas. He would request Prunella Scales to read Thomas's 'Adlestrop'. 'At this point you come into it,' he advised me. 'We'll talk about Edward Thomas before I ask you to read your poem, 'Not Adlestrop,' all right?'

Before we went into the studio I asked if he, Sir John, had been influenced by Thomas Hood, by, for instance, the rhythms of 'The Bridge of Sighs'. Sir John gave me a dazzling smile before opening his eyes wide to recite by heart the whole of 'The Bridge of Sighs'. Hearing that poem mediated through his voice Hood sounded utterly Betjemanesque:

> In she plunged boldly
> No matter how coldly
> The rough river ran.
> Over the brink of it
> Picture it — think of it
> Dissolute man!...
>
> Take her up tenderly
> Lift her with care
> Fashioned so slenderly
> Young and so fair.

Soon after, we sat in the harsh TV lights — Sir John, Prunella Scales and I — for a rehearsal. His illness had left him in decline and though he could recite Thomas Hood at length, and accurately, he displayed memory lapses which agitated the producer. The latter began to wonder whether Sir John was now capable of performing as 'an anchor man' for the seven programmes planned. Prunella Scales, who was accustomed to working with Sir John Betjeman, whispered, 'Don't worry, he's always like this at rehearsal. When we actually do it, he'll be brilliant, you'll see.'

During the actual performance before a studio audience Sir John, alas, did lose his place and did bumble rather. He forgot to mention Edward Thomas so I had to ask him, 'Do you like Edward Thomas, his poem 'Adlestrop' for instance?' I did not think these promptings mattered too much. Soon he was asking Prunella Scales to read Thomas's poem and his hesitations, his transparent recoveries, his now obvious vulnerability, surely made him all the more likeable to a viewing audience? Certainly the studio audience warmed to him.

The producer, though, felt the programme was not smooth and professional enough. So the series was cancelled and this pilot programme not shown. I wish they would find a slot for an edited version of it now. Viewers do not want mere slick professionalism and would surely respond to his enthusiasm and to his hesitating, friendly unpredictability.

After that pilot programme many of the studio audience approached Sir John with books to be signed. Books by John Betjeman piled up in front of him. It so happened that on the table lay my own *Collected Poems* from which I had read earlier. John Betjeman, signing book after book, accidentally wrote his signature in mine. Thus I can proudly boast that, in my bookcase, I now have my *Collected Poems* signed by John Betjeman. That should fool one or two collectors!

Dr Billy Graham has long been described as a particularly charismatic evangelist. It was cold that recent May day in Sunderland, when he preached to the 16,000 crowd in the football stadium at Roker Park. Whatever else charisma does for you, it does not keep you warm. 'It's the coldest open air weather I've ever preached in,' Dr Graham complained. He admitted to wearing two pairs of thermal underwear. When you come down from the mountain should you feel so cold?

We use the term 'charisma' nowadays to signify a magical, appealing power that certain individuals emanate. Successful prophets have it, messiahs trade on it, fringe healers depend on it, politicians long for it, evangelists such as Dr Graham (they say) exude it. Such charismatic characters, it would appear, are capable of generating a collective excitement among those who spiritually surrender to them.

Psychoanalysts tell us that we all possess a vestigial longing to discover a god-like personage with unlimited power and wisdom. When we were children we believed our parents to be omniscient and omnipotent. The child is father of the man and our longing to discover our parents as they once seemed to be, becomes more pronounced when we feel defeated and helpless. Then we are most open to the hypnotic power of a seemingly caring charis- matic figure who, we irrationally hope, can solve our problems and our ills. Such a figure may be both father and mother to us. Father-like, authoritatively, he will tell us what we must do and simultaneously, mother-like, he will comfort us, be infinitely sympathetic.

The hypnotist works like that. 'Raise your right arm,' he commands us with masculine sternness. Then in a darkened room, stroking us gently, softening his voice to a lullaby, mother-like, he tells us, 'You're sleepy now, child, very sleepy.'

The psychoanalysts' view that charismatic leaders are able to project both the masculine and feminine components of their personality like hypnotists, seems to me to be plausible. Take Mrs Thatcher, for instance. There are those, a considerable number, who do not believe her to be The Great British Disaster. On the contrary, be they Cabinet subservient or troubled Mrs Smith, our neighbour, they find in her the bossy masculine prototype, our stern Daddy, and, at the same time, when she turns her feminine side towards them, our dear, sweet Mum. In short, just what the patient ordered.

But to get back to Dr William Graham. What I want to know is — what does wearing two sets of thermal underwear do for your charisma?

My favourite religious charismatic was one who lived in twelfth century Yemen. (His name escapes me.) When he proclaimed himself to be the Messiah he was hauled in chains before the King who himself was a lineal descendant of Fatima, the Prophet's daughter. The King, a doubting man evidently, invited the chained fanatic to prove his credentials.

'Maybe perform some miracle?' suggested the King.

The aspiring messiah agreed. 'Cut off my head,' he urged the King confidently. 'Then I'll return to life again.'

The King obliged the charismatic and subsequently, with growing disappointment, waited patiently for the miracle that did not take place.

That cold day in May when Billy Graham wore his two pairs of knickers I leaned over the railings of the lower pond in Golders Hill Park watching the Australian white swan with the black neck. It hardly moved, remaining there in concussed reverie. It was late, almost closing time, and the Park had emptied.

I walked up and around in a horizontal arc towards the main gate. Then I observed, in front of me, a figure sprawled on a wooden bench, swathed in cloth, an old balaclava about his head, a scarf up to his nostrils. If I had been a child I would have known, without a doubt, that here, now, that May evening, I had encountered the primal Bogeyman!

Being an adult, I merely looked around uneasily for other human company. No one else was about. I approached, his eyes were shut and I thought how the night dreams of the sane and of the insane are little different from each other. He did not move and I began to wonder if he were dead. For a moment I watched him as I had the swan earlier. Both so motionless. Then, to my relief, the inert figure stirred and I passed on, leaving the tramp, if tramp he was, to his own dreamings. As I left the park the lamps in West Heath Drive lit up and the earliest dark flowed through the railings; and I wondered if the Bogeyman would stay on that bench all night. Poor old fella.

It is not every day that one's son gets married. Disliking formality, I had not at first been overjoyed when he and his bride, Sue Morris, decided they wanted a religious ceremony followed by a real reception. Weddings, I believed, should be observed quietly. Besides, it meant me wearing my one suit which is a bit hot for June. In the event, the ceremony was touchingly beautiful and the reception an occasion of much pleasure. All the same I was somewhat taken aback that I received so many requests not to make a speech.

Perhaps some present recalled that, once upon a time when I was sour sixteen, I took part in a school debate in which I advocated that the Institution of Marriage was Bankrupt. I have, after my own experience, changed my mind. Balzac, surely, was utterly sensible when he declared that it is as absurd to say that a man can't love one woman all the time as it is to say that a violinist needs several violins to play the same piece of music.

It is a long time (1951) since the *Ham and High* wickedly announced our fugitive wedding. 'Dannie Abse of 50 Belsize Square', the hound reported, 'married Joan Mercer of 50 Belsize Square at Hampstead Registry Office'. Afterwards Joan and I went off to the Blue Danube Club in Swiss Cottage with a few of our slightly drunk friends. It was a really nice occasion: I'm just sorry my son and his bride could not have been there.

I live a guarded life. I rarely have to embark on the intrepid adventure of shopping. On Thursday, though, I needed to post a parcel to the U.S.A. and I discovered I had no money on me. 'I'll just pop into the bank,' I told my wife. 'I won't be long'. She then, unusually, asked me to do some shopping for her at Sainsbury's. 'Just a few items,' she reassured me.

So off I went on my great mission, first to Barclays Bank, then to Golders Green Post Office, then to Sainsbury's. As I walked down Rodborough Road the sun shone down on the debris from Mac-Donalds that had thoughtfully been shoved at happy intervals in the green hedges of front gardens. Seeing me with shopping bag the birds whistled in the trees, delighted.

At Barclays Bank I waited in a morose queue. Nobody smiled. I waited and waited. Eventually I cashed my cheque and left the reverent hushed atmosphere of the bank for the noise of Finchley Road. I walked the length of a cricket pitch before reaching Golders Green Post Office where the queue stretched almost to the door and looked even more depressed. So much so that I felt everybody urgently needed a dose of electro-convulsive therapy. I waited and I waited and I waited. At last I reached the grid where a reasonably civil, civil servant picked up my parcel very slowly. I took my own pulse.

Later I crossed the road to the emporium of Sainsbury's where I cleverly selected the items my wife required, then found I had to join an impossible queue to pay for them. I waited and I waited and I waited and I waited. In Sainsbury's one has to be more patient than a patient. No wonder a row began. Some gent devoid of his motorcar had pushed an old lady aside and a strenuous young woman bottled up with just feminist ardour went into battle against this masculine swine. I agreed with her, but some minutes later I was prepared to certify several members of the queue, especially those ahead of me.

By the time I returned to the safety of my own house the best part of the morning had gone. My wife did not ask me why I had taken so long to do so little. Like a child I suggested simplistically that Barclays Bank, the Post Office, Sainsbury's, etc. should employ more people and give us all a better service. 'Vote to reduce queues,' I said, 'including those in the Job Centres.' 'Isn't it the head man at Sainsbury's whose advice the Prime Minister is going to take about the reorganization of the National Health Service?' my wife asked.

Drug addiction in Britain is a growing problem. That I knew; but I was surprised when I learnt how often the drug addict turns out to be the favourite son of a family. Common to many a drug addict, apparently, is an over-close relationship with his mother. From case histories it is evident that not infrequently the mother of the drug addict has no husband — he may have taken off or died years earlier. Thus the widow or grass widow feels all the more need to be needed by her son who develops, as it were, into a surrogate husband.

If such are the satisfactions of a number of such mothers what are those of their sons? Experts testify how patients tell them quite directly that 'the works' as they call it in the argot, (that is to say, the syringe and needle), is like a breast. 'When the addict is high', Dr Isidore Chein has written, 'he feels that he is together with his mother, long ago, warm, comfortable, happy, at peace; when he injects the opiate solution, he mixes the solution with his blood and bounces the blood-opiate mixture back and forth from syringe to vein and, as he does this, he has fantasies of intercourse.'

Such testimonies may seem outlandish, even repugnant to some. Yet only through such interpretations can the addict's description of a fix be understood. Alexander Trocchi, the Scottish novelist who died recently was an addict and he wrote in Cain's Book: 'When one presses the bulb of the eye-dropper and watches the pale, blood-streaked liquid disappear through the nozzle and into the needle and the vein it is not, not only, a question of feeling good. It's not only a question of kicks. The ritual itself, the powder in the spoon, the little ball of cotton, the matches applied, the bubbling liquid drawn up through the cotton filter into the eye-dropper, the tie round the arm to make a vein stand out, the fix often slow because a man will stand there with the needle in the vein and allow the level in the eye-dropper to waver up and down, up and down, until there is more blood than heroin in the dropper — all this is not for nothing: it is born of a respect for the whole chemistry of alienation. When a man fixes he is turned on almost instantaneously ... you can speak of a flash, a tinily murmured orgasm in the bloodstream, in the central nervous system.'

Trocchi was glamorizing something sad and shabby and sick and I doubt if he understood fully the symbolic significance of what he was saying.

July 1984

A Canterbury Tale Chaucer did not write concerns a consultant surgeon, Mr M.R. Williams FRCS, who allowed his friend, the vet, to assist him during a hernia operation at a local hospital. Mr Williams, who used to teach medical students at St Thomas's Hospital, apparently allowed the vet to make the initial incision and to stitch up afterwards. All this, of course, under his supervision, but the newspapers have reported, 'This revelation has caused serious concern to a shocked medical profession.'

I can imagine the placards in Canterbury: LOCAL VET SHOCK. It is no joke, though, for Mr Williams, already the cemetery side of sixty, has had his retirement date brought forward. I can imagine, too, the patient who, now fully recovered, no doubt pulls up his shirt, lowers his trousers, and boasts, 'Hey, hey, look at this scar. This is what the vet did.'

When I was in South Wales last week it was warm enough to go swimming. And I did — into the dirty waves of Ogmore-by-Sea. Afterwards I had a cup of tea with my friend, Roger Palmer, who works for an air-conditioning firm. The economy in Wales, of course, as everybody knows, is particularly depressed. So one does not ask anyone, 'How's business?' I'm reminded of an old Jewish joke. Mr Cohen complains to Mr Goldstein, 'Goldstein, you never ask me how business is these days.' Goldstein shrugs his shoulders and asks, 'Well, how's business?' Mr Cohen rolls his eyes. 'Don't ask,' he replies.

But Roger Palmer told me *voluntarily* how his firm was doing. 'Business is booming,' he said. 'Fantastic.' I was surprised. That day it was quite hot, but all said and done, South Wales is hardly the South of France. I looked up at the sky. To have air- conditioning put into your villa or slum in Glamorgan does seem somewhat epicurean.

'Oh, it's not for people for the most part,' Roger said scornfully. 'It's for computers.'

I was puzzled until I learnt that computers do not like sticky, muggy weather. So where people work, where they have worked for years, in sometimes muggy conditions, now there stands, or rather sits, a beautiful, spoilt machine. For computers, it seems, are more refined than human beings. They'll go on strike at the hint of thunder. So the air-conditioning business thrives.

Mr Keating telephoned to ask if he could visit me. 'I'm doing a thesis,' he explained. What a sensible fellow, I thought, to undertake a thesis on my work. I warmed to him at once. I would help him. However, I soon gathered that he wanted to interview me only because he had begun writing a thesis on Stevie Smith!

'I would be obliged,' he said, 'if you would give me your impressions of her as a person. I know you shared a platform with Stevie Smith on various occasions. I once heard you both at the Theatre Royal in Stratford East.'

He had heard us both, I pondered, and wanted to write a thesis on Stevie. I cooled towards the fellow in an instant. I claimed, truthfully, little acquaintance with Stevie Smith, but Mr Keating was insistent. Reluctantly I agreed to see him.

I would tell him about another telephone call I had once received that led to my one and only altercation with Stevie Smith. It was from David Carver, the then Secretary of the PEN, who wanted my opinion about the current standing of Robin Skelton's reputation, who, visiting London from Canada, had offered to give a poetry reading for PEN. David Carver had, in any case, it seemed, intended to sponsor a PEN reading some time at the Porchester Hall and was, indeed, on the look-out for an important poet-reader.

'Would Skelton attract a large enough audience?' asked Mr

Carver. 'Do you think it would be better if I asked someone like Stevie Smith instead?'

'Why not both of them?' I suggested.

I knew that Stevie would draw an audience. During the last few years she had become popular partly because of the Poetry and Jazz readings arranged by Jeremy Robson. Stevie was considerably older than the other poets who shared that platform with her. She was almost 70 and looked like a very thin great-aunt about to say 'Don't'. Perhaps the audience had expected, from her appearance, to hear dull hymns to Flowers, Elves and Bees. At first they viewed her with suspicion but soon she was reciting:

> I was much too far out all my life
> And not waving but drowning.

Or surprisingly, she would sing her lines excruciatingly, daringly, off-key. The audience warmed to her, cheered her audacity.

Later David Carver telephoned to say that Stevie wanted to read solo. She had declared that she never read with anyone else!

'Nonsense,' I said. 'I'll persuade her if you like.'

Most poets prefer not to read in tandem but usually agree to do so if pressed. And if Robin Skelton wanted to read, well, why not?

My telephone call to Stevie was a disaster. She was harsh, regally adamant. She did not sound like the Stevie Smith I knew. She seemed to be invaded by some alien personality, one I had never met and I put down the telephone, upset, defeated. So Stevie Smith read at the Porchester Hall, solo. I did not attend her reading.

Some months later I met her at a party and, happily, we became 'friends' again. That was the last time I saw Stevie for, soon after, she became ill, suffering from a brain tumour. In retrospect, I wonder whether her apparent personality change, her uncharacteristic response to my telephone call, was an early sign of her lesion. Probably not. In any case, I can hardly imagine how such a surmise can help Mr Keating one way or another.

*

The man at the bar took the pipe out of his mouth and said to Vernon Scannell, 'Since you're a poet you should know where this comes from.' Then he proudly recited, 'Loveliest of trees...' Vernon

interrupted him with, 'Housman'. The man narrowed his eyes.
'Look,' he said, 'if you can tell me who wrote this I'll buy you a
pint.' He recited more Housman and Vernon Scannell replied,
'A.E. Housman.' The pint glass was soon emptied. 'I'll buy you
another one,' said the pipe-smoking gentleman reciter of poetry,
'if you guess who the author is this time.'

He intoned more lines of verse and yet again Vernon Scannell
interrupted him with a triumphant, 'Housman.' The quiz continued, the prize always being a pint. However, the man who
wanted to recite poetry and confound Vernon Scannell knew only
the work of Housman. He kept on reciting his favourite poet and
as Vernon called out Housman, each time less clearly, pints were
bought for all. Just before closing time, though, I don't think
Vernon heard what lines were being recited, yet clever as Dick, he
mumbled, 'Housman.' And the man was amazed at Vernon's
extraordinary erudition.

It always surprises me how many people, given half a chance,
will with evident pleasure recite the verses they know off by heart.
My own mother, after a couple of wine gums, could be persuaded,
drear of tone and wild of eye, to recite 'Hiawatha' — the whole of
it. Once my mother got going she was hard to stop. 'O the famine
and the fever!' she would howl. 'O the wailing of the children!'

There used to be an annual Festival of Spoken Poetry. It went on
successfully for some thirty years until 1959. The winner that last
year was a beautiful young lady named Betty Mulcahy. Not long
ago I happened to hear Ms Mulcahy read out loud, at a concert, a
poem by Vernon Scannell. The poem, a striking one, was called
'Taken in Adultery'. The Master of Ceremonies who introduced
the reading did so without punctuation. Breathlessly he said,
'Betty Mulcahy, taken in adultery by Vernon Scannell.' That made
a few people raise their eyebrows.

I understand that recently some 1.4 million Americans have been
in London. I should think that figure is correct because I reckon 1.2
million of them have called on me. One of my favourite visitors
told me how many of his compatriots in New Orleans have a high
regard for French culture — that if they weren't Americans they
would like to have been French. I thought of the Frenchman who

once told the Duke of Wellington, 'If I wasn't French I should have liked to have been English.' 'If I wasn't English,' the Iron Duke apparently replied, 'I would like to have been English.'

For years I've been grumbling about British Rail. Not so long ago I used to take my father-in-law to Euston Station for his return journey to Lancashire. I never had to worry about finding him an empty seat. It was, because of the extortionate railway prices, a question of him choosing which empty *carriage* he preferred. I would stand on the platform watching the long, almost empty, train pull away and think, 'When I get home I'll write a crisp letter to Peter Parker saying, "*Why don't you lower the fares?*"' I never did, of course.

Several years later some fantastic genius working for BR had the happy idea that the trains might be used a bit if fares were reduced. And so they have been, despite the intricacy of the Saver Fares — those concessions of Byzantine complexity that any fool who possesses the wisdom of Solomon and the patience of Griselda can easily work out.

Last week I caught, or meant to catch, the 3 p.m. train to Liverpool. At Euston I extracted £17 from my pocket, having no Persil boxes on me and asked for the Inter City Saver. 'No Inter City fares after 3 p.m.,' said the clerk victoriously. I was puzzled; last time I bought a ticket Inter City fares were finished after 4 p.m. 'Yes,' said the clerk, 'that used to be so. Now it's 3 p.m.'

Then I remembered the train left at 3 p.m. so I said, 'Well, the train, in any case, leaves at 3 p.m. so surely I can have an Inter City fare?' The clerk was now almost on the verge of laughter. 'That train used to be at 3 p.m.,' he said, 'but they've changed it to 3.05 p.m. Your timetable is, ha, out of date.' Now came the biggest joke of all. 'The fare is 41.50,' the clerk added with purest joy.

I was not going to pay £41 bleeding 50. I turned angrily away. I'll write a letter, I thought. I'll write a letter to BR asking whether those people employed only to change timetables might be given a little rest at the nearest bloody mental hospital. Gradually my anger subsided. I had to go to Liverpool so there was no choice. I turned back to the ticket office, ready to capitulate. Now, though, a queue had formed. I waited, but I think somebody ahead of me

was also having trouble with the arcane secrets of the Fare Struc-
ture. If I loitered any longer I would miss the 3 p.m. train, I mean
the 3.05 p.m. train, thank heavens. So I raced past the barrier like
Steve Ovett, having decided that I would have to pay on the train.

Eventually the ticket collector appeared. I asked for an Inter-City
ticket. '£17, sir,' he said. 'What a nice fellow', I thought. 'What a
nice, ignorant fellow'. After I had given him the money he sweetly
departed and I opened the newspaper that I had brought with me.
At once, a huge BR advertisement caught my eye: PROSPECTS
FOR THE RAILWAY CUSTOMER LOOK MUCH BETTER.

Inspiration. What is its nature, what does it mean? One dictionary
states that it is an 'influence of the Spirit of God upon the human
mind or soul.' Scriptural writers may well have received divine
assistance in preparing their texts but what about us secular lot?

I have always liked Pasteur's words on scientific inspiration —
'Chance favours the prepared mind,' he remarked. I like, too, a
story I heard recently about a champion golfer who, obviously
inspired, holed in one. 'What luck,' cried one bystander. The golfer
nodded. 'You're right,' he said. 'And the odd thing is that the more
I practise the luckier I get.'

August 1984

The dream was continuously black and white. I can only remember
the corybantic rags of it and what I do recall is absurd — as if
Margaret Thatcher appeared on stage in classical ballet dress with
coal dust on her face and wearing a CND badge. Dreams often are
ridiculous. Didn't Freud once say, 'Dreams are most profound
when they seem most crazy'? But then he believed, like the
prophets and kings of old, that a dream uninterpreted was like a
letter unread.

Some dreams stay with us all our lives though they may be
uncoloured and far from spectacular. For instance, I remember one
dream from thirty-five years ago. A bird alighted on my shoulder,

stayed on my shoulder. Because of this feathered creature I was followed by a horde of cats who, in turn, were followed by a procession of dogs. There is more to my dream than that, several disjointed scenes, but I won't elaborate. I do not wish to bore you. For our dreams, generally, while fascinating to ourselves, usually bore others.

Other people's nightmares are a little more interesting perhaps than their milder dreams — such as the one John Ruskin recorded in his diary and commented on as being the ghastliest nightmare of his life. Ruskin in his oneiric trance observed an old dying surgeon dissecting himself. 'It was worse than dissecting — *tearing*,' wrote Ruskin on December 27th, 1875, 'and with circumstances of horror about the treatment of the head which I will not enter.' Ruskin's castration anxieties often seemed to guide the speedless direction and normal delirium of his dreams. He himself sometimes attributed his horror-film night visions to a lamb chop or some other item of food he had too much enjoyed the previous evening.

The patient had the same name as me: Abse. He was a Lebanese Christian. 'Is Abse a common name in the Middle East?' I asked. Unsmiling, he nodded and told me he had encountered the name in Egypt and Syria as well as in the Lebanon. 'It's an old name,' he said. 'Have you heard of the poet, Abse?' Taken aback, I hesitated. 'The great poet, Abse,' he added. This is my day, I thought, but he continued, 'The great poet, Abse, who lived in the sixth century, at the time of the prophet.'

I swallowed. I looked at him suspiciously. But it was quite evident that he did not know that I too scribbled away, scribble, scribble, scribble. 'The great poet, Antara el Abse,' Mr Abse said. 'I'm not a literary man but Antara is famous among Arabs. He was a robber-prince and was half-black.'

Later I learned from reading an essay by Bernard Lewis in an old *Encounter* that the blacks had been persecuted in the Moslem sixth century world. No wonder Antara wrote:

> Half of me comes from the family of Abse,
> The other half I defend with my sword.

I like that. I wouldn't mind sticking those two lines at the top of my notepaper. Indeed, the more I hear of this Antara el Abse the more I'm willing to claim him as a long-lost ancestor.

Once, it seems, a crowd shrank before a huge wild bull. One man cried to Antara, 'Only Antara can deal with that bull.' Antara el Abse nodded in seeming agreement, then answered, 'Ye-es, but does that bull know I'm Antara?'

The Italian waiter was, you might say, operatic. He ignored our earnest conversation about the miners' sorry predicament and the Government's expensive inflexibility and sang a Verdi phrase or two as he served us. At the next table, the lady, smiling, asked for the bill. He presented it to her as though it were a bouquet of roses. She said, putting on her glasses, 'Does this include service?' He almost pirouetted. 'Yes, madam,' he said, 'it includes service, but not the tip.'

My companions discussed Goethe's dying words, 'Mehr licht.' One of them wondered whether Goethe, in pronouncing his 'More light' was merely requesting greater illumination in order that he might see more clearly the beautiful face of the woman at his bedside. Another, more religiously inclined, suggested that he was trying to tell those in attendance something about the nature of heaven whose gates he was at. After all, there is a legend that in the world to come the light of the moon shall be as the light of the sun and the light of the sun shall be sevenfold.

Why do Last Words interest us at all? Why do they seem more important than say, the utterances of a man or woman on the occasion of a 40th birthday? Do we assume that only at the end of life can a lifetime's vision be summarized in one pithy sentence, be whispered, like a secret, to the near and dear ones at the bedside? Or do we believe that a man faced with death will reveal himself as never before, not wishing in that solemn hour to deceive any-one?

More likely our curiosity springs from the childish belief that a man or woman at Death's portals is well-placed to tell us something of the terrain from which no traveller returns and for which we are, alas, all eventually bound. We who are tourists not yet set out, listen fearfully to a tourist who has almost awesomely arrived.

The fact is, though, that those recorded words of the dying are almost always falsified or just simply manufactured. Goethe, for instance, did not actually whisper, 'Mehr licht.' Instead, he softly requested, 'Open the second shutter so that more light can come in.' But how much more memorable is the fictive, ambiguous, 'More Light.' If Goethe had lived to record his own dying words they would doubtless have been more memorable still!

Spike Milligan once asked me if I knew Gladstone's Dying Words. I shook my head. Putting on a Spike Milligan funny voice Spike Milligan uttered, 'I feel better now.' Perhaps Gladstone did actually expire with those words. For surely the more banal the saying the more likely it is to be true. I do not believe Beethoven's spooky and striking, 'I shall hear in heaven.' I do believe King George V's 'How is the Empire?'

Yesterday I went in search of a haircut. I had put off visiting a barber because...well, who over 40 years of age enjoys visiting a hairdresser?

Each time you submit to the snip snip snip of a triumphant pair of scissors you observe how the hair clinging to the front of the white gown has become more silvery and aged. As if that were not defeating enough, they make you face a mirror, a huge, tactless, devil-mirror. And when the snip snip snip is over they, cockily, hold another swinish mirror to the back of your head, force you to admit to yourself that the bald patch lying there has spread yet again territorially and is freehold.

Why do hairdressers insist on having so many voyeuring mirrors around? Have they, as a breed, like actors, a mirror fetish?

Apart from insulting you with the uncompromising reality of mirrors they also insist upon making complacent conversation.

'Have you had your holiday yet?'

'Not yet.'

Snip snip snip. You know the hairdresser is desperately trying to think of something else to say. So being a nice guy, you help out.

'Have you had *your* holiday yet?'

'Not yet.'

Snip snip snip. You think: Shall I ask her where she's thinking of going when she goes? You desist. You've done your bit.

Snip snip snip. 'Do you work around here?' she asks, inspired.

You have to pay for such fascinating conversations. That big bill could not be just for the haircut. For gone are the days, alas, when a haircut cost half a crown. Now, women often cut men's hair and they do it well, very well. But a high price has to be paid to hire a Delilah.

Certainly an absurdly high price around these parts. Yesterday I went into a hairdressing Unisex emporium in Golders Green Road. It looked fairly classy with potted plants and Radio 2 wall-paper-music. The Delilahs all had clean fingernails. 'How much,' I asked, 'for a trim?' When they told me the price I had to emphasise I wanted a haircut not an operation.

I do not know why, just before I sat down at this desk, Paddy Muir came to mind. I have little in common with him. I have not seen him these many years, not since he and his wife emigrated to Canada. Yet suddenly, for no apparent reason, a minute or so before the telephone sounded, I thought of him. I walked into the hall, picked up the receiver and heard his voice. I felt curiously cold at the back of my neck. It's time, I thought, time to consult oracles, pay attention to inklings and omens. Simply, though, he was in London, and he decided well, why not, he would just telephone me, old mate, to see how I was getting on. Still writing poems are you? 'I've just had a haircut,' I said.

Coincidences. They occur all the time, increasingly, I fancy, as the years pass by, as the pages are blown over. Things happen that we knew would happen before the door opened. The feeling of having been here before. And 'déjà vu' we say, as if the mystery named is the mystery solved. And 'synchronicity' we say, as if that word itself were a diagnosis and an explanation of all coincidences.

Was it Jung who first used the word 'synchronicity' to indicate a meaningful coincidence? But what was meaningful about P. Muir telephoning me 35 minutes ago? And why am I thinking now of another coincidence, one more odd, which concerns a Saturday morning journey across London in 1948 when I was a medical student?

That morning in June, I had set out from my digs in 38 Aberdare Gardens, NW6, carrying a bag and a cricket bat, for Finchley Road underground station. I was on my way to play cricket for Westminster Hospital whose sports ground was located in those of a mental institution in South London. So I had to travel to Charing Cross, change to the Northern Line, continue to South Clapham before taking a final short bus ride.

When I entered the train at Finchley Road I was not thinking of my journey or of cricket but of a telephone conversation I had had the previous day with Louis MacNeice whom, at that time I had not met. I sat down and, soon after, overheard an animated conversation going on about poetry-drama. I looked up in surprise and with some alarm for one of the two men in conversation opposite me looked like Louis MacNeice — or rather, looked like a photograph I had seen of Louis MacNeice in a book.

At Charing Cross Station the man resembling Louis MacNeice got up and quit the carriage at the same time as I did, and on the platform I dared to stammer, 'Excuse me, are you Louis MacNeice?'

'No,' the man said, unsmilingly.

Embarrassed, I moved away as fast as I could and, in adolescent confusion, lost my way. Eventually I discovered the correct platform for trains on the Northern Line travelling south. As I approached, the doors of a waiting train began to close and I spurted forward, managing to extend my cricket bat just in time to prevent the doors shutting completely. All the doors of the train had to open again so, victoriously, if somewhat self-conscious, I strutted into the carriage.

He was sitting opposite me. He was staring at me and at my cricket bat with transparent distaste. I did not look again at Louis MacNeice's doppelganger but gazed at the back of my hand entranced almost all the way to South Clapham where, to my horror, he stood up preparing to exit.

I allowed him to get ahead of me. He shot forward purposefully; I loitered. He walked up the ascending escalator; I rested on its rail with chronic inertia. I pretended not to notice how, when he reached the top, he looked over his shoulder rather wildly.

It must have been all of three minutes before I found him at the bus queue. I had almost decided to walk but the damned bus came trundling in. Because he went downstairs I took my bat and bag upstairs.

Five minutes later when I descended, he was ready to alight also. It was incredible. We had journeyed from Finchley Road Tube Station to this same bus-stop in South Clapham. On the pavement, as the bus moved away, he swivelled towards me, pulled out his wallet, extracted delicately from it a visiting card which he offered me as proof that he was not Louis MacNeice.

'I'm not following you,' I protested vehemently. 'I'm going to play cricket in there.'

I pointed my cricket bat towards the main gates of the hospital. He followed the direction of my bat and read the big sign which indicated that these were the gates of a Mental Asylum.

Mouth open, he walked away with undignified haste.

In those post-war days when I lodged in 38 Aberdare Gardens, I often visited the cafés of Swiss Cottage. Sometimes I encountered there that gifted sculptor, William Turnbull. Last night, while watching the News on television I thought of Bill Turnbull and of a story he once told me.

On the TV screen they showed, as usual, how in Britain now, Violence no longer snores in the armchair but roams the streets. War in Northern Ireland, then war on the mainland — this time police rioting near a colliery. It is no use talking about the law, I thought, justice has its eternal statutes. Then, abruptly, the script was no longer devised by our Prime Minister for the cameras took us to Australia, to a helicopter flying over bolting wild horses. Gunners in this same helicopter were shooting them. Not all these horses died instantly. They were being slaughtered, apparently, because they had infected with TB some of the valuable cattle of the Australian plains.

But what you may ask has this to do with William Turnbull, sculptor? Bill had been in the RAF and one day, while out on exercise, his plane, along with others, flew low over the sea. When the squadron suddenly observed on shore a colony of seals, one of the planes banked down and started shooting them up. Other pilots, daft in their own adrenaline, dived down and soon all the guns were mindlessly firing tak tak tak, just for the hell of it. They fired and fired, the aircrews shouting loud, the guns all blazing. The seals tried to slide into the sea, the rocks and shingle a wriggling, black mass of seals. Then Bill saw it, they all saw it: the foam at the edge of the sea the colour of raw meat, a most disconcerting, shocking red.

Last night, after I turned off the News, as I sat opposite the blank television screen I wondered if Bill Turnbull had seen the shooting from the air of those frightened wild horses. If he did so, I know what he would be remembering and what colour he would be thinking of.

September 1984

At the back of letters I send off to correspondents in the U.S.A. I set down, according to custom, my address. After writing down the number of my house, the name of my street, and then London NW11 8NH, please sir, do I write England or United Kingdom or Great Britain?

England suffices, I suppose, when I write from London. Often, though, I am in Wales and send off letters from Wales. Despite the success of English imperialism, I cannot write Wales, England, for the phantom of Owain Glyndwr would breathe coldly forever down the back of my neck and share my bed. Nor can I write Wales, near England, for that description, however accurate, seems absurd. Yet I have to add some geographical location for the sake of the American mailmen who think Wales merely to be the name of the cemetery where Elizabeth Taylor wants to be buried — when she's dead, that is.

I feel ill at ease setting down United Kingdom — not because of some feminists who would name it United Queendom — but because these days we are so many nations and so disunited. We are living in a state of latent civil war not only in Northern Ireland but on the mainland also. Besides, Americans call us Brits. That suggests perhaps I should write Great Britain.

However when I have added great to Britain I hear distant drums roll and bugles toot. I feel grandiose claiming I am a Great Brit.

Sticking on the stamp in Golders Green Post Office in Finchley Road I would feel obliged to hum to myself, 'Rule Britannia, Britannia Rules the Waves'. I can imagine how, for some reason, people would then move away from me. On the other hand, I probably would get served pronto by the usually yawning Post-Office clerk.

Great Britain? Who first used that appellation? Presumably it was a self-description but I have always understood that we, as a nation, are prone to understatement. Still, Mrs Thatcher talks about making Britain 'Great' again. To which I can only add the Welsh exclamation, 'Ach y fi'. For the very word 'great' in this context brings to my mind, and perhaps to others of my gener- ation, those lunatics, Hitler and Mussolini, who wanted their postal addresses to be A. Hitler, Great Germany, and B. Musso- lini, Great Italy.

There are occasions, of course, when boasting and immodesty are expected. Read the notices of Estate Agents. Their hyperbole matches that of Hollywood. Or look at the blurb of any book. You will find the blurb-writer using the word 'great' unblushingly.

I have just received from Robson Books an advance copy of my autobiography, *A Poet in the Family*, which is now coming out as a paperback ten years after its original publication. On the cover is a photograph of myself and beneath it the inevitable boasting quote. In this case, 'A magnificently conceived work on the auth- or's life' — *Guardian*. (Which it is, Fred, which it verily is!)

However, I have a secret to disclose. When the publisher sent to me for my approval the rough of the cover, the quote beneath my photograph was somewhat briefer. It read, 'Magnificently con- ceived.' My parents, had they been alive, might have wanly smiled at that, or at least raised their eyebrows. But there is a point, as I suggested to Robson Books, where boasting goes too far.

The neighbourhood watch schemes, instigated and encouraged by the police to combat crime, are spreading. They have reached my area. I have been circularised and told the names of the ten wardens who live within a stone's throw of my house. Good luck to them. I understand that through these neighbourhood schemes the crime rate has been drastically reduced. It would be more universally reduced if the Government tackled the unemployment problem with greater commitment.

Nobody likes burglars. Not even other burglars. I have never been able to forget a cartoon I once saw in the *New Yorker* a decade or so ago. It was of a very scared, masked burglar trying to rouse a sleeping couple. The caption read: 'Wake up, wake up. There's a noise downstairs and it's not me!'

Before the American elections are over we may hear more about one Jerry Falwell, whose TV programme 'Old Time Gospel Hour' is so popular in the USA. He tells viewers that nuclear war and apocalypse are at hand. Devout Christians, however, need not worry. They have a wonderful future. 'We don't need to go to bed at night wondering if someone's going to push the button and destroy the planet between now and sunrise,' he declaims. The reason for such complacency, apparently, is that before the holocaust genuine Christians will be taken protectively straight up to Heaven by God, the Father.

It is reported that Jerry Falwell has the ear of Ronald Reagan. Certainly he is urging his mesmerised followers to vote Republican. Perhaps doubting viewers will see the menace and irony in this? Joke: We shall bomb Soviet Russia in five minutes.

Last Sunday, I thought of Jerry Falwell when I visited a nursing home in Kent. As I quit my parked car I saw a group of people, some in shade, some in sunlight. They looked weary and sick. Suddenly one of the denizens was at my side. She was one who had recently 'seen the light'. Now she said to me gently, 'The day of our death is the most beautiful day of our lives.'

I did not say to her that with such a belief she should vote Republican. I did not respond in any way. She had, it would seem, inner peace and serenity whereas I live in this confusing world of 'I don't know'. The woman was smiling at me as I walked on. I know that smile. I have seen it depicted in a painting on the countenance of a bloodily-arrowed St Sebastian.

It is hopeless to argue with those who know the rapture of certainty, as new converts do, be they religious converts, born-again communists, or whatever. For converts find intelligible our unintelligible world, hear sweet dialectical harmony where we listen to dissonance, see a clear pattern where we observe only amorphous mass. And should we present them with contradictory facts how soon these are adapted, fitted, interfused into the harmony or pattern.

All this makes me recall a patient who came into the Casualty Department declaring he was dead. He was certain of this. It was his unshakable belief. When asked if dead men can bleed he replied, 'Of course not.' One of the doctors, then, with a pin drew a little blood on the back of his forearm. The patient stared at it, startled. 'That just goes to show,' he said, 'that dead men do bleed, doctor.'

Research scientists imbued with a relentless spirit of enquiry are a rum lot, admirable though many of them may be. Think of those doctors such as John Hunter who audaciously experimented on themselves for the sake of suffering humankind.

Many watching the TV over-dramatised biography of Sigmund Freud will be reminded of his over-enthusiastic use of cocaine. What a bloodier meal the BBC drama department could have made of another cocaine story: that of the German surgeon August Bier and his assistant Hildenbrandt who, together, initiated the practice of spinal anaesthesia.

It was in the summer of 1898 that Bier suggested to his assistant that they inject cocaine into the spinal fluid before an operation rather than administer a general anaesthetic. First, though, they needed to discover whether this procedure would be effective, would delete the pain of major surgery. It was no use experimenting on animals. The creatures could not give the necessary subjective evidence, could not talk. So they injected cocaine into their own cerebro-spinal fluids before recording their sensations to pain-stimuli with teutonic thoroughness.

For instance, the injection having been given to Hildenbrandt, Bier made an incision in the skin of his assistant's leg, making blood flow. Hildenbrandt blithely remarked that he merely felt the mild pressure of the scalpel. Minutes later Bier grasped a long thick needle and plunged it through the muscles of Hildebrandt's thigh until it grated against the bone. 'I'm feeling nothing,' Hildenbrandt exclaimed delightedly.

Bier lit a cigar and I can imagine how, momentarily, the two men stared at each other before Bier brought down his lit cigar to the skin. His assistant smelt his own flesh burning out but experienced no pain. August Bier picked up a heavy hammer. 'Go ahead,' said Hildenbrandt — in German, of course.

We have our own intrepid scientists in Britain, now, experimenting on themselves. One such is Professor Brindley who works in the Department of Physiology at the Institute of Psychiatry in South East London. With colleagues he has been conducting experiments that could lead to an organic treatment of impotence. He has reported in the *Lancet* that he has injected substances that caused erections lasting two to five hours. Some patients suffered them longer — sorry about that pun — up to forty hours. Such priapism of course is no joking matter. It is a condition terribly distressful as Professor Brindley could testify, for on experimentiing on himself, as well as on other volunteers, he, too, suffered a sustained priapism.

Priapism outside the laboratory is far from common but it can be a most painful side-effect of certain modern drugs. So great credit to the professor because he has now probably discovered an effective therapy for it. For after taking the drug metaraminol he was able to report, 'The smallest dose (0.4 mg) caused conspicuous shrinkage of the penis lasting one and a half hours. During this time it was difficult but not impossible to obtain a psychogenic or reflex erection.'

I shake my head in astonishment. I know that one should be solemn about advances in the treatment of impotence or priapism but I cannot help but smile to myself as I picture the professor sitting in his laboratory, ruler in one hand, stop watch in the other, looking down and excitedly shouting, 'Eureka! Eureka!'

We took our holiday late this year — in the South of France. We had not visited France for more than a decade and my schoolboy French has deteriorated further. I had to leave all conversations to my wife. After all, one must shut up irrevocably if on asking for bread at a restaurant one is served with rabbit.

So I sat on the beach, silent as a monk, reading Peter Ackroyd's biography of T.S. Eliot which had been sent to me for review, thinking how despite that poet's worldly success his life-story was threaded with chapters of ill-health and unhappiness. Or I reclined staring at the sea, thinking of nothing, or remembering my own past (*nostalgie de l'enfance*), or wondering about the invisible colour that rests between the last and first of the rainbow. Or I simply looked about me at the topless ones with pleasure and occasional priapism.

Of course, making conversation in English, in England, can be difficult — real conversation I mean, the kind of creative conversation where 'one can feel at home'. How can one talk, for instance, to those who have specialized so much that they have little interest outside their specialty — e.g., nuclear physics? We are living in an age of increasing specialization, technology and cultural barbarism. No wonder most conversations are clichéd and tedious.

I am not suggesting that my own interests and knowledge are wide. I am ignorant of so many things. Dance, for instance. I am simply not interested in the ballet. Once, at a Foyle's Literary Lunch I was placed next to Dame Ninette de Valois. I tried hard to think of something to say to that beautiful old lady. The soup bowl was empty and still we had not exchanged more than a smile and a 'how-do-you-do'. Desperate, I blurted out, 'I'm afraid I know nothing about Dance.' Then I stupidly added, 'But I am interested in Football.'

Dame Ninette de Valois stared at her soup plate, obviously troubled. At last the soup plates were whisked away and she turned to me and said triumphantly, 'I know little of Poetry. But I danced for Yeats. You see, he chanted his poems and I danced to them.'

Ninette de Valois. Would that, I wonder, be a French name?

Of all reported conversations the one between William Blake and the portrait painter, Thomas Phillips, amuses me most. Their talk touched on angels. Now Blake believed, without doubt, that angels descended literally for the great painters and sat for their portraits.

'We hear much,' said Phillips, 'of the grandeur of Michelangelo; from the engravings I should say he's been over-rated; he could not paint an angel as well as Raphael.'

'He's not over-rated, Sir,' replied Blake. 'And he could paint an angel better than Raphael.'

'But you've never seen paintings of Michelangelo. Perhaps your friends' opinions have deceived you.'

'I speak from the opinion of a friend who could not be mistaken,' Blake stated. 'I mean the Archangel Gabriel... I was reading Young's *Night Thoughts* and I came to the passage "Who can paint an Angel?" And a voice answered "Michelangelo. I know. I sat for him. I am the Archangel Gabriel."'

Blake went on to explain that he knew it truly was the Archangel when he looked from whence the voice came and saw a shining shape with bright wings much diffused in light. Blake continued, 'As I looked the shape dilated more and more: he waved his hands, the roof of my study opened; he ascended into heaven.'

Thomas Phillips marvelled at this wild story. And so he should have done. It would be a hell of a thing, would it not, to find Blake sitting next to one at a Foyle's Literary Lunch?

Nostalgie de l'enfance. I heard someone in the street whistling 'Danny Boy'. At once I recalled from the gone years my mother's voice singing to me the words of that melancholy song.

> The summer's gone and the last rose is falling
> Tis you, tis you, must go and I must bide.

An appropriate song for this moody time of the year. The white rose is withering. So many white things have fallen away: the white blossom of spring; the white flowers, the white paired butterflies of summer. Gone this 1984. Shall there be some more white things, snow perhaps, later?

Already, while walking the streets of Hampstead these fading evenings, after the balmy airs of Southern France, I turn my collar up, I see my breath smoke in the air. In the distance, I fancy that I can observe The Ghost of Winter walking this way. Under the furthest lamp-post look how he turns towards us to reveal his utterly pale face.

October 1984

I want to record two recent enounters, one with Eddie whom no doubt I shall soon forget, the other with Emile whom I shall remember always.

In a Hampstead pub I was asked by one of the bar-lolling denizens ('I'm Eddie,' he said) about the dangers of the asbestos fall-out from the great fire at Cricklewood. Six weeks ago, it was reported that one and a half tons of asbestos debris fountained up into the air and was gently scattered over clandestine places in the borough of Brent. My new-found friend of quarter of an hour was not sanguine. 'The prevailing winds,' he said, 'come from the South West towards Hampstead. That flaming fire was less than a mile away as the black crow flies.'

Further conversation with Eddie revealed that he was not only a gloomy fellow who knew there were no frontiers for flying asbestos between Brent and Camden but one who also had no faith in his own body physiology. Of course, that is true of all hypochondriacs: they do not trust their own bodies. They know their health depends precariously on the amazing balancing machinery of billions and billions and billions of complicated body cells. Sod's law declares to them that something is sure to go wrong if not on Monday, then on Tuesday, especially if there are fires in Cricklewood.

I do not mock hypochondriacs however often they put out their tongues at the mirror or stare with peculiar sadness at their own faeces in the lavatory bowl. I was once a medical student and all medical students become temporary hypochondriacs. When I first walked the wards at Westminster Hospital and observed a patient recovering from a coronary I secretly took my own pulse. When I gazed at the chest X-ray on the illuminated, oblong screen and saw there the mischievous shadow of a neoplasm, back in my own room, later, I listened with my new stethoscope to my own chest. When the consultant neurologist, Dr Meadows, examined a lady with multiple sclerosis and declared how, twenty years earlier, she had experienced a transient blindness, I began to feel my own eyes go out of focus. And soon after leaving the operating theatre, having watched for the first time an appendix being removed, I suddenly suffered an inordinate amount of painful wind in my right iliac fossa. Perhaps the only time I felt entirely healthy was when I was doing my midwifery!

So I shall not mock hypochondriacs. I shall not mock Hampstead Eddie. I shall not mock myself. I live even nearer to the Cricklewood Conflagration than he does and asbestos fallout is a serious matter. For there is no known safe exposure limit to the blue or brown variety. Doctors are aware, though, that there is a powerful synergistic effect between these asbestos fibres and tobacco smoke.

'So if those exposed to such asbestos give up smoking, Eddie,' I said, 'after eighteen months their statistical chances of suffering a lung cancer would be reduced by more than ten times'.

'They should have signs — "No Smoking in Hampstead",' the barmaid said who had overheard our conversation.

Eddie dragged at his cigarette with anxious vehemence and then began to cough. When I left the pub I could not help but notice which way the wind was blowing.

I had arranged to visit a College of Education at Stoke-on-Trent in the afternoon and then drive a further ninety miles to the University town where I was scheduled to give a poetry reading in the evening. I was beginning to feel sorry that I had agreed to undertake such an arduous jaunt especially when a Dr Margaret Smith of the English Department at the University telephoned me and asked me to be there at 6 p.m. I could not be there that early.

'We'd like to give you dinner first,' she said. 'The reading will be at 8 p.m.'

Reluctantly I agreed to meet her at the forecourt of the local railway station at the compromise time of 6.45 p.m. Leaving Stoke I already felt somewhat tired as a result of the morning drive up the growling M1 and M6 from Golders Green and from the holding forth in the afternoon classroom. And now I had to drive much too fast into the sunset to keep my appointment with Dr Smith.

Amazingly, though, I arrived at the station at 6.45 p.m. exactly. A short young woman (Dr Smith) and a tall younger man (a student called Emile) strolled lazily towards me as I climbed stiffly out of my car. They did not know how many lorry drivers I had cursed, how I had taken various bends on two wheels. I stood there slightly shaking, proud of my punctuality, but as exhausted as a stunt man's understudy. I needed a wash and a rest. It was years since I had left Golders Green.

Dr Smith insisted, 'First come to the restaurant and eat, then we'll take you to The Garth Hotel which is near the University.' I allowed her to persuade me. The table was waiting. I did not know the waiter was not waiting. He had the soul of a snail and took hours to reach our table. At 7.30 p.m. I had spooned one avocado pear and sipped a glass of white wine. 'I do need to go to the hotel and sort myself out before the reading,' I sighed.

So Emile was commanded to take me to The Garth Hotel (so near the University where the reading was to take place) while Dr Smith paid the bill. She would meet me in ten minutes time. Emile would jump into my car and direct me to the hotel pronto.

Alas, Emile lost his way. We turned right, we turned left, we turned left again, and soon, at 8 p.m. we had returned from whence we had started. At that moment my audience at the University were, no doubt, settling themselves.

'Christ, Emile,' I said, 'I've travelled a helluva way and fast to get here on time.'

Emile, a born pedestrian if ever there was one, blamed the one way system. He stated that he knew the wrong turning taken, so we set off again. Once more he lost his way. At 8.10 pm. he cried out triumphantly, 'It's just around the corner. I know where I am.' I drove the car speedily around he corner where he shouted, 'There it is.' It looked more like a dismal, sow-coloured pub. I parked the car aghast, thinking, 'God, they could have found me a better place to stay than this.'

But there was no time to lose. We pushed the doors open into the noise of a jukebox. Above its harsh soundings Emile declared masterfully to the man behind the bar busily engaged serving a couple, 'This is Dr Dannie Abse. There's a room here booked for him.' The barman gestured to the stairs that started from a distant alcove. I ran towards these carrying my bag, leaving Emile standing. I ran up the stairs to a corridor, to a door, opened it. Surprise, surprise, here was peace, a spacious bedroom, a sleepy-looking, tidy double bed. I looked at my watch: 8.15. They would have to wait, I decided.

I tested the bed, pulled back the eiderdown and sheets. I needed a wash, I needed a pee. No washbasin, though over a Windsor chair I espied a towel. I took the towel and investigated the corridor that owned yet another door which I opened. There was, as the estate agents say, a well-appointed bathroom, scented soap, every convenience.

Back in my room I changed my sticky shirt, put my pyjamas under the pillow, threw the towel accurately towards the chair, pulled out the books I needed to read from, then in laundered glory, descended the stairs into the shadowy alcove where Emile loitered anxiously, biting his nails. 'It's gone quarter past,' he accused me.

'Don't get lost this time,' I responded, knowing the University was near at hand.

In the car once more we turned right, turned left, screeched around several corners. Emile, unbelievably, had lost his way yet again. As we hesitated at one crossroads, wondering whether to go left or right I noticed opposite me a sign on a building which read The Garth Hotel.

'Emile,' I asked, in what a cliché-loving writer would describe as a strangled voice, 'Emile, didn't Dr Smith say that my hotel was The Garth?'

'Yes,' said Emile.

'Where the hell did you take me?'

'I must have made a mistake. But there's no time for you to register now. We must get to the University.'

'Emile, you schlemiel,' I said, 'I've got to go back and get my case, my pyjamas, my toothbrush, shaving stuff, Christ.'

I thought how I must have gone into somebody's private bedroom, somebody's private bathroom, tested somebody's private bed, used somebody's private towel, etc., etc. Probably the room was the publican's own pride and joy. If I didn't go back to that sow-coloured pub now I would never be able to find the place again. We arrived back there this time fortunately without mishap. Emile waited in the car, somewhat white-faced. I ran into the pub. I did not look at the barman. I zipped into the alcove and up the stairs. I ran down the corridor and into the bedroom. Thank heavens nobody was occupying it. I collected my pyjamas and my bag and returned down the stairs, sprinted to the door and into the car. We arrived at the University and at the next stroke it was 8.40 p.m. precisely.

There is something wrong with me. These days I hardly ever dream Walter Mitty daydreams. No longer, as the number 13 bus trundles through autumn and Swiss Cottage do I bring down my conker against my opponent's to become the Conker King. Between two bus stops, approaching Lord's as I sit upstairs, I no longer replay the old remarkable game of cricket when, with a broken arm, I hit a six to make Glamorgan the champion County. How many elegiac years have passed since that same bus magically transformed itself into a nightclub, smokily lit, bare-armed, while I played the piano and sang, better than Fats Waller, 'Aint Misbehavin' while the audience listened enraptured until some fool shouted in my left ear, as if I were deaf, 'Any fares please?'

It hardly happens any more. It did last week, though, after a telephone call inviting me to be an auctioneer, along with David Benedictus, Humphrey Burton and Melvyn Bragg, in aid of Amnesty Interntional. 'An auction of prints by Auerbach, Kitaj, Elisabeth Frink, Josef Herman, Joe Tilson, Milein Cosman and many others,' I was told. 'At noon, Saturday October 27th at the Friends' Meeting House in Hampstead.' But I had to be elsewhere on that date.

After I put the phone down I slipped, in the old way, into reverie. In no time at all there I was, a hero, high up there on the rostrum, hoarse and shouting (oddly), 'How much for her beautiful head, how much for her beautiful legs, how much for her red-buried heart? C'mon bid, bid, bid. I'll give you a hammer of ebony, nails of silver, too, and a varnished plank of pine to hit the nails right through. So bid, bid, bid and going, going, gone, says the little pink worm.'

'What's the matter with you?' asked my wife.

'I, er,' I said.

Amnesty International. I stopped daydreaming and thought instead of the reality of why such an organization exists. It is hard, if one lives in comfortable liberty, to think for long of all the damp, dark, dangerous dungeons of the world wherein lie so many political prisoners. I recently had a visit from a Polish friend who told me of the plight of a poet I know who had supported Solidarity like so many others. He is not in a cell and yet he is not truly at liberty either. A man not allowed to work whether in a colliery or at a desk is not fully at liberty. There are many ways of condemning a man.

So many important European poets have been subjected to grim social pressures which we writers in Britain have largely escaped. Lorca was murdered, Mayakovsky committed suicide, Mandelstam disappeared, Hernandez died in a Franco prison, Celan survived a Nazi concentration camp, Brecht was exiled, Pasternak in disgrace. Of course, some poets survived and later made unforgettable direct or indirect artefacts of their experience. The best poet now writing in Poland, Zbigniew Herbert, has written, 'I think that the war created all the problems of my writing: what a man is in the face of death, how he behaves in the presence of a totalitarian threat...'

Mandelstam's wife spoke of one way to react when threatened. 'I often wondered,' she wrote, 'whether it is right to scream when you are being beaten and trampled underfoot. Isn't it better to face one's tormentors in a stance of satanic pride, answering them with contemptuous silence? I decided that it is better to scream. This pitiful sound, which sometimes, goodness knows how, reaches into the remotest prison cell, is a concentrated expression of the last vestige of human dignity. It is a man's way of leaving a trace, of telling people how he lived and died. By his screams he asserts his right to live, sends a message to the outside world demanding help and calling for resistance. If nothing is left one must scream. Silence is the real crime against humanity.'

What the coercive authorities prefer most, of course, is silence. But screaming messages do come through rather like that of Dan Pagis who survived annihilation by Hitler and who later composed this brief poem called 'Written in Pencil in the Sealed Railway car':

> here in the carload
> i am eve
> with abel my son
> if you see my other son

cain son of man
tell him i

There are many silences and not all are of the grave. 'Silence everybody,' says the worst and last Auctioneer. Totalitarian societies meanwhile, take a lease on that irrevocable silence and would not have those articulate ever forget it. Another Polish poet, Tymoteusz Karpowicz, has said it better than I can in this 'Lesson of Silence':

> Whenever a butterfly
> happened to fold
> too violently its wings —
> there was a call: silence, please!
>
> As soon as one feather
> of a startled bird
> jostled against a ray —
> there was a call: silence, please!
>
> In that way we were taught
> how to walk without noise
> the elephant on his drum,
> man on his earth.
>
> The trees were rising
> mute above the fields
> as rises the hair
> of the horror-stricken.

November 1984

Every other Thursday morning I sit down at my desk to write the next instalment of my 1984 Diary. After cleaning my teeth, after picking up the letters from the hall-mat, after eating my buttered toast, drinking my two cups of tea (milk with one sugar, since I know you are all agog to know), after indulging in another enormously commonplace activities that any Cabinet Minister would immediately transcribe into his diaries for posterity, I reach my desk and the blank page on which I will write Abse's 1984.

At this moment, since unvarnished truth in diaries must be told, my mind is full of other writers' journals. For before going to bed last night (I sleep on the right-hand side of a double bed) I watched on TV an admirably produced, adapted and well-acted film feature of Boswell's *London Diary*, unboundedly open in its communication; and not ten minutes ago while reading *The Times* over breakfast (and mumbling yet again, Why don't we take the *Guardian*?) I alighted on a book review of *The Castle Diaries* by Woodrow Wyatt of bow-tie fame.

Apparently, these diaries, even abridged, contain a half a million words. Wyatt suggests that should a research student in some distant future pick his way through the unabridged version lodged in one or another University Library, then the student should promptly be certified as insane. In kinder mood, Woodrow Wyatt adds that 'there are some nuggets to be extracted' and with blithe pincers he pulls them out one by one for our delectation. Barbara Castle's hatred of Callaghan — 'Frankly I believe Jim Callaghan is capable of anything'; Harold Wilson's drinking habits — 'I think he had been taking comfort in his brandy again'; Roy Jenkins's ataraxic presence — 'My private tête-à-tête with Roy took place one lunch at No 11. Why do I feel constrained at these intimate talks?' Nuggets, every one of them Mr Wyatt assures us.

Perhaps they are. I remember the *Crossman Diaries, Volume III.* Wonderful nuggets there: 'I had a horrible office lunch of particularly disgusting sandwiches';'...at 2 a.m. my stomach evacuated totally...'; 'I lunched at the Ritz with Peregrine Worsthorne'; and pure gold this — 'before Cabinet I had a frantic message that Tony Crosland wanted to lunch with me. I took him to lunch. (I don't know why he doesn't take me, perhaps because he doesn't have a club.) So off we went to the Athenaeum where I gave him grouse and claret.'

Politicians such as Crossman and Castle believe that their red-hot diary insertions will one day be of historical value. 'Back to a late reception at Lancaster House for the Commonwealth Prime Ministers' Conference. George Brown was rolling round (sic) distressingly sozzled.' (Castle); 'I went off to put up plaques at a couple of health centres and then I drove to Coventry to address the annual dinner of The College of Midwives with Doris Butterworth, Jolly Jack's wife, who is their President, in the chair.'

(Crossman).

Why do so many people, other than politicians, keep diaries? I suspect that the majority of them are unsure of their identities and perhaps feel themselves, too often, to be half-dead like convicts in a prison. Diary-keeping, then, can be a therapeutic exercise, a prescription to prove to themselves that they are alive. Like the imperative diary pages of a prisoner their words proclaim, 'I am here, I am alive, I thought this, I did that.'

So meaningful can diary-keeping be that its author's life may be changed by it. It can become a dangerous activity. Even Boswell realized that he might have sought out certain adventures in order that he could claim them for his diary. Those who succumb to such temptations are rather like those tourists with busy cameras who only visit Venice, say, in order to return with snapshots of themselves standing amongst the pigeons of St Mark's Square or in front of the Doge's Palace. They may not have enjoyed the pleasurable offerings of Venice but, by damn, they have wonderful souvenirs in their albums.

Diary-keeping, though, can work as a moral force. It has been asserted that by the act of confessing their sins Catholics are not only allowed consolation but the very prospect of confession is an effective prophylactic. It is embarrassing for them to whisper to the priest yet again that, on Monday, they coveted their neighbour's wife, on Tuesday they masturbated, and that, on Wednesday, they committed adultery. In the same way the diarist may not wish to confess to his diary one more act of meanness and of spite and so behaves himself instead. Velleities do not become desires and desires do not become overt acts because of the power of the word on a page.

It is not comfortable, though, to be with one who obsessionally keeps a diary. Lately I was in Lancashire with the Welsh poet, Gillian Clarke. I was telling her about a cartoon I had seen concerning Reagan and Mondale. The cartoon showed Reagan with his Cabinet — Reagan was asleep. It also showed Mondale with his Cabinet — the Cabinet were asleep. 'It was that Republican Bob Hope who remarked that Mondale had had a charisma by-pass operation,' I added. Gillian laughed and said, 'I'll put that in my diary.' When I told her later about an incident involving a common friend of ours she said, 'Oh yes, I'll definitely put that in my diary tonight.' Because Gillian seemed to keep her midnight diary with such implacable regularity I began to feel bugged. I found myself thereafter being cautious about what I said, what I did.

Some writers, of course, bug themselves. The Goncourt brothers recorded how Victor Hugo 'always has a note book in his pocket and if, in conversation with you, he happens to express the tiniest thought, to put forward the smallest idea, he promptly turns away from you, takes out his note book and writes down what he has just said.' Thanks to the Goncourts, practised buggers, Hugo, the self-bugger, was bugged.

If I kept a diary with the conscientious ardour of Gillian Clarke or Virginia Woolf, say, who kept diaries between 1915-1941, thirty volumes of them, I think I would feel guilty. In a diary a writer is talking to himself: in other forms of prose, even autobiography, the writer is speaking to others. And it is a writer's job, is it not, to address others, however few these may seem to be? Virginia Woolf felt guilty when she devoted herself to her diary rather as I would if, instead of working, I slouched off in scowling truancy, on rainy weekday afternoons, to the Odeon. Virginia Woolf scolded herself for 'the lawless exercise' of writing diaries, for not addressing herself to the much more difficult task of shaping a novel.

Yet, of course, most diaries presuppose another reader. For instance, when André Gide confesses in his journals to using a chamber pot one night, why does he add firmly that this is not his usual habit? Gide knows perfectly well what his nocturnal micturating habits are, so whom is he addressing? I believe firmly that the diarist is one who likes to have secrets but he hopes that one day, maybe tomorrow, maybe centuries hence, those secrets will be whispered to others — the more the better.

Moreover, when his diaries are finally published — I was here, I was a great fellow — he is not so open to the wrath of his critics as novelists, poets, and autobiographers are. Diaries pretend to be spontaneous effusions, to be defenceless, unpremeditated scribblings and as such are not only self-indulgent but beg the indulgence of reader and critic. As I do now.

Excitement. It is not every day that one receives an invitation to visit Turkey. It seemed that Cevat Capan, a celebrated Turkish writer, had translated a whole battery of 20th century British poets and that his one-man anthology is soon to be published. So the dynamic Mrs Yildiz Arda of the Turk-Ingiliz Kultur Dernegi, plus the British Council, asked me to deliver lectures at several Turkish universities on post-war British poetry and, in addition, to read from my own work at the Turco-British Associations in Istanbul and Ankara.

I expressed doubts. After all I'm not too well understood in Golders Green. Besides, my pigeon-Welsh is better than my Turkish. 'You'll find your audiences will understand English poetry better than the denizens of Golders Green,' I was told somewhat drily.

I could not imagine Turkey. Soon enough, at Heathrow, I was boarding a magic Turkish carpet powered by a Boeing engine and three and a half hours later I alighted, blinking, in Istanbul. Already the wounded sunset shifted its coloured mobiles over the Bosphorus. I stood there, somewhat concussed, as the waters in slow knots passed under the gigantic bridge that spans Europe and Asia.

The bridge resembled, in a magnified way, the Severn Bridge — it was designed by the same engineer. 'The eighth bridge?' I suggested brilliantly, though nobody, of course, raised a diplomatic smile. 'It's their faulty English,' I consoled myself.

Next morning, before you could say Abse Pasha, my generous hosts whisked me off to view the Topkapi Palace, the oldest of the remaining palaces in the world, the Harem section of it alone containing 400 rooms, many of which faced pleasant small inner courts. It doesn't look too much like Cardiff Castle.

In the Harem building I imagined all those hand-picked, dark-eyed concubines, the Sultan yawning, lying back on cushions, spitting sherbert, while musicians plucked and blew. Wasn't this, as Yeats fancied, the country of animal sensuality? But suppose the Sultan had an Oedipus complex, or was mournfully impotent. How terrible, then, to be living there in the torture of so much available, voluptuous femininity. 'An aged man is but a paltry thing, A tattered coat upon a stick...'

'Stop it,' I said. Think prose, I told myself. Imagine, rather, Byzantium trees made of gold and silver with artificial birds singing, imagine the ghosts of the mosaic workers, the illuminators of sacred books, the craftsmen of jewellery, and leave the concubines alone. My hosts moved our caravans, the dogs barked and soon enough I arrived, shoeless, in the serene hush of the Blue Mosque, and later into that of St Sophia. So much enclosed space under huge semi-domes. So much to inspect closely and to relish.

In Istanbul the lectures and readings did not prompt complaints. Nobody threw knives or Turkish Delight. Afterwards, when I was taken out to dinner, we had to pass down a narrow, dimly lit alleyway. There a man stood waving the oncoming traffic of people to one side, for he was guarding two cats who were copulating under the one lamp-post. I was surprised at their outrageous sensuality. I always thought cats to be secretive creatures. I have heard their oriental cries, of course, but never seen them fastened to each other. Maybe English cats, so well-bred, are more reticent than their Turkish counterparts?

We walked on and I asked Mike Winter, one of the British Council representatives in Istanbul, whether he thought that the anonymous cat-guard was simply a kind, conscientious lover of cats — or was he just a voyeur? Before he could reply one of our party known as Ginger, an American lady married to a Turk, related how only weeks earlier she had encountered another two cats copulating and a man had stood there throwing stones at these feline lovers. She had suggested that the stone thrower desist, leave the cats alone, and that nature should be allowed healthily to take its course.

'But it's not healthy, it's two male cats,' the man protested, picking up another stone.

At the first University I visited in Ankara, before I delivered my lecture, a lunch was arranged to which all the English Faculty professors, associate professors etc. were invited. I sat opposite the Dean who told me with evident satisfaction, 'We've had Elizabeth Jane Howard, Arnold Wesker and Margaret Drabble before you. If Shakespeare was alive we'd have him too.'

At Ankara I was worked hard but I did have one afternoon to visit the Hittite Museum. There I gazed at primitive implements, at messages from pre-recorded history as well as at recondite writings on ancient stone. I recalled a Hittite ritual prescription against pestilence which I had once read in one of my favourite books, *Ancient Near Eastern Texts*, edited by James B. Pritchard —

a book to take to Roy Plomley's Desert Island: 'These are the words of Uhha-muwas, the Arzawaman. If people are dying in the country and if some god of the enemy is to blame then drive up one ram. Twine together blue wool, red wool, yellow wool, black wool and white wool, make it into a crown and crown the ram with it. Drive the ram on to the road leading to the enemy and while doing so speak as follows: whatever god from the enemy-land has caused this plague — see! how we drive this crowned ram to pacify thee, o god. We drive the crowned ram towards the enemy.' It's the sort of thing we normally chant at football matches, especially in Turkey after we sing 'Eight-nil, Eight-nil.'

That same night I went to a party given by Frank Taylor, the British Council representative in Ankara. There I met a dramatist recently released from prison and learnt something of the darker, more averted side of Turkey. But the Life and Soul of the party proved to be the French Cultural Attaché. He shone, he sparkled like a diamond in floodlight, he wittily discussed the national characteristics of the Turks, the Dutch, the Russians. He also dilated on the ignorance of the peasants in Eastern Turkey. Why did I want to defend them, why did I argue I wonder? To illustrate my point I told the old joke of a Londoner who stopped his car in deepest Somerset to ask the way to Bristol. 'Is it that way?' he asked. 'Oi don't know,' replied the countryman. 'Is it the other way then?' Again the Somerset man shook his head, saying 'Oi don't know.' 'Well, is it straight on?' 'Oi don't know.' Exasperated, our city slicker sneered, 'You don't know much, do you?' Slowly the Somerset man replied, 'That may be so. But I baint be lost.'

Flying back to Istanbul, to the generous care of Yildiz Arda, I bought the *Turkish Daily News*, the only English newspaper in Turkey. Already I knew something of its reputation, how for instance it was bravely unafraid to criticize the government's monetarist policies which had not only *not* cured inflation but had also led to a deterioration in general living standards. *The Daily News* also had a less enviable reputation for misprints. Someone, I can't remember who, had told me how after the attempted assassination of Reagan the *Daily News* reported that the President had been under the surgeon's wife for six hours.

Now, though, in the plane, I spotted very few misprints — less than you would find on an average day in the *Guardian*. I read with interest the world League Table of Worker's wages per hour expressed in terms of dollars:

Norway	9.66	Japan	6.28
Belgium	9.14	France	6.07
Switzerland	8.65	Britain	5.46
USA	8.60	Spain	3.87
Canada	8.50	Hong Kong	1.65
Denmark	7.97	Taiwan	1.64
Sweden	7.91	Portugal	1.28
Australia	7.85	Turkey	1.19
West Germany	7.54	India	0.71
Italy	6.35	China	0.26

Afterwards I turned to the inside page and was amazed to read there how a certain inhabitant of Ankara, lost in deepest Eastern Turkey, asked his way to Bitlis. 'Right? Left? Straight on?' 'Don't know.' 'You don't know much, do you?' 'No, but I'm not lost.' Somebody at the party obviously worked for the paper, and, hard up for copy, had used my joke. I had a terrific sense of triumph. I had visited Turkey and, as you see, had anonymously left my mark. Well done, me. Not many poets do that.

December 1984

I am trying to look back over the bumpy months of 1984, but I continue too fast in reverse, for I keep thinking of 1974. In May of that year I was about to quit my temporary job in the U.S.A. as Writer-In-Residence at Princeton University. Then I was asked to stay on.

I hesitated. It had been pleasurable living in Princeton — a locus not unlike Hampstead, with its duplicate of an Everyman cinema, ready at a blink to show *Blue Angel* or *The Battleship Potemkin*, with its own coffee houses such as you'd find opposite Hampstead Tube station, alleyways such as Perrins Court, similar notices in the 'High Street', pinned on to the back of pavement trees. In addition, of course, adjacent to that 'High Street' were, as in an architect's dream, imitation Oxford Colleges.

Yes, it was pleasant there, but I missed Britain too much. How easy it was to be a patriot abroad: to take pride in a BBC that countenanced no advertisements; to boast of our other cultural institutions and of our more serious newspapers; above all, despite Northern Ireland, to state that Britain was, more or less, a caring society, believing in the ideal of full employment and somewhat concerned about its aged and its sick.

'Look at our National Health Service,' I'd say to American friends. 'Why, look at our police force even. They aren't armed as yours are. And they are respected, kept on a short leash.'

True, that 1973-4 winter, there had been the disconsolate aggro and discomfort of the three day week which I had missed. But that was over now. Britain was on the road to becoming almost itself. The U.S.A. with all its private affluence had outrageous disadvantages. Even in agreeable, middle-class Princeton, one experienced, occasionally, a taste of the other America.

For instance, in February, my young son suffered a worrying earache, presumably the result of a potent infection. So I telephoned the local Ear, Nose and Throat specialist. His secretary responded, 'He'll see your son in two weeks.'

I explained that the boy had a high temperature. 'Sorry, he's very busy,' his secretary said. I asserted that I was a British doctor, that my young son probably had an acute otitis media and would my American colleague therefore examine him urgently as I had no instrument to examine his eardrums?

The secretary went away. I listened to the silence of the telephone receiver. She returned eventually to say, 'Since you're a doctor he'll see your son next week, on Tuesday.' I fumed. I thought I must get hold of some antibiotics. I thought that if this could happen in civilized Princeton then what would happen out there in the American sticks? 'At home, with the National Health Service,' I pondered, 'sick youngsters would not be kept waiting like this.'

I declined the generous invitation to remain in the USA. Though grateful for my experience of Princeton, I returned home and was glad to be back in caring Britain. But now, in 1984, I ask myself, 'Am I at home? If so, who has come to occupy it like a vandal? Who has set class against class, North against South? Who sanctions the scandal of increasing unemployment so that the spirit of hooliganism stalks the land? Who is dismantling our National Health Service? Whose police are these, disguised in their metallic accoutrements, combating the wrath of miners and their families?'

In Yorkshire, in Durham, in Ayrshire, in South Wales, in Kent, violence is being done to whole communities. And these sleepy people have now come awake. As Duncan Bush has put it in the current issue of *Poetry Wales* , 'The villages are no longer aggregates of dwellings privatized by television but communities again, the rented videos and tapes back in the shop...and meetings

> in workmen's clubs and miners' welfare
> halls, just as it had been once, communities
> beleagured but the closer
> the intenser for it, with resources
> now distributed to need, and organised to last,
> the dance floors stacked
> with foodstuffs like a dockside, as if
> an atavistic common memory, an inheritance
> perhaps long thought romantic,
> like the old men's proud and bitter
> tales of 1926, was now being learnt again
> in grandchildren and
> great-grandchildren of their bloodline...'

Thatcher's Britain is a different country from the one I returned to in 1974. Extremists, whether they be Scargills, Benns, Norman Tebbits or Margaret Thatchers may, in opposition, play a valuable part in the evolution of society. But, given power, such fanatical ideologues as these tend to smash all that is fragile. Embattled as they are, they see enemies everywhere; they use the language of the lunatic asylum and speak, for instance, of 'The Enemy Within'.

Once, as a result of the Falklands War, Neil Kinnock called Margaret Thatcher 'bloodthirsty'. Afterwards he apologized. And so he should have done — for not being subtle enough.

*

One thing unchanged since 1974 is the operation of the literary mafia. As usual we are having those lists — The Best Books of 1984 — that permit some of my best friends to give a puff to some of my other best friends. Most of the books of poems recommended are boring, most of the novels lousy, most of the non-fiction not worth a candle.

My guess is that the best novel published in Britain during 1984 was one I happened on in Princeton in 1974: *The Wife of Martin Guerre* by Janet Lewis. It is a minor classic. When I returned home I recommended it to several publishers without success. Last summer Penguin published it. No madam, no sir, I do not know Janet Lewis.

I think the best short short story I read during 1984 was a feminist one. It concerns Beruriah and can be found in the Agoda of the Babylonian Talmud. It seems that Rabbi Jose met Beruriah walking on the road. 'Which way to the city of Lud?' asked the Rabbi. And Beruriah replied, 'You Galilean fool, don't our sages say, don't talk too long with a woman. You should have asked me, "Which way to Lud?"'

The best parable I came across in 1984 was one related in a lecture by Richard Ellmann who declared it was much loved by James Joyce. It is about an old man who, earlier this century, lived in the Blasket Islands (off the South West coast of Ireland) and who had not even visited the mainland.

One day he did so and, at a bazaar, came across a small hand-mirror — something he'd never seen before. He looked at it with wonder. He stared at it, stared again, then muttered softly, 'Oh father, father!' Seeing how much poignant pleasure he received from gazing into this small looking-glass they let him take it away. Now and then he would take it out of his pocket, stare into it, smile and say, 'Father.'

Then he rowed back to the Blaskets, jealously guarding his precious possession, and would not show it to his wife who became suspicious. What did he have in his pocket?

One hot day when they were both working in the fields, he hung his jacket over the hedge. She then took her opportunity to pull the object out of his pocket and gazed at it curiously. 'Ach' she cried, throwing it away, 'it's only an old woman.'

My last patient at the chest clinic this year seemed to be more interested in his piles than in his chest. I told him how Galen, in the 2nd century, had treated anal bleeding. 'With a stone of India,' I continued, 'worn at the neck, an emerald in the navel and a black leg of a toad tucked under his armpit.'

'You're jokin', doctor,' said my patient.

Perhaps I was. After all, there are those who speak secrets they do not know, nor are they aware they have spoken them.

March-April 1985

It seems much more than three months since I looked out of the bedroom window and the leprous snow on the London pavement, on hedges, front garden lawns, trees, rooftops, hurt my eyes intolerably. I was ill. I drew the noise of the curtains and went back to bed, closed my eyes. I had never suffered a headache like this. Headache, photophobia, fever. Surely not a meningitis? No neck rigidity, so perhaps it was merely a severe influenza with meningism, an irritation of the meninges, the coverings of the brain, rather than a frank inflammation of these?

I stayed behind my eyelids and eventually fell asleep, woke, half-dreamed, blanks, slept, woke, headache, turned my head towards the wall because even the light breaking through the barrier of the drawn curtains bruised my eyes. I wished I could fall asleep properly, deeply, refreshingly, wake up free of this unrelenting headache.

Next morning I felt no better. I sat up in bed while Joan took my temperature. 101. It would probably climb higher by the evening. 'I'd better call Dr Ross,' Joan said. I dissuaded her. I told her the diagnosis: not meningism merely, but a viral meningitis or, as the text-book called it Benign Lymphocytic Meningitis. Where the hell had I picked up the virus? Headache, photophobia, fever, anorexia. Turkey? No, that visit had been several months ago. How long did meningeal viruses take to incubate? I wondered, too, if that episode, early in the new year, when I had rescued a mouse from Caitlin's soft pawings had significance. One medical authority curiously suggested that mice may harbour viruses that can cause meningitis. But I had simply banished the cat to the living room, opened the door of the kitchen, and with a brush, gently, guided the shocked mouse into freezing 1985.

'It can't be TB meningitis,' I said to Joan. 'I've seen too many TB patients over the years. I must be resistant to TB. It's a viral meningitis.'

'Let's see what Dr Ross says,' Joan advised.

What was the point? There was no specific treatment for viral meningitis. Ross would come, would take my temperature, perhaps test my reflexes, then admit me to hospital. There they would extract a cubic inch or so of my cerebro-spinal fluid (a lumbar puncture) and send the fluid which would be as clear as gin to the laboratory and, after weeks, the diagnosis of benign lymphocytic meningitis would be confirmed. They called the condition benign because patients almost always survive it. It didn't *feel* benign. Headache, photophobia, dreaming blanks, time passing, analgesics, darkness, light, darkness, fever, analgesics.

Several days later Joan called in Dr Ross because, if anything, I was worse. After he'd examined me, listened to my short story of symptoms, Ross said, 'You'll have to go to hospital. What about the Royal Free in Hampstead? That's the nearest.'

'I don't fancy a lumbar puncture,' I grumbled.

In addition I did not want to lose Joan's sympathetic and tactful care — to exchange that for the more impersonal concern of hospital routine.

'There's only one place for you,' insisted Ross. 'Hospital. I know the neurologist at the Royal Free. He's first class. I'll telephone him now.'

Soon enough I lay in bed in a darkened emergency room at the Royal Free — the temperature high, the punishing headache and photophobia unchanged. One of the nurses said, 'Could you manage to walk down to the X-ray Department by yourself for a brain scan and chest X-ray? I could get a porter to wheel you there, but that may take a long time as we're short-staffed.' (Did you hear, Mrs Thatcher?)

It was a long walk to the X-ray Department. Eventually I arrived, handed in a slip of a form, waited with the other haggard-looking patients on long benches. Later I was wheeled back to a room which had again been darkened and listened through my headache to a patient next door who kept on shouting out terrible cries in a language I could not understand.

Eventually I was seen by the neurologist who believed the diagnosis to be Benign Lyphocytic Meningitis. A lumber puncture was done and I didn't enjoy it at all. Ten days later my fever seemed to have abated and I asked them all to allow me to go back to the care of my wife who could make for me 'some very special Welsh tomato soup which was absolutely essential for my full recovery!'

When I returned home my temperature also returned. I had hoped to sit quietly in the armchair in the bedroom, listening to the radio, perhaps feeling better each day. When I was released from the Royal Free the consultant neurologist had said, 'It'll take some time for you to be fully recovered. You'll probably get depressed. Don't worry, that's a normal sequel to a meningitis. And don't go and see a psychiatrist. Just come to my outpatients. OK? Mind you don't get a relapse once you leave here.'

But that's what happened: a relapse. I lay in bed again — headache, photophobia, dreaming blanks, time passing, occasional visitors, Dr Ross, darkness, light, day, night, fever, and always Joan on call, near and kind and reassuring.

A true scientist would have listed his symptoms in precise detail, not impressionistically as I have done. Perhaps I should have followed the example of that great neurologist and first modern experimental gerontologist, Charles Brown-Sequard. He remained a scientist even to his last days in 1894 when, stricken with a right-sided haemorrhage of the brain, he continued to itemize precisely his own symptoms, correctly diagnosing his illness and its bleak prognosis — as if he were observing another patient. The next day he was dead.

At least I should have heeded the comment of my friend Sigi Nissel who is the second violinist of the Amadeus Quartet and who, as a result, frequently travels all over the world. One day, during a game of chess with him, I said, 'Sigi, you must get so bored of hotel bedrooms and travelling, travelling all the time. So many aeroplanes, so many airports, so many railway stations, trains, car rides, connections, it must be boring. I'd be bored, fed up to here.'

'I'm never bored.'

'C'mon. Never?'

'Never. Never. I used to get bored. But not for some years now.'

'You must let me into your secret,' I said cynically.

He hesitated. 'You don't know this,' he continued, 'but some years ago I had a brain tumour. I was operated on. In the event it proved to be a benign growth and I was left with no residual symptoms. Since then I'm never bored. I can play music and I can travel. I'm just grateful for each day.'

Chastened, I returned my gaze to the chess board, listened to the silence, then moved a pawn.

I should be grateful too. I have not experienced any depression such as the neurologist at the Royal Free prophesied. For a couple of weeks I had been worried whether the cerebral nerves were affected. I had a toothache, a jawache, then an earache and finally some difficulty in focusing my eyes properly. But all these symptoms passed. I'm back to my old routines of working in London at the chest clinic on Mondays and Tuesdays, returning sometimes to Ogmore, reading, playing chess, and as a matter of fact I am now having a particularly productive period of writing poems. So all's well and all manner of things.

Today I walked past my Uncle Joe's house and saw the notice outside: TO BE SOLD. Injurious Time. Strangers will come to live there and his name on the brass plate, Dr Joseph Shepherd, will be scandalously removed. In future, when I walk this way, I know I shall not cross the road with averted eyes but hesitate. And all deaths remind one of one's own.

> Ay, but to die, and go we know not where;
> To lie in cold obstruction and to rot;
> This sensible warm motion to become
> A kneaded clod; and the delighted spirit
> To bathe in fiery floods, or to reside
> In thrilling region of thick-ribbed ice;
> To be imprison'd in the viewless winds.
> And blown with restless violence round about
> The pendant world; or to be worse than worst

Of those that lawless and uncertain thoughts
Imagine howling: 'tis too horrible!

Of all my uncles and aunts who have departed this world to become speechless and disgraced, I miss Joe the most. Had he been alive when I had my viral meningitis he would certainly have been summoned to my bedside. He was a most skilled GP. A physician who, unlike so many others, kept up to date with medical advances and who, besides, read widely in disciplines other than medicine.

Over the years I referred a number of patients to him, including a few poets and their wives. I think Joe delighted in having slightly off-beat patients. Most of them were well-heeled, living locally, but he also treated a number of working-class Irishmen. 'Why do you have so many Irishmen from Kilburn coming to you, uncle?' 'Word of mouth,' he would reply before telling me a riveting anecdote about one or another of them. One story he told me was surely material for a Zola or a Guy de Maupassant. It concerned a short-statured, wiry Irishman who, Joe decided, needed an abdominal operation.

Patrick, sitting up on the couch, after the clinical examination, said, 'Well, if you think it desperately necessary, doctor.' The patient then asserted that he wanted the operation to be done privately. He was not interested in the National Health Service. Joe, believing that his patient could ill-afford private surgery, tried to dissuade him.

'Money's no object,' declared Patrick. 'Sure, it's no problem at all. I want the best and most corrigible surgeon in the land.'

Joe, curious now about the apparently limitless wealth of his patient, expressed surprise that plumbing was such a lucrative business. Patrick looked discomforted. He cleared his throat. At length he asked, 'You've taken the solemn oath, haven't you, doctor, like all doctors? Whatever I say here is entirely confidential, isn't it?'

Joe assured him that this was so, then his patient admitted, 'I'm not a plumber, doctor. I told a lie. That was the heart of falsehood. I'm a burglar.'

My uncle, poker-faced, recommended the noted surgeon, Dickson Wright of St Mary's Hospital, to undertake the operation. 'I'll phone him right away,' Joe said. Patrick nodded and my uncle turned the pages of the Medical Directory seeking Dickson Wright's home telephone number. Before dialling it, he repeated the number out loud and his patient cried, 'Dija say Cunningham? A fig! Is it a Cunningham number? Why be damn, that St John's Wood, isn't it? My beat's St John's Wood.'

'Your beat?'

'My practice, doctor. It's agreed between us. We do not trespass on each other's territory. What road does this surgeon live in?'

When Joe told him the street his patient stood up as if affronted. When he told him the number of the house Patrick said, 'I only did him two weeks ago. I've still got his pestilent stuff.'

Joe telephoned Dickson Wright. Yes, he had been burgled recently and yes, he had lost a lot of silver and how did Joe know?

'Do you want all your property returned?' asked Joe. 'Because if you do you'll have to operate for free.'

And so it came to pass...Patrick left St Mary's Hospital a healthier man and Dickson Wright had all his silver returned. I wish I could continue Joe's story by writing, 'Soon after — long enough for a man to convalesce from an abdominal operation — Dickson Wright's house was burgled again,' but such an addendum would, alas, belong to the lying vice of fiction.

May 1985

It is common practise nowadays to sell books at poetry readings. Organizers provide a table and ask the poet to bring books with him. Ordering such books, direct from a publisher, can be tricky. For instance, I telephone Tiptree where Hutchinson keep their warehouse. 'My name is Dannie Abse. I've ordered books from you before. May I have another sixty copies of my *Collected Poems* please?'

'That's ABSE, isn't it?'

'Yes.'

'And you want *The Collected Poems*?'

'Right.'

'What's the name of the author?'

'Dannie Abse.'

'You want six copies of *The Collected Poems of Dannie Abse.*'

'Sixty copies.'

'Just a minute.'

I hold on. I wait until the voice returns. 'OK, now what is it you want?'

Three weeks later a parcel arrives from Tiptree. I open up the box and inside it I discover sixty copies of *The Collected Poems of Kingsley Amis*! On the telephone I seem to have difficulty in making myself understood. When I demand that they take back Mr Amis's when they deliver the sixty copies of *my Collected Poems*, they argue that it cannot be done. 'We only deliver, not take back.' I settle for them sending me sixty copies of my book and privately decide to return the Kingsley Amis volumes to the Editorial Department at Fitzroy Square. This I do, though heavy is this light-weight poet to carry, and eventually the second box of books arrives at my home from Tiptree. They have come too late for the poetry reading; no matter, there will be other readings and I open the box in the hall. Soon I'm shouting, 'Joan. Joan, for Chrissake, come and look at this.' Tiptree have sent me sixty copies of *The Collected Poems* of the Pope.

Because we are all different, because we are not clones, because we all react differently in some measure to the assault of diseases and drugs, medicine is not a science, it cannot be. It has to rely on generalizations, not laws. Not only are we not identical, but the germs that attack us are also individual. It has been said that there are as many B coli germs in the intestines as there are stars in the sky and under an ordinary microscope these bacteria appear to be the same. But a more sophisticated scrutiny, through an electron microscope, proves otherwise.

I've sent my new book of poems to Anthony Whittome at Hutchinson today. It contains work over five years. I've called the book *Ask the Bloody Horse* because I don't know and still don't know, where I'm going. I should have liked to put, as an epigraph, a quotation by Martin Buber: 'All journeys have secret destinations of which the traveller is unaware.' Alas, Charles Causley has done exactly that in one of his volumes. Instead I have prefaced the book with:

> While Freud was tracing the river to its source
> he met Itzig unsteadily riding.
> 'Where are you going?' he asked that wild-eyed rider.
> 'Don't ask me,' said Itzig, 'ask the bloody horse.'

Simply I've adapted the old joke about the novice horseman Itzig. Apparently it was Freud's favourite joke, presumably because he perceived the horse to be an emblem of the unconscious and recognized the truth of Itzig's response. Hence I introduced Freud into the quatrain. The best jokes, I think, often turn out to be humorous parables. Anyway, what is writ, is writ — Would it were worthier!

Fraser Steele has invited me to contribute to the Poet on Poet Radio 4 series he is producing. I was tempted to recycle the lecture I gave at the Poetry Society — *The Dread of Sylvia Plath*. On second thoughts, I decided to be less lazy. I have let Fraser know that I would like to write a piece on D.H. Lawrence. I've chosen Lawrence because I think that, generally, he is still under-estimated as a poet.

Years ago, when I was a medical student, I happened on his poems for the first time and responded at once to 'The Ship of Death' and 'Bavarian Gentians'. I did not know then, being untutored, that these poems were among his last, were by a man dying of pulmonary tuberculosis. Re-reading these poems, aware of the fact, I find I am even more deeply touched now than I was then.

What a double-streaked man Lawrence was. His poems reveal it over and over again — at one moment he's gentle and patient, at another he is shrill, irascible. He was ambivalent about so many things, not least sex. That's why I like that early poem of his, one that critics do not much remark upon, and which begins, 'She said as well to me: Why are you ashamed?...' That poem not only shows, dramatically and precisely, Lawrence's ambiguous sexual preoccupations but articulates, characteristically enough, his vivid awareness of the mystery and, indeed, divinity of life — human and non-human life. When Keith Sagar writes, 'His vision becomes increasingly sacramental,' it is not entirely true. It is there from the beginning in the earliest poems, blurred, myopic, as in such bad poems as 'Mystic Blue' — the secretive, living dark (its blueness) was there then but abstract, not wonderfully concrete as the dying Lawrence was later to order it in 'Bavarian Gentians'.

I was about to leave the Tate Gallery when Mark Gertler's painting 'Merry-Go-Round' made me hesitate. It intrigued me: the background of night, the tense, open-mouthed figures in the artificial light whose enjoyment, if it were such, was akin to that of spectators at a horror film. Gertler painted it in 1916 and no doubt was making some allegorical statement about the First World War.

On the way home I kept thinking of Gertler's painting, its ambiguity, the terror in it, and then I recalled Rilke's poem about a Merry-Go-Round at night. How typical, I thought, of Rilke to focus on such an image, interested as he was in the mediation of the invisible to the visible. ('The Angel of the Duino Elegies,' he wrote, 'is the being who vouces for the recognition of a higher degree of reality in the invisible, terrible to us because we ... still cling to the visible.') Yes, the Merry-Go-Round at night was a given metaphor for Rilke: fairground spectators have the optical illusion of night's invisible creatures becoming tangible, as the roundabout turns them from darkness into light.

It was years since I had read Rilke's poem. When I arrived home I picked out Rilke's poems from the bookshelf. I read J.B. Leishman's translation of da Karussell (I have no German, alas) and was astonished to discover I had misremembered the poem, that the Merry-Go-Round Rilke portrayed was not even one revolving at night! Somehow I must have merged Gertler's vision with my own weak remembrance of Rilke's poem. Doodling, I sat down to write the translation I though I had remembered:

> The roof turns, the brassy merry-go-round crashes
> out music. Gaudy horses gallop tail to snout,
> inhabit the phantasmagoria of light
> substantial as smoke. Then each one vanishes.
>
> Some pull carriages. Some children, frightened, hold tight
> the reins as they arrive and disappear

chased by a scarlet lion that seems to sneer
and snarl. And here's a unicorn painted white.

Look! From another world this strange, lit retinue.
A boy on a steer, whooping, loud as dynamite —
a sheriff, no doubt, though dressed in sailor-blue.
And here comes the unicorn painted white.

Faster! The children spellbound, the animals prance,
and this is happiness, this no-man's land
where nothing's forbidden. And hardly a glance
at parents who smile, who *think* they understand

as the scarlet lion leaps into the night
and here comes the unicorn painted white.

The red-haired woman, with here fiancé lingering a yard behind, approached me. It seemed she had once been in a BBC schools programme I had conducted. Her fiancé nodded. 'I was only fifteen then,' said the redhead.

So were all the other children. I remebered the occasion well because my own daughter, Susanna, took part in the programme. The scheme was that I would read a poem of my own choosing, one, say, by Hardy, or by Ted Hughes, and afterwards the young-sters would comment, pronounce on why they liked the poem or disliked it. The producer, Stuart Evans, commended, 'You will act as an active chairman,' and I asked if Susanna could join the group for if she did so I knew there would be no awkward, accumulating silences in the studio.

'But she's older than fifteen, isn't she?' asked Stuart.

'No,' I said, 'she's fifteen, a mature-looking, lipsticked fifteen, but fifteen nevertheless.'

Stuart agreed, providing no one knew that I was her father. 'It wouldn't be fair to the others if they knew,' he argued. So in due course, anonymously but loudly, Susanna joined the schoolboys and girls in the studio, including apparently this red-haired lady who now stood before me. After the programme Susanna had hung back until all the others had departed, then I drove her home, saying, 'I think it went quite well, don't you?'

'Fine,' Susanna had replied, 'but all the other kids thought you were very perculiar, Dad.'

'Perculiar?' I said, mortified.

'Well, you did keep winking at me all the time.'

Memory. Proust was right when he averred that most of our days are forgotten, unremembered, and could be stored, as it were, in a book for some vast library, in a book that no reader will ever ask for, that will never be taken down.

July 1985

Dear Norman,

I read your poem about triangles with interest. Perhaps you should allow it to be part of a geometric sequence? In exchange, Norman Kreitman, I offer you this Diagram to Explain Religion:

Draw a large circle not quite complete. Allow two apertures, each a centimetre wide, east and west, for exits and entrances. Within, sketch houses, trees, gasworks, grass. Also scrupulous soldiers bayoneting each other. Above these, trapeze artists. Above these, vultures. Above these, clouds. Above these, aeroplanes. Also other creatures, other things of this world, leaving spaces, inches of whiteness, so that all that breathes may breathe.

Outside the circumference make no pencil mark, despite Old Masters who claimed familiarity with the shapes of angels, demons, dissident unicorns, etc. This is how it is. Sometimes, through the aperture in the east, sometimes from the west, the modest whiteness outside slips into the aerobic whiteness inside. Watch carefully. When you see this happen, when you see the differences in the white, then write at the bottom of the page that signature you once forged in Sleep's Visiting Book.

All that's good,

Dannie

Dear Francis Bacon,

Let me tell you something about that particular painting that has so influenced you, a painting, indeed, most seminal for many other contemporary painters.

I am in possession of a secret, one that I have never divulged before. Your master, you may recall, was slain by a coronary in the solitude of his studio the very morning he hoped to finish this masterpiece. What you do not know is that the Angel of Death was about to leave softly, as usual, but he could not help gaze first at the canvas on the easel, at the contained black uproar on the canvas. With slow, such strange slow recognition, he stood there amazed. He bent down, excited, plucked the paint-brush from the recumbent's wax-work hand. He rose. Com-pelled, he approached the easel, completed the dark picture with hurried, moonless-dark brushstrokes. Note how this, the most melancholy, most macabre painting extant, remains unsigned...I take it you will not broadcast this secret. But having just been to your exhibition at the Tate I thought you would like to know.

As ever,
Dannie Abse

The biopsy proved that President Reagan has an intestinal neoplasm. Hence the telephone call from the *Sunday Express*. The *Express* spoke with the voice of Lady Olga Maitland, that well-known CND basher and gossip columnist. I was surprised to hear from her.

Lady O.M. 'In January 1984, you looked into your Orwellian crystal ball and wrote in the *Ham and High* that President Reagan would suffer a bowel cancer.'

D.A. 'Mmm?'

Lady O.M. 'The first suggestion that the President had anything suspicious at all was after a routine medical check-up in May 1984. So how did you know? Have you psychic powers?

D.A. 'Mmm.'

Lady O.M. 'How did you come to the conclusion he would suffer from bowel cancer?'

D.A. 'I have a cat — we call her Caitlin. She told me.'

Lady O.M. 'Seriously. How did you fathom it?'

D.A. I'm not going to tell you. Why should I let you into my secrets?'

Lady O.M. 'Mmm?'

Dissatisfied with my response (I should perhaps have talked about Reagan's frustrated sadistic anal drives which, through neuro-transmitters, led to mitotic changes in the cells of the mu-cous membrane, etc.), Lady Olga telephoned my relatives to dis-cover whether I was a true psychic.

Leo's wife, Marjorie, eventually killed the *Express* story. For when Lady O.M. telephoned her she snorted, 'Dannie foretell the future? You're jokin' — he can't predict who's going to win a match at Cardiff Arms Park.'

Since the *Express* phoned I've had a call from *The Times*. Now I sit by the telephone waiting for the CIA.

August-September 1985

Passionately held political convictions are likely to unhinge one who sets himself up as a literary critic, especially if he lacks a sense of humour. Certainly I was mildly irritated by John Barnie's review of *Wales in Verse*, an anthology I had edited for the Secker series. Despite remarking that it was 'an enjoyable anthology' Mr Barnie concentrated on attacking my brief inconsequential introduction rather than referring to the main text. True, he did focus on Anthony Conran's poem, 'Elegy for the Welsh Dead in the Falkland Islands, 1982' only to suggest, 'In his short introduction, Abse is at pains, it seems to me, to diminish the impact of a poem like this for his English readers.'

Why should I have wished to have done that? The poem is a bitter one, the only successful poem I know written about the war in the Falklands, and it so happens that I liked it not only as a poem but was, and am, in close sympathy with what is being said. My own view about the Falklands war is no different now from that which I expressed at the time in *Authors Take Sides on the Falklands (See Appednix 1)* when, along with others, in that summer of 1982, I was asked: 'Are you for or against our Government's response to the Argentinian annexation of the Falkland Islands?'

Indeed, when Anthony Conran sent me his poem to read he made it clear that it was for my private perusal. He felt the poem, if published, might wound susceptible relatives of the Welsh casualties. I persuaded him otherwise and he allowed me to publish the poem first in *Wales in Verse*. I count that a privilege.

*

Letters from America indicate that my poetry tour next month will be alarmingly strenuous: as far west as Iowa, as far north as Chicago, as far south as Texas. It's the travelling I dread most. Apart from readings I shall be obliged to give a lecture or two at medical schools — the relationship of Literature and Medicine. I have given very few formal lectures and I suspect I'm not very good at it.

Of course it is better to improvise, or at least seemingly improvise, like those lectures delivered, yes *delivered*, years ago by Dr Ernest Lloyd at Westminster Hospital when I was a medical student but which I still vividly remember. Ernie Lloyd resembled Lloyd George; he took him, I think, as a model, and even barbered his long white hair in the same fashion. Ernie did not wear a cloak but it would have become him. He would commence (not begin) his histrionic lectures on Cardiac Diseases by throwing out his left hand towards the ceiling, pause ceremonially, then with hand still elevated, stare steadily over his spectacles at his now curious student audience. Suddenly, he would shout in Welsh-English, as if announcing the Emperor of the World, *The heart, ladies and gentlemen, the old heart.* And slowly, inch by inch, lovely ham that he was, he would bring his left hand down until it reached his left chest where he would open and close it rhythmically as he continued, 'beats eighty times a minute, minute in, minute out, hour in, hour out, week in, week out, month in, month out, year in, year out...the old heart.'

After this prolegomenon he would lean forward as if to tell us some arcane, naughty secret. 'Have you ever heard a mitral murmur, boys, have you?' he would say softly. 'It's like the wind rustling through the golden corn. You think I'm being poetic? Why, when you listen with your stethoscope to the old heart, boys, you are listening to a kind of poetry.'

How many Abse family stories have I listened to over the years about cousins who played practical jokes on other cousins, (of hilarious invention, of course) of uncles roaring with laughter at the discomfiture of other uncles and aunts who had been benignly fooled by them? Perhaps playing practical jokes is in the Abse genes, a family trait, but ever since I read W.H. Auden's essay 'The

Joker in the Pack' I have paused before assuming the role of manipulative practical joker. Auden argues that every practical joke has a sinister element, that the joker is not only interested in unattractive power but has an identity problem. Fearful of being a brummagem he can only cry out, 'I am' when he tears the mask from his face as he laughs at his put-down victim. 'The practical joker,' Auden writes 'desires to make others obey without being aware of his existence until the moment of his theophany when he says, "Behold the god whose puppets you have been and behold, he does not look like a god but is a human being just like yourselves."'

But I would argue with Auden when he continues, 'even the most harmless practical joke is an expression of the joker's contempt for those he deceives'. I don't believe that. For instance — this may sound a bald remark — I am full of admiration for my wife and yet, once every two years, I become a fully-fledged Abse and play a practical joke on her.

A few mornings ago I was presenting a pre-recorded *Poetry Please* on Radio 4. I could not turn on the radio for, at that moment, I was at the clinic talking to a patient who had contracted a yeast-like fungus lung disease while out in Arizona — coccidioidomycosis. However I knew that Joan would probably be listening to the programme so, after the patient left, on impulse I telephoned home to ask:

'Ees Dr Abs zere, plis?'

'No, I'm afraid he's not here at present,' Joan replied.

'Ah. Uh. Ees that Mrs Abs?'

'Yes, it is. Can I help you?'

'Uh. Ah. I just vanted to say that I vos listening to *Poetry Plis* and I thought your husband vas Vunderful. *Simply vunderful.*'

'How kind of you to phone,' said Joan.

'Uh. Ah. You vill tell him of my admiration.'

'Certainly. Thank you.'

'And it's a vise vife, wouldn't you say, who knows her own husband, plis!'

Oddly, two days later, yesterday (my birthday), my brother Leo, wishing on my birthday to be fraternal, telephoned me.

'Dannie Abse?'

'Speaking,' I said, recognizing at once Leo's unmistakable Welsh accent, though for some reason he was trying to pretend he was a telephone operator.

'Will you take a reverse call from Ankara?' he said.

'Yes, Leo,' I replied.

Leo, who is now sixty-eight, told me that on the Friday he would publicly announce his intention to retire at the next General Election. This morning, September 28th, *The Times* is on my desk and I read Leo's speech: 'I have no intention of joining the ranks of ageing politicians who, Reagan-like, maniacally deny the ageing process and death itself. It is time to get a younger standard bearer in the constituency to give support to Neil Kinnock's premiership.'

It worries me that he speaks in such a resigned fashion; indeed my conversations with him recently are too much about Time passing and our eventual certain assignments with Thanatos. Leo has confessed in his book *Private Member* how the first year in the House of Commons was one of the most painful of his life: 'The nights after I left the Commons for my lonely hotel room were full of nightmares and terror: seemingly for hours I would, in a twilight world between dream and wakefulness be gripped by vertigo. The whole room would spin round me, now slowly, now like some ghastly merry-go-round totally out of control, and again and again my attempts to impose order and stillness on the whirling furniture would fail. I was unbalanced and had lost my bearings.'

I think leaving the Commons may be equally disturbing for him. After all, so much of his life has revolved around politics. He has been an MP since 1958 and before that he had been a Cardiff councillor. When he was twenty-one, before he had had the opportunity to vote himself, he had been adopted as a Labour councillor for one of the Cardiff wards. I was a fourteen year old schoolboy then and was soon chanting:

> Vote vote vote for Leo Abse
> Kick old Whitey in the pants.

Leo is one of the most remarkable individuals I have ever known. What startles those who do not know him is his proclivity to offer ceaseless Freudian explanations for argued beliefs or particular actions. It naturally upsets them! He has worn psycho-analytical spectacles for scores of years. When we both lived in our parents' house in Cardiff he had, pinned up on his bedroom wall, a reproduction of Giorgione's 'La Tempesta'. 'It shouldn't have been called 'The Tempest',' he argued. 'It's post-coital. Look how calm and serene the scene. The storm has passed; the man is dressed now and the naked woman is feeding her child. Look how between them flows the river which represents Time, does it not, flowing on to eternity eternally. And note in the foreground how the column is broken, a spent penis symbol. Right?'

Unpredictable, original, irritating, tactless, extremely efficient, quick to understand a problem and to suggest a sensible solution, it must have been vexing for him to have watched fellow MPs, less gifted, though more tactful, some associated with Cardiff like James Callaghan or George Thomas, achieve honours and positions of power while he remained a backbencher. Yet, as Michael Foot once said to me, 'Leo did more to raise the quality of life for many in Britain through his private bills than did the government under Wilson's long tenancy at 10 Downing Street.'

When Leo entered parliament, Aneurin Bevan advised him to 'cultivate irreverence'. Leo never needed that advice. On the contrary, a dose of foreign office caution might have been more corrective for him. But a man's character, of course, is his fate, and Leo, quite rightly, had to be and must continue to be, himself. He will continue for the next two years anyway to impugn overtly the motives of his fellow MPs, inform them man to man, that their actions are an expression of auto-erotic narcissism or repressed homosexuality or — as he once said to a bewildered Richard Crossman — 'The trouble with you, Dick, you're an obsessional; it's all to do with your early potty training.'

Leo's judgement of people, or rather his sometimes bizarre reasons for prejudice for or against them, must make his auditor wonder. Not long ago I asked him what he thought of Robert Maxwell who, of course, years ago, had been a Labour MP. Leo hesitated. 'Didn't know him too well. But I didn't care for him.'

'Why not?'

'Well... he opened doors for me. He'd rush ahead, right, to open a door, you know. By being so subservient he must have experienced a feeling of power. No, didn't care for him. Right?'

When Leo was elected in 1958, I met him soon after at the Palace of Westminster. He was wearing a polo-necked sweater and a suede jacket. He looked boyish, not like a dignified MP at all, nor had he assumed then the flamboyant clothes so characteristic of him some years later.

'How do you like being an MP?' I asked, as he let me into the deserted medieval Westminster Hall.

'I'm forty,' he said. 'Life begins at forty! One should change the direction of one's life at forty.'

As we stood there grinning, suddenly the chimes of Big Ben struck the hour clear and near. Nine times. We waited silently and Leo ceased smiling. 'You know,' he continued softly, solemnly, 'ever since I've been a small boy I've dreamed of this moment, to be standing here as an MP and listening to Big Ben chime like that. I've achieved my ambition.'

'Well,' I said, 'what next, Leo? Have you further ambitions?'

'No, no,' he said.

'Wouldn't you like to be a minister?'

'No, no,' he said with utter seriousness. 'To be a backbencher, that's all that I wanted. That's enough, that's all I want. One can, with luck, be of use as a backbencher.'

He seemed overcome. He did not speak further and I was moved because I could see he was moved. As we continued to walk together silently I recalled how Freud had achieved his boyhood ambition of visiting Athens, of standing before the Parthenon and had felt unaccountably depressed. Later he recognized the source of his depression — he felt unworthy, as if he had been guilty of parricide. I did not guess Leo's own uncertainties. He always appeared to be so confident, so buoyant. If I had had an inkling of his true state of mind I might have referred to Freud's paper. Leo then, of course, had not yet written *Private Member* in which he echoed Freud by writing, 'All achievements bring guilt, and those most yearned for in childhood, on attainment, bring the heaviest neurotic burdens.'

Leo is a superb orator. He has certainly been unashamed of high rhetoric ever since he first uttered in public. I see him now, twenty-one years of age, standing on the raised platform of the drab, small, misnamed Sunshine Hall in the district of Canton, Cardiff, addressing forty or so individuals in wet, smelly raincoats and pronouncing, 'It is given to man to live but once and he should so live, that dying he may say, all my life and all my strength have been devoted to the finest cause in the world: the enlightenment and liberation of mankind.'

I was fourteen years of age and thrilled to hear such oratory. Later, when I read poetry seriously I could see the relationship between such oratory and certain modes of verse. For instance, Walt Whitman:

> Not a grave of the murder'd for freedom but grows seed for
> freedom,
> in its turn to bear seed,
> Which the winds carry afar and resow, and the rains and the
> snows nourish.
> Not a disembodied spirit can the weapon of tyrants let loose
> But it stalks invisibly over the earth, whispering, counselling,
> cautioning,
> Liberty, let others despair of you — I never despair of you.
>
> Is the house shut? is the master away?
> Nevertheless, be ready, be not weary of watching,
> He will soon return, his messengers come anon.

Could this not have been spoken by some brilliant orator at a political meeting? It is as much oratory as it is poetry while remaining recognizably the latter. It breaks the rules of poetry: it does not crystallize, it does not avoid generalizations, it relies on abstract words like 'Liberty'. And like oratory, rational and lucid as its meaning is, the hypnotic rhythms needle their way beyond the conscious mind.

Donald Davie, in his essay 'The Rhetoric of Emotion' would have us believe that there is a difference between the rhetoric of poetry and that of oratory. The orator, he suggests, endeavours to provoke emotion in order to make his auditors act, whereas in rhetorical literature the emotional inflammation is the end in itself. This, no doubt, is true for many rhetorical poets, Swinburne, Yeats, Dylan Thomas among them, but not for others and certainly not for many of the contributors to the first anthology of poetry I ever read voluntarily as a schoolboy, *Poems for Spain*. That was a time when Spain was the bloodiest arena in Europe and many an honest man or woman was appalled by Britain's Non-Intervention policy. The poets, then, like orators, were telling us 'a future of dust advances' and were trying to persuade people to act.

Most poets in Britain now avoid such large-gestured rhetoric. So, for that matter, with few exceptions, do our members of Parliament. Their speeches are cliché-ridden, modest, atrophic, grey, and they conclude with 'At the end of the day.' I suggested to Leo that this is because they were not brought up on the Bible: they did not have in their bloodstream, as it were, the enchanting cadences and parallelisms of the King James's Bible, unlike the old-time orators: Lloyd George, Churchill, Aneurin Bevan.

'The majority of MPs don't read anything,' Leo said, 'apart from sociological and economic textbooks.'

Perhaps the eschewing of rhetoric by post-war poets and MPs is because of the distrust of demagogy. Rhetoric — Hitler, Mussolini, Oswald Mosley — had been put to unprincipled use. As Ferdinand Brunetière declared in the nineteenth century: 'Where reasoning wanders, and reason even blenches there does rhetoric come and found its empire. It lays hold of an entire province of the human mind, not the least vast and inaccessible, and impenetrable to the demonstrations of erudition and the inductions of metaphysic; it establishes itself there and reigns in sovereign sway.' Throughout history monsters like Hitler have known how to calculate the effects of their bacterial rhetoric.

Why did the poets of the 1950s, the Movement poets, opt for a neutral tone and a cool accountant diction? Was it only a dialectical contradiction of its opposite — the verbal strategies of Dylan Thomas and the then fashionable excesses of neoromanticism? Perhaps it was also, unconsciously, a rebellion against the fashions of oratory — the age of Churchill was over and we had been led to the very edge of the chasm. Even the eloquent poets of that time seemed to distrust eloquence! Here's Emanuel Litvinoff, a war poet writing post-war — 'The Orator':

> ...His rich voice sweetened on corpses.
> Deep and thrilling, he could meet their praise
> With lush and laurelled dignities, raise

Verbal cenotaphs to close their violence.
The brave thunder of his guns in war
Shamed the inglorious reproach of grief.

What did it matter if his metaphors
Were frayed and mildewed like a sack of rags?
He knew the magic of old spells could bind
A power of hate upon his ancient curses,
And he could patch and mend his purple cloak
To prove the repetition of events.

Walking in space he dread to touch the ground
And lose his pain in commonplace commotion,
Rather would he be a bronze bell ringing
Carillons for victory and harvest or,
Better still, toll the bruised silence
Falling like ash on the spent field of war.

Yet when all's said and done, as Leo recently declared in a lecture at Oxford (he could have quoted Cicero), 'Rhetoric can inspire, persuade and finally move men into the cause of justice and prompt them into action that improves our lot and theirs.'

October-November 1985

Iowa City was a pleasant surprise: a river as wide as the Taff in Cardiff flowed right through the campus.

As Paul Zimmer let Joan and me into the hotel foyer we stumbled into Gerald Stern, a poet of some renown in the U.S.A.

'Are you all right now, Gerry?' asked Paul Zimmer. 'I know you've still got a bullet in your jaw.'

'Yeh,' replied Gerald Stern. 'The surgeon decided to leave it there. I'm OK except that when I go through security at the airport the bells ring, the buzzers buzz and all the lights go on.'

Poetry Readings, it seems, can be dangerous in the U.S.A. I have not heard of any poet on the circuit being shot in Britain though not a few perhaps, deserve to be. Gerald Stern was scheduled to read with Daniel Hoffman in Philadelphia. He had flown from Iowa City into Newark, New Jersey, where he had been met by one of the organizers of the prospective reading. Stern, very much a verbal man as I was to discover, perhaps distracted the driver with his lively conversation. Anyway, she soon lost her way. Newark, New Jersey, is not a good place to lose your way in. It makes Merthyr on a winter's night look like a garden city. As the driver hesitated at traffic lights, wondering whether to go right or left, a group of black youths appeared waving guns, demanding money. One of the youths, possibly smashed, without warning suddenly emptied his wild revolver and one of the bullets lodged in Gerald Stern's jaw.

'Hey,' said Gerald Stern lightly, 'I never made that reading with Daniel Hoffman but I'm coming to yours tomorrow!'

The lift, or rather the elevator, took Joan and me to our spacious room. I looked out of the window at this other America, so far from Newark, New Jersey. We could see the river. The trees were wonderfully rusted into colour — mustard, gold, brown, ochre, crimson — more spectacularly than they would be at home. One leaf fell slowly, as if on a stage set, and the river flowed on through the expensively-mounted opera landscape.

Rochester, NY. After our brief sojourn at Penn State, Joan and I temporarily parted ways. She drove the hired car to Washington, while I took a flight to Rochester where I was scheduled to give one talk and two readings over several days.

The first reading was to be at the medical school. So on Wednesday afternoon I was led into a large lecture room. Above me, row above row, sat medical students, a few doctors in white coats, other faculty staff. On the blackboard had been chalked: DON'T FORGET YOUR ANATOMY EXAMINATION IS TOMORROW. I decided that apart from reading poems relating to my own medical experience, it would be appropriate to read a page or two from my autobiography, *A Poet in the Family,* where I described my first reactions to working in the Dissecting Room. Those particular prose passages I had never read out loud before.

I had described how I had shared a cadaver with another nineteen year old medical student, one named Russell Barton, and how we had investigated that forlorn corpse, pried into its bloodless meat, dug into its sour formaldehyde-smelling material with our scalpels. The body we dissected seemed so anonymous. I continued, 'The neck, say, exposed with all its muscles and its vessels mimicking a coloured plate in an anatomy book seemed, soon enough, never to have belonged to a live person...the hand, or rather the resemblance of a hand, had never held, it seemed, another hand in greeting or in tenderness, had never clenched a fist in anger, had never held a pen to sign an authentic name. For this thing — as the weeks, the months, passed by — this decreasing thing, visibly losing its divine proportions, this residue, this so-called trunk of a body, this legless, armless, headless thing had never had a name surely?'

My reading of this prose passage from A *Poet in the Family* called forth several responses from some of the audience. One doctor related how when he had been a student his partner in dissection could not bear to behold the corpse's face. When he was working on the body he put a cloth over it. Faceless, it was more anony-mous. 'Guess what this student became?' said the doctor. 'A tho-racic surgeon. When he operates he still does not see the face.'

A Catholic priest who had been in the lecture room told me that the previous year, when the Anatomy course was concluded, he arranged a service to be conducted at his church for the dead bodies that had been dissected. 'Because of that anonymity you justly spoke about,' he said. 'I wanted to put that right so I invited the students to come to the service and the relatives of the cadavers. Towards the end of the service I ordered the Anatomy attendant from the Dissecting Room to read out the register, one by one, of the dead. The names of the cadavers. Do you know, many of the students cried when they heard that plangent roll-call?'

In the evening I gave a poetry reading for the English Depart-ment and gave medical matters a miss. Some people from the town attended and one of them, when the reading was over, lingered behind until I was free. 'Do you remember me, Dannie?' he asked. He had an English voice. 'I'm sorry,' I said as I stared at the short, smiling, grey-haired man in front of me. He interrupted me. 'Why should you remember?' he said. 'It's forty years since we met. I'm in private practice here in Rochester. I'm a psychiatrist. My name's Russell Barton.'

Chicago. I was startled and pleased to see John F. Nims, the ex-editor of *Poetry* (Chicago) at the reading. He had once declared that 'poetry readings are to our time what the Black Plague was to the fourteenth century'. A letter of his had been printed in the

Winter 1984/85 issue of the *American Scholar* in which he had quoted from Trollope's *Barchester Towers* changing 'Preaching clergyman' to 'visiting poet' and substituting 'poetry readings' for 'sermons'.

'There is, perhaps, no greater hardship inflicted on mankind in civilised and free countries, than the necessity of listening to poetry readings. No one but a visiting poet has, in these realms, the power of compelling an audience to sit silent and to be tormented. No one but a visiting poet can revel in platitudes, truisms, and untruisms, and yet receive as his undisputed privilege, the same respectful demeanour as though words of impassioned eloquence, or persuasive logic, fell from his lips.... A Member of Parliament can be laughed down or counted out. Town councillors can be tabooed. But no-one can rid himself of the visiting poet...that anxious longing for escape, which is the common consequence of poetry readings.... But you must excuse me, my insufficient young poet, if I yawn over your imperfect sentences, your repeated phrases, your false pathos, your drawlings and denouncings, your humming and hawing, your oh-ing and ah-ing.'

Nevertheless, there he sat, John Nims, demonstrating once again how for friendship's sake a man will suffer and endure many things. However, by now, living in Chicago with all those oh-ing and ah-ing poets passing through, John must have vigorous antibodies against the Black Plague racing through his bloodstream. Joe Paresi, who came to my other reading in Chicago (he's the present editor of *Poetry*), looked pretty fit too.

Philadelphia. After a long dream-like flight from Houston I was cheered at the barrier by seeing my real world again, for there, waiting, was Joan accompanied by Daniel Hoffman. Dan had arranged a reading for me at the University of Pennsylvania — Ezra Pound's and William Carlos Williams's student stamping-ground.

Next day, before the evening reading, suasible, we went with Dan and Liz Hoffman to catch the current Ars Medica exhibition: 'Art, medicine and the human condition' as it was importantly named. Well, St Luke is the patron saint of physicians and of painters. Tradition proclaims that he painted a portrait of the Virgin Mary and no doubt he practised alternative medicine.

A large section of the exhibition was devoted to Anatomy, a

subfusc topic that does not usually preoccupy my thoughts but which, lately, I seem to have had a dose of. As I inspected 'Blood-letting Manikin, 1517', 'Removal of the Pia Mater and a Cross Section of the Brain, 1541', 'The Anatomy Lesson of Dr Pieter Paaw, 1615' and 'Muscle Man, 1739', I found myself imagining the on-lookers at a 16th and 17th century public dissection. For at that time such dissections of human bodies were public ceremonies, spe-cially sanctioned by the Church, and the invited spectators would have included priests as well as physicians and artists. Such an occasion was part of a festival, a kind of necrophilic Strip Show. Of course, they were also questing for the seat of the soul. After that failure, the festival would continue; actors would be called in to present a decorous play or musicians hired to play cathartic music.

And speaking of necrophilia, one of the most memorable images in the exhibition was surely Munch's 'Death and the Maiden' — a naked buxom lady dancing with an actively sexual skeleton. Haunting, too, was a woodcut by Munch, 'Visit of Condolence'. In the background a bed in which lies, under the bedsheets, a dead woman. To the left, close to us, a door has been opened by the widower, allowing entrance to visitors who have handkerchiefs held to their faces. They are not weeping. Rather it seems they are assaulted by the smell of the odious, but no doubt, well-beloved, corpse.

How odd that is: in paintings, in prints, we are rarely directed towards an olfactory reality. All those beautiful painted flowers have no scent other than the paint itself.

November-December 1985

I was answering the letters that had accumulated while I was in the U.S.A. when the telephone sounded. It was Gavin Ewart. 'I enjoyed reading your piece in the *Poetry Review*,' Gavin said. 'That man, Norman Maw, I used to know him.'

In August I had quickly written a piece for the *Poetry Review* about a reading I had given in the Lake District and the behaviour of the, er, imposing gentleman who had chaired that reading (See Appendix 2). Gavin was now puzzling me, for he continued to opine on someone called Norman Maw.

'Norman Maw?' I asked.

'Yes, your chairman,' Gavin said.

Only later, when I received the *Poetry Review* did I realize that Gavin's posh accent had changed Moore to Maw. Not that it made any difference: I did not know anyone called Norman Moore either. The description I had given of that Lake District reading was totally truthful but I had invented the name of the chairman. In fact, as I spoke to Gavin Ewart on the telephone, not only had I forgotten the name that I had invented, but I was even under the impression that I had omitted the name of the chairman altogether, leaving that gentleman anonymous.

'Did you say Norman Maw?' I asked.

'Norman Maw,' agreed Gavin.

'I don't know him,' I said.

'Yes you do,' Gavin insisted. 'So do I.'

I held the phone to my ear, feeling jet-lagged.

'Anyway, I enjoyed reading the piece — I just wanted to tell you that. And that I, too, know Norman Maw.'

'Norman Maw?'

'Yes, your chairman.'

'My chairman? Gavin, I didn't actually give the name of the chairman in that *Poetry Review* piece, did I?'

'Oh yes you did,' said Gavin. 'I have it here. Norman Maw. I could tell you stories about him myself.'

'But Gavin, I avoided giving the name of that chairman.'

'Norman Maw,' said Gavin resolutely.

'I don't think it was Norman Maw,' I said.

'Yes it was,' said Gavin. 'It says so here in the *Poetry Review*. I knew him quite well. I was interested to learn that he's now living in the Lake District. I didn't know that.'

While we were in the U.S.A. our bright-eyed friend Hans Keller died. We shall miss him. As I'm writing this I hear his distinctive voice, his accent, the way he stated an opinion, one never tentative, utterly certain of its truth. Hans loved arguing, or to be more exact, 'fighting verbally'. Didn't he once remark, ' I am a fighter — but don't want to maim or kill anybody — which is a disadvantage!' He was remarkable in many ways — not least in that he could write a radio talk or a long complex lecture in his head. And then, when it came to its delivery, he only had to remember it.

Mozart, he told me, found the writing down of his compositions the least interesting aspect of his work. He was a clerk to himself and only had to remember his music and transcribe it. Mozart would listen, in fact, to other men's music while simultaneously he recorded his own!

Hans's favourite preoccupations were music, football and the theories and modifications of psychoanalytic psychiatry. In discussions of these subjects he was electrically alive. Even when he was quiet, when he carefully listened — often to the answer of a question he himself had posed — he seemed full of static electricity.

Brian Glanville once wrote that 'all goalkeepers are crazy'. By that, of course, he didn't mean they were psychotic. Simply, they tended to be more eccentric, more 'characters' than the rest of the team. Hans, when young, played football in goal — though remembering his wiry, matchstick frame which ever since I first knew him (1950?) had its Giacometti aspect, it was hard to imagine him punching out a ball from, say, a bustling corner.

At the BBC, where he worked for so many years, I'm sure he behaved rather like an international goalkeeper. Apart from opera he was in charge of all music. No doubt the BBC Managers had their problems with him. He did not want Radio 3 to become what it now is — a predominantly music programme. He was not in favour of cultural apartheid; he believed in mixed and contrasting planning. When Hans's views were labelled as eccentric, he replied, characteristically, with a question: 'In relation to which centre?'

He identified himself with the true heroes who took up maverick positions, like Freud, and who, at the time, appeared to be glaringly eccentric. He poured witty scorn on mediocrity.

In November 1938 as a teenager in Vienna, a Jewish boy, he was one of the victims of the Kristallnacht pogroms. He, like so many others, was beaten up, arrested, beaten up again, mentally tortured — on the sixth day of his imprisonment told 'Tomorrow at 6 a.m.

you will be castrated and at 8 o'clock you will be executed.' He tells of these gruesome experiences in his one book which he entitled *1975 (1984 minus 9).* A volume too little known. These experiences, I'm sure, left him with deep psychic wounds, but they also allowed him, as he himself asserted, the recurring awareness and grateful elation of being alive.

I think Hans overestimated my knowledge — I mean knowledge of a transcendental kind. He would ask me questions, metaphysical questions and he seemed to expect me to provide concrete, logical answers. Did he fancy that because I was a poet I was privy to certain supernal verities? I suspect he believed music itself was a secret language that had evolved over the milleniums from celestial discourse! Hans, as musician and critical interpreter, surely not only attempted to discover the names of the demons and of the gods, but quested, in a secular way, for what lay hidden behind the hidden, the revelation of the metadivine.

Now comes news of other casualties: Robert Graves, Philip Larkin, Geoffrey Grigson.

I met Robert Graves but once and in *A Strong Dose of Myself* (Hutchinson, 1983) I wrote an account of the meeting which I doubt Mr Graves would have enjoyed. But I liked, and continue to like his poetry. He composed poems in the central English lyric tradition and he used a conservative diction and a logical syntax without display, though not without the power to surprise. His was an essentially romantic sensibility, with belief in phantoms and miracle; in the terrifying and terrific supernatural; in his interest in myth as a surviving, operativepower even in our so-called rational societies; and in his enduring preoccupation with the creative and destructive element that waxes and wanes in the man-woman relationship.

Indeed, almost one-third of Robert Graves's poems refer to this relationship. In 1963 he opined: 'My theme was always the practical impossibility, transcended only by miracle, of absolute love continuing between man and woman.' He seemed to believe in the mythographic story of woman as the lover and the destroyer of man. As Ronald Gaskill has put it — 'the story of man drawn inescapably to woman by her beauty, immolated in the act of love and finally supplanted by her son.'

Unlike D.H. Lawrence, Graves did not dwell on the physicality of man-woman love. With Graves one seldom senses a man and woman most and least themselves, coupling beneath the sheets. Rather we encounter the emotions of lovers or ex-lovers, and usually they are fully-clothed and courtly always, and civilized always, even in dismissal and disappointment. (Not surprisingly Graves called D.H. Lawrence a 'wretch', a man who is sick, muddle-headed and sex-mad). When we do discover Robert Graves's lovers in bed as in the poem 'Never Such Love' they are groping for words rather than for each other:

> Turned together and, as is customary,
> For words of rapture groping they
> 'Never such love,' swore 'ever before was.'
> Contrast with all loves that had failed or staled
> Registered their own as love indeed.

I hardly knew Larkin either. We met only at the Poetry Book Society committee meetings. As a chairman he was always courteous, always considerate, relieving argumentative tensions with humorous one-liners. He did not seem shy, though I'm sure he was.

In committee, he had a problem with his deafness. In earlier years he suffered, I understand, from a dire stammer. There was no trace of that handicap at the PBS meetings. Apparently that crippling stammer had dramatically cleared up when his father died. He was suddenly free to say what he wished. Yet later he suffered another kind of block. He could not write poetry.

> They fuck you up, your mum and dad.
> They may not mean to, but they do.

From all accounts Philip's father, the Coventry City Treasurer, had been a most dominating, authoritative figure, mercilessly tidy and solemn. According to Noel Hughes who had been at school with Philip Larkin, he, Sdney Larkin, went on visits to pre-war Germany and was struck by 'qualities of decisiveness and vigour in German public administration that compelled his admiration'.

Sooner or later someone will write a biography of Philip Larkin.

My guess is that the biographer will not have to be a crude Jake Balokowsky to discover that Sidney Larkin was an unambiguous, fervent Nazi sympathizer.

How much did Philip model himself on his father? I do not mean politically, although Philip Larkin's own knee-jerk, right-wing views I find deplorable enough. (How absurd and näive of Craig Raine to write in today's *Guardian*, 'The nice thing about Larkin is that he was a reactionary.')

However much I admire Philip Larkin's poetry it was his social attitudes that made me feel distanced from him. It was predictable that when the PBS had to shift from the Arts Council's sheltering roof to either the care of the National Book League or to the Poetry Society, Philip supported the NBL because of its larger economic resources and despite its 'non-record' concerning poetry.

'I'm for the Big Battalions,' Philip argued, not being ironic, as of course Voltaire had been when he wrote, 'On dit que Dieu est toujours pour les gros bataillons.' The Big Battalions are what I've never been for. It's not for nothing that Cardiff City FC are now right at the bottom of Division Three!

It is good to be back in Ogmore. Because of the American trip we have not been here since October 6th. This time of the year one can take an oxygen walk to Southerndown without seeing anyone — for company there's only the sheep, the crows and the gulls, and perhaps an occasional self-absorbed, solitary dog. This morning we took the sand route at first, for the tide was right; then we climbed up and over the rocks to the high, breath-holding cliffs. We observed a sheep utterly motionless. It seemed to be reading a red danger sign on which was written DANGEROUS CLIFFS. To mis-quote Shelley: there is only one better walk in the world than from Ogmore to Southerndown and that is the walk from Southerndown to Ogmore. The return journey is especially good to take at dusk when one can watch the slow Western mobile sunsets below the aeroplane vapour-trails.

In the 1930s, when we lived in Cardiff, our car, a Riley, seemed to know only one route. It would go instinctively to Ogmore-by-sea. My father only had to sit in the driving seat, turn on the ignition, and off it would go along the A48, up Tumble Down Dick, through Cowbridge, up and down Crack Hill, all of the twenty-three miles to the sea, the sea at Ogmore. Every half sunny Sunday, every holiday, the car knew we wanted to play cricket on the sands of Hardee's Bay while its boss, my father, fished near the mouth of the river for dabs, salmon bass, and ghosts.

Not only my immediate family homed back to Ogmore. Uncles and aunts, fat and thin, cousins short and tall, from Cardiff, Swansea, Ammanford, singing in their closed saloons, 'Stormy Weather' and 'She was a Good Girl until I took her to a Dance' returned to meet and quarrel and take a dip in the unstable Ogmore estuary.

My sister, Huldah, once confided that she had lost her virginity in one of the secret caves of Ogmore while my Uncle Max, unaware, played the violin on the rocks nearby, and cousins and their friends munched gritty tomato sandwiches and stared at the incoming, loosely-chained sea.

Not everybody in the Abse family is stuck on Ogmore. I have an American nephew, Nathan. When he was ten he came to stay with us at Ogmore. His voice was inordinately deep and husky and Virginian. He arrived after nightfall, gave the slate-black emptiness of Ogmore the once over, heard the sheep munching in the dark, then gazing towards the funfair's shimmering lights across the bay of distant Porthcawl, said, 'Hey, man, let's take off for civilization.'

I wish we could stay here longer. I'm fed up with driving up and down the M4, from and to London. But I don't see any solution to that. In the new year we shall still be making the same tedious journeys. No matter, now, as I breathe out the air of London and breathe in the air of Ogmore I know it's all worth it. I walk beside the cutlery-glinting sea, consoled by the sound of the waves' irregularities, by the pitch and tone of them, the 'sssh' of shingle, the way the sea slaps on rocks or shuffles sinking into the sand that sizzles as the tide recedes. And there, quite near really, the steamers pass, slow and hushed, around the breath-holding cliffs on their seamless way to the ports of Barry, Cardiff, Newport and, in dream, further, mysteriously, into 1986.

January-February 1986

Both Joan and I have been reading Jeffrey Masson's book *The Assault on Truth*. Until given the sack, Masson worked on the archives at Freud's house in Maresfield Gardens, Hampstead. He discovered documents and letters which led him to write this rather scandalous volume.

Masson believes that trauma, sexual abuse or rape of a child by father or relative, lies at the root of most mental illness. This aetiological hypothesis Freud advocated in 1896 but discarded when he realized that his patients' rememberings of such assaults were but once-forgotten fantasies.

When Joan and I joined Carole and Jeremy Robson for an Indian meal our conversation circled around Masson's book, the details of which, particularly his description of the unnecessary iatrogenic, physical sufferings endured by Freud's patient, Emma Eckstein, had deeply shocked my wife. Indeed after the onion bhajis had been consumed, Joan and I were engaged in a too vigorous argument about Freud with the Robsons looking on, somewhat troubled.

Aware of their uneasy silence, I wanted to say to Joan in my middle class way, 'not in front of the neighbours, kid'. But her blood was up, as my mother would have put it. Thus, our verbal private aggression (assaults) continued until I, narked, found myself moving to a Hans Keller, barely forgivable, infuriating conclusion. 'I won't argue with you further, Joan, because 1. you are absolutely wrong and 2. because I am absolutely right.' I saw Carole and Jeremy simultaneously thrust their forks into their buttered chicken.

Paul and Susanna proudly visited us with their baby. More than a quarter of a century ago I had listened to Susanna's heartbeat before she had been born. A month ago, I put my right ear to Susanna's own tight, convex abdomen and heard the fast heartbeat of her child to be. I listened with a kind of muted excitement as if I had been privileged to hear the secret of the future. When I raised my head and could no longer hear that vibrant masterpiece the conversation between Keren and Joan continued. They were discussing the events in Northern Ireland and I felt as if I had plunged my face into ice-cold water.

Anyhow, here Susanna was with my first grandchild in her arms, the baby emperor herself. I gazed into her colourless, unfocussed eyes. Her sight was still inward.

Paul told me that in April they intend to get married. They have been living together for several years but now it seems my son-out-of-law intends to become my son-in-law and they will make an honest grandfather out of me.

The Roll Call was to take place on Monday, February 17th, in the stone arena on the waterfront of the National Theatre from dawn to dusk. The names to be called belonged to some of the 10,000 Soviet Jews who had applied for and had been refused emigration visas. One name missing, fortunately, from that list would now be Anatole Scharansky.

When Tom Stoppard wrote asking if I would join one hundred or so others in reading a page of that register I had to accept. I had reservations, of course: I knew that many of these 'refuseniks' were religious zealots who, if they reached Israel, as was their imperative wish, would swell the numbers of those opposed to tolerant and more rational policies. On the other hand, I was aware, too, how, having applied for visas, these Jews whatever their religious and political affiliations, were subject to arbitrary arrest, to searchings and to beatings, to all kinds of discrimation and harrassment.

They had endured such humiliations for many years and were willing to endure them still, so how could one refuse to read for one and a half minutes a list of names to a microphone in the open air and to a TV camera on a cold February day?

I was sent a page to read. It began *Veronika Dubrovskaya*. And after her name was written the length of time she had been waiting for a visa: seven years. I looked down the list:

Rakhil Dulman — Seven years
Zinaida Kanskaya — Six years
Svetlana Kaplan — Seven years

There were twenty names in all. So that Monday afternoon I left the chest clinic early and by 3.30 p.m. I was waiting with Brian Magee, Alan Silitoe, Alfred Marks, Adrian Mitchell, and Sian Phillips, to take my turn and step forward to the microphone. Strewn on the stone arena in front of me were many carnations, more and more being added, each one representing a person who had applied for an exit visa and who was still forlornly waiting. The names of these individuals were read out continuously, one after one — a steady rhythm of names — for between, say, Adrian Mitchell and Alan Silitoe announcing their lists, elsewhere, over another microphone, other names were being called by drama students. One after one after one, regular as the beat of a metronome, the long cast was identified, had been identified since dawn, and was still being called out now while, below, cold, the River Thames flowed on.

'*Veronika Dubrovskaya* — seven years; *Fanya Dukhovnaya* — seven years.' And then, to my horror, I observed that somehow the photocopy print had, for some reason, become smudged so that the letters were out of focus and a number of the names quite unreadable. To fill up the gap in the list I quickly invented names. Did I say '*Alexy Karamazov* — eight years, *Ivan Ilyich* — seven years'?

I'm not sure, now, what Russian names I uttered, but soon the list became clear again and I was back to the real world of characters, not fiction:

Svetlana Kaplan — seven years
Yan Kaplan — seven years
Yuliya Kapustina — five years.

But what of the real names, half-erased, unreadable, that I did not call out? Who were they? Who are they? Where are they today?

It was a game, of course. Who, of all people in history would you have liked to dine with most? I did not hesitate long. Dismissing half-naked Helen of Troy, I plumped for Shakespeare. Yet if he spoke (no doubt eloquently) over our pizza, given his strong Elizabethan accent, would I have understood him? But think of the questions one could ask:

'Will, do you agree with Wordsworth that the sonnets unlocked your heart?'

'Mmmmm?'

'How autobiographical are the sonnets?'

'Mmmm.'

'Can I have your opinion of the Earl of Southampton?'

'Mmmm.'

'Will, is that hair of yours a natural red?'

'Mmmm?'

'Will, during the plague in London of 1592 did you slope off to Italy?'

'Mmmm?'

'Will, Shakespearean scholars of today are very interested in the nature of your sexual appetites.'

'Mmm?'

'Would you like a cappucino to follow your pizza?'

'Mmmm.'

I must stop daydreaming. I agree with Stephen Booth's irrefutable assertion that William Shakespeare was almost certainly homosexual, bisexual or heterosexual.

March-April 1986

On my way back to the clinic I was startled to see ahead of me the doppelganger of a publisher's rep whom I used to encounter in the Welsh bookshop in Cecil Court. It could not be he for that rep had died several years ago. Frankly, I had never found him very congenial and as he, or rather the image of him, proceeded towards me I was surprised how he stared unsmilingly into my eyes as if awaiting recognition. I felt the cold at the back of my neck as he passed by silently.

Perhaps the wine taken over lunch, not excessive, had affected me more than I realized?

But sometimes, even the most sober of us and the most healthy of us, find it difficult to distinguish between illusion and reality.

And not just man but the creatures too. If the Greeks are to be believed did not a certain stallion attempt to mount a mare painted by Apelles?!

What is real? What is not real? Hercules, startled by the lifelike quality of Daedalus's statue of himself, is reported to have thrown a stone at it. And when Byron visited Athens in 1810, his companion, Hobhouse, overheard Greek workmen refusing to carry a statue to Lord Elgin's ship for they believed they heard the statue sobbing at the prospect of exile.

But to meet one assumed dead walking down familiar Goodge Street at two o'clock of an afternoon does provoke feelings that are uncompanionable. The word 'uncanny' comes to mind. I suppose what makes an incident feel uncanny is when we can provide no plausible, mechanistic, *satisfying* explanation for it.

I find it interesting that the word for 'uncanny' in Arabic or Hebrew signifies also the daemonic.

We decided to dine out to celebrate the arrival of an advance copy of my new book of poems, *Ask the Bloody Horse*. We chose to eat at The Cosmo in Swiss Cottage. Joan and I had not visited that Viennese café for years but suddenly, in nostalgic mood, we wanted to make a return journey to 1949. In the post-war years, when I was a medical student, instead of studying in my 'digs' in Aberdare Gardens, NW6, Boyd's *Textbook of Pathology* or Hamilton Bailey's *Physical Signs in Clinical Surgery* I often spent an evening gossiping and arguing with other Cosmo habitués.

Because of the refugees who had come to live in small rooms scattered across Swiss Cottage, this area had become a corner of Vienna with a distinct café life. Soon, young British writers, artists, musicians and burglars, joined the refugees and found the party-going, cigarette-smoke laden atmosphere of The Cosmo congenial. Generally Joan — then Joan Mercer — and I sat in the annexe over one cup of coffee all night but there were occasions when the annexe was too full and its occupants overflowed into the large main restaurant where they had laid white linen table-cloths over the tables in order to encourage their clientele to eat something!

It was to the main restaurant that we now repaired. It had hardly changed. There was something old-fashioned about the place, something outmoded, as if the clock had stopped not so much in 1949 but in pre-war Vienna. On the walls were prints by Topolski and one had the feeling of not being in England. It was probable that the ageing waiters, despite their white coats, white shirts, black bow ties, were really chess players in disguise. The menu, too, was unaltered and surely unalterable, written down, as it were, with the permanence of the Ten Commandments. Thou shalt eat Rheinischer Sauerbraten with Dumplings and Red Cabbage or Wiener Schnitzel or Zwiebel Hockbraten or Zwiebel Rosbraten Viennoise, or Karlsbraten Veal Goulash.

The man (surely a successful refugee?) at the next table was already commanding his dinner. The waiter stood, pad and biro in hand, poised like a cat to spring on whatever sentence our next-door-table neighbour would utter.

'Uh-huh,' he finally asked, 'is it veal goulash?'

'Of course it's real,' the waiter said, baffled.

'I said veal not real,' he pronounced. 'If it's not veal I don't vant it.'

'It's veal, sir,' the chess player, disguised as a waiter, said.

'It's not pork?'

'No.'

'I don't vant pork.'

'It's not pork.'

'Pork I don't vant.'

'If it's written on the menu, veal, sir, it's veal. If it's written pork, it's pork.'

The customer once more read through the menu and the waiter waited.

'I'll have veal goulash,' he finally said.

It was odd to gaze around the restaurant and observe not one person known to us. Where were the novelists, youthful once more, Peter Brent, Bernice Rubens, Peter Vansittart? Where the sculptor, Bill Turnbull? Would not Emanuel Litvinoff, Cherry Marshall and Rudi Nassauer come in at any minute? Was Ivor M in jail again? Were Keith Sawbridge, Fred Goldsmith and Old Bondy next door in the annexe arguing the toss? I recalled Jack Ashman, somewhat manic, and Theodore Bikel with his guitar — and the prettier faces of Penny, Noa, Betty, Jacky, Peter the Girl, Nina Shelley. I looked out of the window. Across the road where once had stood the elegant facades of fire-blitzed houses reigned instead W.H. Smith and MacDonalds.

Soon Joan and I were talking about the most remarkable ghost of The Cosmo, Elias Canetti. Canetti, some twenty years older than us, used to insist we called him Canetti, not Elias, since he did not care for his first name. But was that merely a rationalization? His own heroes, Stendhal, Kafka, Musil, among them, were hardly called, by us, Henri, Franz, and Bobby! He was a lord spiritually and lords have no first names. His unswerving courtesy, his evident erudition, did not diminish his formidable aura and presence.

Joan said, 'I wouldn't have dared to join his table unless signalled to do so. He was so formidable. Of course, I was only twenty-three years old.'

Canetti would sit in The Cosmo regularly, often with pen in hand. When questioned on what he was writing he made it clear that it was a masterpiece. He had been working, he told us, on a book about Crowds and Power for more than a decade. When asked when he would publish it he quite seriously commented that there was plenty of time, that he did not wish to make the mistake Freud had done — contradict himself. 'I have to be sure,' he would say passionately. If ever a man believed he would one day receive the Nobel Prize for Literature that man was Elias Canetti. And he was right. Meanwhile we read the only book of Canetti's then available in English— his early novel *Auto-Da-Fé*— and we found it strangely memorable.

Joan, however formidable she found the middle-aged Canetti, did not think his conversation as remarkable as I did. Interesting, yes, but not remarkable.

'Why do you find it *so* illumiating?' she once asked me.

I could not, at that moment, quote anything particularly pithy. I recounted, instead, the story Canetti had told me the previous evening, about his meeting with Graham Greene: how Greene had expressed his admiration for *Auto-Da Fé*; how he would be grateful if Canetti would sign his copy of the book for him. Canetti, it seemed, as he sat in his chair, observed a wall of books opposite him and noted how his own novel had been placed right at the bottom — 'Right-hand side, in the servile position of Z,' exclaimed Canetti. Meanwhile, as Canetti took in the insignificant, inferior and therefore to him insulting position of his book, Greene scrambled about in search of it, up, down, right, left, centre, and though on his knees, could not locate Canetti's novel. And Canetti pretended he did not know where to look either.

'So what?' Joan had justly asked, after I had retold that anecdote.

I pondered. The story had depended so much on Canetti's own animated engagement with it as he had re-lived the incident, and how, with startling skill, he had mimicked Graham Greene's voice, mannerisms, posture, hesitations. In his telling of the story, Canetti had given his auditor a comical glimpse of a trivial power struggle, human rivalry.

'Next time Canetti says something wonderful,' Joan had said drily, 'let me know.'

A few evenings later, I joined Canetti at his table in the Cosmo annexe. As I listened to him, I realized how much I was impressed by the fact that he knew so many writers, had met so many whom I respected. Was I dazzled by the name-dropping as well as by his stunning erudition? It was more than that: he had the gift of making whomever he was with in conversation feel important.

> There is nothing so small but my tenderness paints
> It large on a background of gold.

He had the habit of holding his head to one side in a listening posture. He was acoustically aware, as most people aren't, to each word spoken, however trivial. 'Respect for others,' he believed, 'begins with not ignoring their words.' And so he listened to my youthful vapourings as if I spoke with the wisdom of Solomon. He paid attention as a great physician would. And he responded to a comment, to an idea proposed, often excitedly, vividly articulate.

Just before we quit The Cosmo at closing time — we had been talking about paranoia — Canetti remarked, 'But the man suffering from paranoia is correct. Someone *is* standing behind the door pumping invisible gas through the keyhole. For we're dying, right now, all of us, a little every minute.'

Later that night, long after midnight, when I went back to the flat in Belsize Square that I shared with Joan, she was asleep.

Soon I was lying in the dark thinking of Canetti's remark about paranoia and when Joan's regular, soft breathing altered I assumed she had woken up.

'Joan,' I whispered.

She stirred. 'You know what Canetti said,' I continued. She moved restlessly away to the other side of the bed.

'Canetti said,' I repeated.

'What?'Joan said, suddenly awake. 'What? What's the matter?'

'Canetti said that the man suffering from paranoia is correct,' I continued, 'someone *is* standing behind that door pumping invisible gas through the keyhole.'

The room was silent. Then Joan said, 'Christ, you woke me up, just to tell me *that*?'

Because of the publication of *Ask the Bloody Horse* Donald Sturrock has been making a short film about me for BBC2's *Bookmark* programme. Yesterday, when we had more or less finished this project, I asked him what writer would he be focusing on next?

'Any suggestions?' he countered.

I mentioned Canetti. At once I realized that that was a barren idea. Canetti would not allow himself to be interviewed on television. I suspect he would judge it to be too vulgar an enterprise. I recall how, during that Swiss Cottage period, he would express contempt for C. Day Lewis simply because that poet pot-boilered detective stories under another name — as if by doing so, words so legitimate in the confines of a poet's vocabulary, had somehow been sullied and betrayed. I think Canetti had an attitude towards words similar to that the Kabbalists once had for the holy Hebrew alphabet.

Once, in the Cosmo, I happened to share a table with W., an ex-Leavisite critic who had become a 'commercial' novelist and who had recently begun to contribute articles to the *Evening Standard*. After W. quit, Canetti joined me and passionately declared, 'You shouldn't talk to that man. He's worthless. Have you seen his articles, how he uses words? You'll be polluted by people like that.'

It seemed to me then no less than now, that the notion that journalism could corrupt a serious writer was a romantic cliché and unlike many clichés, did not even encapsulate a truth. I know I don't feel corrupted! Yet I continue to understand Canetti's concern for words — some would say abnormal concern. Words do seem to own divine attributes; one can believe they are the source of revelation and that if one could discover some secret combination of them one would attain eternal beatitude. They are like gods in a way, immortal and dangerous. We summon them to help us, to curse and to praise; they allow us some measure of understanding within them, and, beyond their definitions, there is only mystery and silence.

All writers are in thraldom to them and await word-attacks when sometimes, as if from nowhere, a poem results. If such given words do not arrange themselves coherently — I do not mean logically — then the artefact that results seems merely pathological.

Canetti has confessed to very odd 'word-attacks'. 'I recall that in England, during the war,' he wrote, 'I filled page after page with German words. They had nothing to do with what I was working on. Nor did they join together into any sentences...They would suddenly take me by storm and I would cover a few pages with words, as fast as lightning. When I sensed that such a word-attack was imminent I would lock myself in as though to work...I must add that I felt extremely happy during such a fit. Since then, there has been no doubt for me that words are charged with a special kind of passion.... They suddenly spring forth and demand their rights.'

To pack them into a mere detective novel then, or worse, into an inconsequential article for the *Evening Standard,* was, for Canetti, surely to demean the gods themselves and to sell them into dark bondage as slaves.

I recall meeting Peter Williams in the infant's playground at Marlborough Road School, Cardiff, 'I'm six,' I said. He replied, 'I'm seven and I'm growing fast.' When I told him my name he told me his. Then he started boasting about his father.

'He knows everything,' Peter Williams said.

'Gosh,' I said, 'Bet he doesn't know my father.'

'Course he does,' Peter Williams said with the seriousness of authority.

'Go on,' I said.

'I'll tell you his name if you like,' said Peter.

'You don't know that,' I said.

'I do because my father knows him. He knows everything.'

'What's my father's name then?' I challenged him.

Peter Williams hesitated. 'Mr Abse,' he said. And I looked at him awed. Fancy having a father who knew everything.

When I went home and told my father that Peter Williams's father knew him my Dad said, 'Who?'

I related our conversation in the school playground and I couldn't understand then why my parents both laughed as if they were at the Music Hall.

I do not know why Peter Williams, aged seven, came to mind during the wedding ceremony for Paul Gogarty and Susanna Abse at the Registry Office yesterday. Perhaps it was because of my grandchild who slept through it all. The couple had agreed that Gogarty would be the child's surname if it were a boy, Abse if a girl. And now they were getting married the baby girl would still retain Abse as a surname. Her full name would be Larne, Kate, Gogarty, Abse. I like Gogarty as a first name. I can see myself calling her Goggers. But nobody in the playground when she's six will be able to fool her quite in the same way as Peter Williams fooled me.

May 1986

During the early 1960s I received the first note from one who signed himself 'The Master'. He had pencilled on a grubby half page, torn from a slumbering, green-lined exercise book, his peremptory message: 'I have just returned your novel, *Some Corner of an English Field*, to my local library. It shows greater control, tautness, economy than your earlier work; but you must ensure, in the passing years, that when you embark on writing prose it performs no disservice to the reputation of your poetry. Yours sincerely, "The Master".'

Who was this headmaster who patted me on the head? Wouldn't it have been more in keeping with anonymity if he had abused me? Called me upstart crow, rude groom, buckram gentleman, painted monster? I examined the postmark on the cheap, creased envelope:

Beaconsfield. Who lived there? Disraeli had been dead these many years, so had the poet Edmund Waller. (I did not know, then, that Colonel Gadaffi's favourite spot in England was Beaconsfield. He had spent several months in England while a young soldier on a signals course.) So who of the 10,000 denizens of Georgian Beaconsfield had sent me that report?

Some months later I published a group of poems in a literary magazine and again the small office-brown shiny envelope with its postmark of Beaconsfield arrived. Within, I discovered the same grubby piece of paper, the same scrawl on it, the same signature and cognomen. Regularly, for several years after that, whenever I contributed to a magazine or broadcast on the radio or had a play produced, or published a book, I would usually receive a benign review from the anonymous Master of Beaconsfield. I did not welcome his unsolicited comments for I found his very anonymity disturbing but I had to acknowledge that his reviews had a rare degree of percipience and, indeed, an elegance of style. His notes became letters and his letters were *composed*.

Then, one Saturday morning, I suddenly discovered who this wigged and stocking-faced Master was, for Joan happened to read a letter in the *New Statesman* by a certain novelist — or should I say, rather, an ex-novelist. And the address he disclosed was Beaconsfield.

'Didn't you used to know him?' Joan asked.

He was a novelist of the Thirties generation. When I had been a sixth form schoolboy in Cardiff I had read his contributions to John Lehmann's *Penguin New Writing* Later, after I came to London to study medicine, I met him several times in the pubs of Soho and in the busy cafés of Swiss Cottage. Once, before I had published anything anywhere, he invited me to send him poems for a new magazine he proposed to edit. I did so and he accepted them. In the event, the magazine, to my disappointment, never appeared and, oddly, he too disappeared — not only in person but as the years were to demonstrate, as a novelist too. Some time later I heard he had become a window cleaner and lived in Kilburn. Now, it was possible, he was domiciled in Beaconsfield.

'I didn't know him very well,' I told Joan, 'but he was always kind to me. Do you really think he could be "The Master?"'

I decided to write to him — simply: 'Dear Master, I noted your address in the NS. It's been too many years since I've seen you. I trust all goes well and all manner of things. Best, Dannie.'

If he truly had been the author of those innominate letters he would not be baffled by my note. His response came quickly, the recognizable brown envelope, the tatty piece of paper. 'You are a very clever detective. I should have posted my letters to you far from Beaconsfield. The Master.'

That staccato note struck me as being very strange. One would have expected him, unmasked, to have been more chatty, personal perhaps, and certainly to have signed it with his real name. When I did not receive more letters from him, over the next year, I assumed that he felt no longer compelled to overlook my published work now that I knew his real identity. Not so; in September 1967, I contributed to a symposium published in *Encounter* called 'Intellectuals and Just Causes' which referred to the recent war in the Middle East between Arabs and Israelis. (Probably *Encounter* are organizing a similar feature, at present, following last week's Reagan bombing of Libya.) As a result of my contribution I received a shocking, anti-Semitic letter from 'The Master'. He praised Hitler and justified the murder of the Jews in Europe before allowing himself a more personal fusillade of insults. His letter revealed how deeply sick he was and so I had better not, even now, reveal his true name.

I ignored his sad, sodding letter and I did not hear from him again until 1974 when I published an autobiography, *A Poet in the Family*. This time he wrote at length, and blandly. After amiable comments about my book he dwelt on memories of his own early upbringing and adolescence. He concluded his twelve-page letter by sending me his best wishes and signed it once more 'The Master'. I thought, until this morning, that was the last and final signal from Beaconsfield, but among the few letters arrived by the first post were a few forwarded on to me from the BBC as a consequence of my short film in *Bookmark*. One envelope, brown, cheap, creased, which I opened proved to be empty. Had my correspondent simply forgotten to include the letter he had written? Or was this the ultimate in symbolic anonymity? I read my name *typed* on the envelope, c/o BBC and the original postmark — Northampton, a place as 'The Master' might have said himself, quite far from Beaconsfield.

I don't know. *I don't know.*

This morning (May 4th) an East wind was blowing so vigorously in Ogmore that our wooden gate had been thrust open. From the bedroom window I could see that a ewe with two lambs had trespassed into our garden. They were munching the daffodils and narcissi, a nice, forbidden, wicked breakfast. I rushed downstairs, still in my pyjamas, to shoo them out.

As I closed the gate behind them I thought more of the East wind than the sheep. Probably it was bearing invisible death-seeds from Chernobyl. Perhaps radioactive raindrops were sipped from the daffodil cups by the ewe and the lambs. Information, so far, is meagre. In any case, who can believe the complacent, stealthy, reassuring voices of experts and politicians? How much has been covered up before, how much will be told to us now? Will radioactive iodine be taken up by small, thirsty thyroid glands? What about my new granddaughter and all those like her from Ogmore-by-sea to the Ukraine and beyond where Prometheus is still chained to his rock while the vulture eats his liver?

Last Friday in Cardiff, I visited Llandaff Cathedral. I just happened to be nearby, so popped in as I used to as a boy, passing the yellow celandines beneath the yew tree. Inside soaring spaces of worship — Jewish, Moslem or Christian — I feel not just secular but utterly estranged like one without history or memory. Once more, numb, I observed Epstein's dominating aluminium Resurrected Christ.And it was springtime, springtime in the real world and all seemingly dead things were coming alive again though a cancer sailed in from Chernobyl.

Inside the Cathedral, I ambled towards the Lady Chapel reredos where, on either side of the sculpted Madonna, six niches are filled with gold-leafed wreaths of wild flowers. In Welsh, dozens of flowers are named after the Virgin, as is proper in a nation that reveres the Mam of the family. The marigold is called Gold Mair — Mary's Gold; the buttercup, Mary's sweat; the briar rose, Mary's briar; the foxglove, Mary's thimble; the monkshood, Mary's slipper; the cowslip, Mary's primrose; and the snowdrop, Mary's taper. Tapr Mair.

If a man believed in a deity, any deity, goddess, god or God, he would, in that Cathedral, have prayed in English or Welsh or no language at all, for the neutralization of the death wind. And in Ogmore, this morning, as I stood in my pyjamas while the opera-dramatic clouds, grey, cream, or frowning darker, tracked so visibly westwards, my own lips moved.

And I wonder now, once again, in the name of the God others believe in, how much longer will so-called civilized nations absurdly pile up unusable nuclear weapons and to what hell will Man be consigned if, accidentally or purposefully, radioactive winds sail in from places other than Chernobyl.

In our X-ray Department the radiographer, in the spirit of scientific enquiry, had gathered some rainwater and placed it on an underdeveloped chest X-ray film overnight to see if Chernobyl had arrived. He drew a blank.

'I left it too late,' he said, seemingly disappointed!

I think the Chernobyl accident will enduringly change perceptions of nuclear power, civil and military, yet no doubt people in Britain soon will cease to be intensely anxious about radiation dangers. They are, at present, much concerned. Several patients, this morning sent to the X-ray Department, were anxious about the extra radiation involved even in such a simple investigation as a chest X-ray.

After the morning clinic I had lunch with Tony Whittome, my editor at Hutchinson, to discuss the production of this book. We hardly spoke of Chernobyl.

'What about an index for the *Journals?*' I asked, aware how people browsing in bookshops sometimes read an index to see who was in, who was out.

I thought of those memoirs published a few years ago in the U.S.A. which focused particularly on the New York literati. In the index, opposite NORMAN MAILER, the author had mischievously had printed, 'Hi, Norman!' It might be fun to have an inventive index, I thought.

Tony Whittome related how Hutchinson had been sued on one occasion because of an entry in an index. 'We sent the manuscript out to the printer and, at the same time, delivered a copy to the lawyers for them to look over for libel. They advised us strongly to drop a name from page 182. A certain individual on that page had been characterized as a big gangster. So that man, maligned, became anonymous. Only we forgot about the index. Opposite page 182 there remained the villain's name, resoundingly clear and bold.'

I once asked my eldest brother, Wilfred, his opinion about a new book on contemporary trends in psychoanalysis.

'Am I in the index?' he queried.

'No,' I replied.

'Then it can't be any good,' he said with confidence.

Recently I saw my own name listed in the index of a volume about contemporary poetry: pages 66-67 I noted with some plea-sure, believing that the author had devoted a couple of pages to my work. Alas, when I turned to page 66 I found the last word printed on it was Dannie and the first word on page 67 was Abse. The list then continued without further reference to me or my work. It turned out to be a lousy book anyway!

I awoke at dawn and could not sleep again. I heard the bird-orchestra tuning up, one avian instrument after another. Closing my eyes I deliberately conjured up tranquillizing scenes. To that background of bird-rehearsal I turned on my own internal video of Ogmore-by-sea. This failing, I switched instead to Golders Hill Park.

I know no better small park in London, especially in May, than Golders Hill Park and after breakfast I walked there, past the empty bandstand towards the flower garden. I saw, then, how limited my dawn imagination had been — grey compared with these brazen colours. Beyond a bed of bold, uniform-red tulips, standing stiffly at attention, with dying daffodils in between, another plot, a whole military brigade on parade, hundreds of them, waiting for a brass band to strike up — yellow red, yellow purple, purple red. It was the pacific magnolia tree though, that rooted me. It spread horizontally, an epithalamion of full blossom with a few, just a few of its large, gorgeously creamy petals scattered on the paved pathway near my feet. Under the tree, a wooden park bench invited the visitor to sit and ponder. But surely no one would dare rest on it unless he or she were utterly beautiful, if not immortal!

As I hesitated, a blackbird alighted on a branch, half hidden by blossom, and began to play solo. I turned, then, wishing once more that I had the gift to praise, to praise more profoundly, before walking home, awake.

You ask me to tell you the end of the story. I do not know the end of the story. Mostly we collide with shadows. History itself is a public memory and like all memories unreliable. What should one person tell from the ant-heap but the intermittent recollection of his own days, and that, of course, only an approximation, a translation, a blurred tune on a comb, handwriting on blotting paper?

Part Three:
New Journals 1987-93

1987

For the last five years I have been only a part-time doctor working in the same chest clinic. Now, these occasional sessions have come to an end and, at present, I visit the clinic only one morning a week to report on X-rays. Nowadays I rarely see patients and I find the whole Monday morning engagement boring, especially as almost all the X-rays are routine and normal. It is like having to read the same paragraph in a book over and over and over. My contract to visit the clinic is only for a year which, perhaps, is just as well.

This morning, though, was lightened because of a hilarious, sad scene enacted in the X-ray Department. The radiographer there, Pat, was speechlessly embarrassed. He had said to a patient, 'Go into that cubicle, please, and strip to the waist.' When the patient emerged fully gowned the radiographer remarked, 'There was no need to put that gown on — it's meant for a woman.' The patient hesitated, then replied somewhat stridently, 'But I am a woman.'

The first signs of Spring: no daffodils, not even one crocus yet, just a feeling suggested by the February light that something is approaching Wales. A season. But we are off to catch the end of Summer in Australia and I have been packing my bags. I try to imagine Australia, particularly Fremantle, Perth, our first destination. I can't; instead I pick up a newspaper and read that Sagittarius, whom I used to read decades ago in the *New Statesman* has died. The obituary reprints her send-up of W.S. Landor's epigram:

> I, for the love of peace, engaged in strife;
> Dreamed dreams and by no hard experience learned.
> I warmed both hands before the fire of life
> And got my fingers seriously burned.

I laugh, and soon after we are on our way to Heathrow. Somebody, I notice, has written on a wall Tony loves QPR. Why am I bothered all the way to the airport whether or not it was Tony himself who wrote that? I try to think of the Writers' Conference at the Perth Festival, of Thomas Keneally, Peter Porter, Rodney Hall and other Australian writers who will be there. As we take off in a Qantas jumbo I suggest to my wife, Joan, that they've invited us and Eva Figes because we can all read newspapers upside-down. 'Why else?' asks Joan. She turns to read a book. I stare at the novel I've bought for the plane, Kingsley Amis's *The Old Devils*. I give up after 34 pages, deciding that the Booker judges deserved a medal for finishing the book.

When Americans visit London, out of politeness we ask them what they think of the place. We don't actually listen to their replies. We don't give a bugger what they think. But when Americans ask us what we think of New York they appear to be genuinely interested in our opinion. They can be dismayed by a too frank response. So I've hit on a standard brief answer that seems to satisfy everyone. 'It's like no other place on earth,' I say. So when the reporter, pen in hand, asked me what I thought of Australia as I was leaving the Fremantle Arts Centre I didn't disappoint him by saying, 'Well, I've only been here, standing on this vast continent for 48 hours.' Instead I said, 'It's like no place on earth.' He accompanied me through the heat of Western Australia in case I should drop any more genuine remarks. But I could smell the sea nearby and I decided on a quick swim. 'Any sharks on the coast here?' I asked the reporter. He smiled and told me I needn't worry. Just then, I swear to you, around the corner advanced a one-legged man in shorts.

One event scheduled to take place in Perth was the so-called Poets' Lunch, financed by a wine company. Poets were commanded to write and then recite a villanelle in praise of wine. I had written only one villanelle in my life. I'd started it in 1957 and finished it in 1984 and now they wanted one in a matter of days. No wonder I hesitated but Joan said in a Yah-Boo voice, 'The others will provide one so you can't refuse.' So, challenged and wondering if I didn't finish it what will the neighbours think, I eventually, at the Wentworth Plaza Hotel — it seemed more like a barmitzvah than a poets' gathering — fortified by splendid liquid refreshment, recited into a microphone:

> Now praise Australian plonk, not that of France,
> that turns whingeing ockers into demigods,
> that makes dancers schpeak and poets dance.

Let booze amuse, let publishers advance
a dollar or two to broke Australian bards
who praise home-made plonk not that of France.

Look, here's Matilda waltzing in a trance
with Bacchus, swearing red's white, evens odds.
Drunken dancers schpeak and poets dance.

French wine est bon but this heavy red enchants.
Drink up! It's like the nectar of the gods.
So praise Australian plonk not that of France.

Burgundy, Bordeaux, Chablis, these have no chance
compared with grapes from antipodean clods
whereon dancers schpeak and poets dance.

Quick — a straitjacket and an ambulance
for this pommy Homer who nods and nods
to praise Australian plonk not that of France
and thinks dancers schpeak and poets dance.

After the Writers' Festival which was to last a week, we were going
to fly to Sydney and then later on go to the Canberra Word Festival
where, with Eva Figes, we would join Melvyn Bragg and Penelope
Lively. But first the Director of the Fremantle Arts Centre, Ian
Templeman, had arranged for me to give a couple of poetry
readings and Joan to lecture in two small inland settlements —
Boddington, an expanding community where they had struck
gold, and Corrigin, a farming community, contracting because of
dire economic difficulties. Both were several hours from Perth
towards the bush. 'It'll be interesting for you,' Ian assured us. 'It's
a different Australia from Perth, Sydney, Canberra. We'll arrange
for a tour manager to drive you there and see that all's well.'

The tour manager proved to be Bryn Griffiths who, years ago,
had regularly arranged his own poet's lunch at the Flask pub in
NW3. ''ello, cobber, mun,' I greeted him. He drove us to Corrigin
singing Sospan Fach while we observed enlarged, coloured birds,
cockatoos or parrots, flying above the gum trees, and a dead
kangaroo at the roadside.

Two hours later the road narrowed — room only for one vehicle.
The terrain was very flat and the strip of road, Roman-straight,

pointed to Forever. On either side, red gravelly dust had been blown onto the macadam turning that stripe purple. A purple stripe between broad ribbons of red while laterally, outside these, the blond fields shorn of their wheat boasted occasional stunted green trees under a relentlessly blue sky. It seemed unreal. Our car hurtled through a dream.

At Corrigin, I shall always remember seeing a marmalade kitten playing with a farmer's pet kangaroo, and at Boddington they proudly showed to us their small rodeo stadium. I kept pretending not to hear the small boy who, every few minutes, falsetto, kept pestering me, 'Come and pat our pig, Mr Abse. Come and pat our pig.'

In Corrigin, parched Bryn Griffiths swigged some water and immediately spat it out, suggesting it was contaminated with fertiliser. It seemed innocuous enough to me. But the last evening, after nightfall, antipodean hospitality allowed us a barbacue in a private garden and not water but innumerable bottles of best Australian wine. Bryn Griffiths went to it with a Welsh fervour and we left him there still hymning villanelle praises of individual brands of red and white. We looked up at a different sky, at the Southern Cross and all the flung stars. I was aware that not too many miles away, further inland, everything became nameless, edging towards the sinister rock desert that went on and on and on.

Next day Bryn drove us back to Perth. Again the sun was oven-hot and our tour manager wasn't feeling so good. 'That water at Corrigin,' he complained quite seriously. 'Duw, it did for me.' We drove the way we had come, back through the dream of a landscape, past the dead kangaroo. We were a long way from home, a long way from the sleet falling into the sea at Ogmore.

The British Council had arranged that on the way back home we should touch down in Singapore for a few days so that Joan could present her 'Voices in the Gallery' programme at Singapore's National Gallery and I could lecture and read at the University and at a school. We arranged to stay at the famous Raffles hotel.

'While we're in Singapore,' Joan said, 'we must buy presents to bring home.'

'Must get a dress or something for you too,' I said uxoriously.

At the airport I saw just the thing, an exotic oriental dress worn by a young woman who passed by. 'That would look splendid on Joan,' I thought. We walked on to collect our luggage and I was dismayed to pass two more young women each wearing the identical dress that I had admired, that I had hoped to purchase for Joan. Everywhere I looked there were these women wearing the same damned thing. They were all air hostesses working for Singapore Airways.

We liked Raffles hotel where we discovered James Fenton, about to leave for the Philippines. I particularly enjoyed my Raffles breakfasts: a wonderful, curious mixture of bacon, lychees and latkas. Very good! Breakfast had substantially to engine my day for I am far from adventurous in my diet, and I did not know what would be coming my way later. Whisper it not in Ashkelon but one lunchtime I furtively slipped away to MacDonald's. Hallelujah!

I can vouch, though, for Chinese cakes. I discovered them in abundance after my school session. The headmistress had invited me to her rooms for tea. There, awaiting us, were a glittering array of small cakes which I was promptly offered. I took one and devoured it with pleasure. Soon after tea was served and tinkling conversation, I was offered a second small rich cake. I took it but when, minutes later, I was offered a third, I declined.

'No,no, please, Dr Abse, have another one. They are so teeny.'

I sensed it would not be polite to refuse this insistent, dainty, Chinese lady. I devoured it slowly. We spoke of England and daffodils and Wordsworth before, eagle-eyed, she suddenly pushed the tray of cakes towards me. Evidently she had been watching my Adam's apple and, realising that I had allowed the last morsel of the last cake to descend down my oesophagus, she was ready and bright with confectionery reinforcements.

'This teeny, teeny cake has its own very characteristic flavour,' she said. 'And it's so teeny. You must try it. It's quite different from the others.'

I examined the proffered cake with some apprehension. It was no smaller than the others. Worse, when I finished it, and was wondering how soon I could now make my exit, she cried out, 'Oh dear. Oh dear dear, you can't leave without tasting one of my favourites. That one...'.

'No, no, thank you.'

'Please, oh please. It's so teeny. Just this little, little, teeny one. Oh, you must.'

You have it, if it's your favourite, I thought. 'Really, I...'

'Oh do. You will relish it so. And the British Council car will be here so soon to take you away.'

'Well...er... perhaps we could share it,' I said gloomily.

When I had finished it she threw both her hands up in the air before letting them fall disconsolately. 'Oh dear,' she said. 'Oh dear.'

'What's the matter?' I asked, alarmed.

'That one. That teeny teeny one there. I forgot. In fact, I didn't see it. That really is my favourite. Oh please, Dr Abse, please please. I do want you to taste my absolute favourite before you go. And it's so teeny, teeny.'

Returning home we discovered that Bridgend, my father's home-town (some six miles from Ogmore-by-sea) has been dubbed Sin City. While we were in Singapore the citizens of Bridgend awoke to see banners hoisted across the main shopping streets on which were writ the words: GOD HAS A CASE AGAINST THIS TOWN. Soon after, a free newspaper, *The Cornerstone*, produced by Evangelical Christians, was dropped through all letter boxes. It carried a bold headline: SHAME ON YOU BRIDGEND.

When Cary Archard drove the six miles to visit us at Ogmore I asked him what I had been missing in Bridgend. I didn't know the place was so interesting. As far as I knew, those respectable, ineptly named night clubs — for instance, Flamingo Road, Shimmers, Crossways, and Astons — were hardly swinging places.

'There's something in it,' said Cary. 'Satan himself wouldn't feel too safe going home late on Saturday night in Bridgend.'

It is a moonless Sunday night here, now, in Ogmore. The village is utterly quiet. The occasional amber of the lamp-posts fumbles the lane's darkness down towards the darkness of the sea. Far away, in the ink of the Bristol Channel, the lighthouses flash compulsively on and off: incandescent, nervous, exclamation

Across the estuary, across the bay, the lights of Porthcawl shiver and above all and everything, the usual awesome black vacuity of sky suspends the stars and more stars and yet more stars still. Satan, if he's hereabouts, is asleep.

Satan, I think, has taken note of Builth Wells. A disciple of his has been vandalising the statue of the Builth Wells poet, T. Harri Jones, who once called himself 'the poor man's Dylan Thomas.' Maybe that is what enraged Satan. It is more than twenty years since T.H. Jones was found drowned in an Australian swimming pool; but the poet deservedly continues to gain a posthumous reputation in Wales. A statue of him was commissioned — though why the sculptor, Ben Jones, elected to portray him nude is a mystery. Anyway there, bang in the middle of Builth, the statue asserts itself, big, white and conspicuous.

No wonder Satan had his bit of fun. He sent forth one of his disciples — a Bridgend man? — to proceed stealthily through the darkness of night armed with a hammer. The rotter hammered Harri's penis off. Quite rightly the Builth worthies decided to pay the sculptor to fashion another penis for T.H. Jones. And so it was stuck on. Alas, once again, in the light of morning, the folk of Builth have seen Satan's insistent power — poor Harri's statue has been castrated once more. And now I hear the rumour that they are going to take away T.H. Jones's shamed statue and hide him in a garage. If that is so, Satan wins.

The concert to raise funds for the Ystalyfera Heritage Society was over. The pretty harpist with the pretty name of Delyth who had sung Welsh songs so soulfully and plucked on her harp (made in Japan) so skilfully, left for Swansea. The rest of us retired to one of the Swansea Valley's re-upholstered hostelries. There two old men were engaged in a fierce argument in Welsh. The barmaid whispered to this monoglot, 'They're on about the meaning of life.' I listened further and identified some names which revealed to me that they were talking about rugby!

Soon after, a very short man wearing a cap — I think it was Lloyd George who said that the Welsh may generally be of short stature but in Wales we measure a man from his neck up — sidled up to me.

'Excuse me,' he said, 'but I think I've seen your brother on television.'

'Leo,' I said, 'yes, very likely.'

He stuck his chest out. 'I'm in the media too,' he said proudly. I smiled in millimetres. He waited there obviously expecting me to do more than smile, to congratulate him perhaps.

'Only local, mind,' he pronounced.

'What?' I asked, doing my best. 'Local TV? Radio? Swansea Sound?'

'No no,' he said. 'Newspapers.'

'Oh,' I said, trying hard. 'Daily? Weekly?'

'No, oh no,' he said at last. 'I'm a newsagent. Got a shop up the road.'

1988

Some useless facts stay in my mind. I daresay many people know that Lake Titicaca is half in Bolivia and half in Peru and is half the size of Wales; but who knows that quite a few tortoises die of diphtheria or that the Eskimoes have 37 words for snow? I could not remember where I had read that Thomas Bowdler was buried in the graveyard of All Saints Church at the Mumbles, Swansea — the same Bowdler who, in 1818, edited ten volumes of Shakespeare and deleted everything 'which cannot with propriety be read aloud to the family'.

So since Joan and I happened to be in Swansea and passing by the church, I thought we could spend a respectable morbid moment or two with the great Deleter.

'Are you sure Bowdler was buried here?' said doubting Joan.

I searched east among the lopsided gravestones while Joan searched west. Then I went north, Joan south; but without success. Had I got it wrong?

On returning home I consulted Margaret Drabble's *Oxford Companion to English Literature*. No hint there of where Bowdler's skeleton lies. No trace either in Meic Stephens's *Oxford Companion to the Literature of Wales*. But eureka! *The Shell Guide to Britain* confirmed that Bowdler's last resting place was at All Saints Church at the Mumbles. So what had happened to Bowdler's grave. Had we not searched diligently enough? Or had his grave been bowdlerised, deleted?

When I learned that some of my poems had been translated into Czech by Miroslav Holub I was delighted — even more so when I received an invitation through the British Council to visit Czechoslovakia with my wife, to read and talk about my poems at Prague, Olomouc, Brno and Bratislava. 'That faraway place — as Chamberlain called Czechoslovakia — ' I told my wife, 'is less than two hours away by plane.'

We were leaving our house at Ogmore-by-sea, to travel to London and then on to Prague, when we saw something we shall never forget all our lives. As we gazed down at the estuary, at the river's snail-trailing exit into the sea, I expected once more to be pleasured by the magnificent view. I have stood there and seen, on occasions, sea-mists like cannon-smoke or ectoplasm mysteriously moving, creeping over the marram-greened, tall sand-dunes; I have seen sunsets that not even Turner could paint. But this was different.

The sun was behind us that windy day, and travelling towards us at 30 m.p.h. we observed a blown vertical wall of rain. In front of it a rainbow advanced at the same speed becoming more and more distinct as it bore down towards us. Soon one arch of the bow fell on our side of the river, the other arch on the far sand dunes. Just then, as we silently looked on, a seagull (not a dove) flew right through the highest part of the bow. 'I expect that seagull's no longer white,' I said to my wife. The sighting of that hurtling rainbow seemed a strong prolegomenon to our visit to Czechoslovakia. An omen? Were we blessed or cursed?

In London, Joan tripped on the pavement and rose with a developing black eye. In Prague, they might have thought me to be a wife-beater. When we journeyed to Olomouc, where I was to give a poetry reading at the university, the head of the English department collapsed and had to be taken to hospital just as we arrived. At our next stop, in Bratislava, our splendid, pretty interpreter contracted a virus and a coffin cough. She led us, noisy as a chest clinic, into a restaurant where the waiter who took our order never returned. Not because of virus-fear, not because of being carted off by the secret police, but because he had tipped a pan of boiling water over himself. When we returned to Prague for our journey home, a dense fog descended so that our plane could not take off. By now my wife's black eye had become all the colours of the rainbow.

Our visit to Prague happened to coincide with a remarkable and successful celebration of British music. When we weren't working we were whisked off to concerts, sometimes two concerts a day: the Hilliard Ensemble, the Nash Ensemble, concerts in St James's Church, in the Basilica of St George, in the St Agnes Convent, and at the Dvorak Hall with the Royal Liverpool Philharmonic Orchestra. The music was fine but the clapping was something else. If ever I have another play on I want the house papered with Czechs. They have very strong hands. They clapped like bloody 'ell — not only after Holst, Elgar and Benjamin Britten but after Nicholas Maw too.

Not at the opera though. The audiences there are not necessarily music lovers. Factory workers etc. seem to be bussed in and they all, Zen addicts to a man, clapped with one hand. As a new-found Czech friend remarked, 'We go to the opera and the dentist twice a year.' The most popular musician in Czechoslovakia, though, seems to be John Lennon. The only graffito we observed during our stay in Prague was 'We love John Lennon', and at Olomouc one wall shouted 'Lennon Lives'. He has become a symbol of liberty and peace. Or maybe someone couldn't spell Lenin.

If the sighting of a speeding rainbow in Wales startled us, so, too, did the scene in Prague when we visited Kafka's house in the Golden Lane. This is within the precincts of the Castle. The tiny medieval houses in the Lane have been authentically restored to become a vision of a modern madman. They resemble a strange, sloping film set from *The Cabinet of Dr Caligari*. Incredibly, as we turned the corner into the Lane, ahead of us, walking past Kafka's small house, we observed a lady dwarf. 'Nobody will believe this,' my wife remarked. When I told the British cultural attaché, Jim Potts, about the dwarf in the Golden Lane he said, 'I don't believe you.'

Jim Potts had every reason to be in a buoyant mood. Everything he had helped to organise, from the Music Festival to the British Council Byron Exhibition (Michael Foot was on his way to Prague to lecture on Byron) was a great success. And, for my part, I had only admiration for the proficiency of the students studying English at the universities I visited and the dedication of their teachers. But Jim Potts seemed downcast one day. 'I have to attend a performance of *Manfred* in Czech,' he said. I could see that he was underpaid. To cheer him up, I told him my favourite Byron story. 'About Byron and the parrot,' I said. Jim Potts continued to look glum. 'Lady Caroline,' I explained, 'his mistress, was bitten on the big toe by a parrot. Byron, a man of action, immediately picked up the bird and when he hurled the creature across the room it squawked out, "Johnny!"' I could see that story convincingly cheered up Jim Potts. He was now anxious, positively happy, to rush away to hear *Manfred* in Czech.

The Czech poets I met gave the impression of being maturely respectable, clean-fingernailed people who would not be particularly admiring of Byron's libidinous behaviour. The only poet I met who acted in a stereotyped Romantic-poet manner was one in Slovakia. In a publisher's office, lunchtime, it was evident he had not read my 1933 brilliant school essay on 'The Evils of Alcohol'. He carried with him a petrol-can full of new, fermenting wine which he poured into my glass from time to time or on to the publisher's plush carpet as he affably swayed and reeled. 'I write with my hands up,' he kept saying to me, much to the embarrassment of the tied and suited editors in attendance. He said other things too, in Slovak, but these were not repeated and my translator's cough worsened. After lunch we became friends and shook hands. He had an enthusiastic, strong grip and it took about half an hour before the blood returned to my fingers: Czechoslovaks have very strong hands.

In the back pages of the Sunday newspapers and weekly journals there has been much discussion of T.S. Eliot's anti-Semitism. This follows the publication of a book by Christopher Ricks called *T.S. Eliot and Prejudice.*

Leonard Woolf (a Jew) once remarked that T.S.Eliot was 'only slightly anti-Semitic'. I am reminded of how Sir Adolph Abrahams on his ward rounds at Westminster Hospital used to forbid medical students to utter the words 'slight' and 'slightly'. I recall how once, after examining a woman, I had told Sir Adolph that the paitient has a slight swelling in her abdomen. 'Slight,' he said imperiously. 'Slight! Either a woman is pregnant or not pregnant. She cannot be slightly pregnant boy.'

In the early Fifties, at the inaugural poetry-reading of the Institute of Contemporary Arts in London, I happened to be sitting a yard away from T.S. Eliot. The chairman, Herbert Reed, called upon Emanuel Litvinoff to read. Litvinoff touched his spectacles, then announced 'To T.S. Eliot' and the audience settled back complacently, expecting to hear a text in homage to Eliot. Instead, Litvinoff declaimed a frontally passionate poem about T.S. Eliot's anti-Semitism:

> I am not one accepted in your parish.
> Bleistein is my relative and I share
> the protozoic slime of Shylock, a page
> in Sturmer, and, underneath the cities,
> a billet somewhat lower than the rats.
> Blood in the sewers. Pieces of our flesh
> Float with the ordure on the Vistula.
> You had a sermon but it was not this...

The poem continued in the same passionate, biting tone and when Litvinoff sat down a wailing arose as if from a battlefield. Some hurled abuse at Litvinoff while, enraged, Stephen Spender rose, tall, to defend Eliot stridently against the charge of anti-Semitism. Anarchist Herbert Read banged a coercive hammer on the table to impose order! Meanwhile, Eliot leaned forward, his head on his hands, muttering over and over, 'It's a good poem, it's a good poem.'

Eliot, in the early Thirties, had been a sick man and it was during this period that he expressed his racial prejudices more blatantly. His eighteen years of impossible marriage to a neurotic woman who, in her later derangement, became a paid-up member of the British Union of Fascists, caused him so much distress that he compared himself to Prometheus whose liver was perpetually gnawed by the vulture. Escaping from the torment of his domestic life, he lectured in the U.S.A. and at the University of Virginia delivered a diatribe against the America that was 'worm-eaten by liberalism' and 'invaded by foreign races'. He specifically deprecated the presence of free-thinking Jews.

But after the war — in 1954 — T.S. Eliot commented on anti-Semitism in the Soviet Union: 'I have long held that any country which denies the rights of its own nationals — and most especially the Jews — will sooner or later have to pay the full price for so doing; and even the "uninvolved" people whom it governs will have to expiate the crime of having allowed such a government to lead them.'

By 1954, of course, History had turned over certain monstrous bloody pages which carried names such as Auschwitz, Belsen, Dachau, and Eliot had read them. That is why, I believe, Eliot contrite, hearing Litvinoff's accusatory poem, leant forward, head in hands, muttering the assent of 'It's a good poem.'

A local railway strike at Manchester Piccadilly station meant we could not catch our intended train. We could still keep our appointment if we took a long distance bus. So Joan prepared some sandwiches for lunch and we joined the queue at Golders Green bus yard. When the double-decker Manchester bus arrived from Victoria it was, unsurprisingly, almost full. We clambered upstairs, Joan first. She walked forward to the partly occupied front seat on the right and I found a space some distance behind her.

Before long I leaned back only to discover that the back of the seat was rickety, half broken. No wonder others had avoided this part of the seat. We were progressing up the M1 when the seat gave way. The man next to me said, 'Hopeless, isn't it?' Some minutes later Joan swivelled her head around and smiled, unaware of my discomfort. She pointed to the sandwiches she had brought with her. I shook my head. We travelled several miles more before I decided it would be impossible to sit in this unsupported posture all the way to Manchester. I looked behind me. To the left of the gangway I spotted a potential space next to a large young woman who, imperialistically had spread herself comfortably over the whole seat. I rose and made my way down the gangway.

'Excuse me,' I said, standing over her. 'I'm afraid that the seat I was sitting in is broken. So may I?'

She did not move her hulks. I repeated myself more forcefully. Sullenly she shifted her big bum to make scarce room for me; but before long she began muttering, 'I can't bear sitting next to people.'

'I'm sorry,' I said, feeling a bit clipped, 'I would prefer to have more space too.'

She gazed out of the window, momentarily quiet. I thought she had decided to accept the contamination of my presence. Joan looked round again, She was obviously puzzled to note the seat I had been occupying was now empty.

Soon the muttering began again: 'I can't bear it, I can't bear it, I can't bear it.' She glared at me. 'I can't bear it,' she repeated.

'Too bad,' I said callously.

'If you don't move,' she said, after pondering for a quiet minute, 'I'll scream.'

It was my turn to ponder! Christ, if she started screaming what would people think? I could not stand up and say 'She's as neurotic as hell.' I looked behind me: there was only one unoccupied seat at the back of the bus. Another young woman sat there — a blonde, heavily made up: white powdered face, thick crimson lipstick, and Egyptian blue eyelids.

'Yes, I'll scream,' the fat girl said.

I rose again. I walked down the gangway again and sat next to the painted blonde doll who regarded me with some alarm. 'My boyfriend is sitting downstairs,' she promptly insisted. She had obviously observed me zigzag from seat to seat. I tried to explain why I had moved originally, then, overcome with the injustice of it all, gave up. I sat as far away from her as I could. Then Joan swivelled round again to focus stochastically on the empty space next to the fat girl. She must have been utterly startled to discover I was now adjacent to — on the face of it — a hot boudoir blonde. What happened next was hardly believable. The bus halted nowhere. We were on the motorway, the M1. A hostess dashed up the stairs and said in a panic, 'Don't panic. Nobody to panic. Leave all your belongings and come down the stairs. AT ONCE! Everybody off the bus!'

Then she shot back down the stairs as if chased by a swarm of bees. We all hurriedly filed out, the fat young lady, the painted blonde, Joan, and all the rest of the passengers upstairs. We joined the passengers already waiting on the edge of the motorway. I heard the word 'fire'. The man next to me said, 'I was sitting behind the driver, an' he says to me, me a passenger, "Do you 'appen to know where the fire extinguisher is kept?"'

The pyrogenetic bus was stationary and would remain so. Eventually we learned that another bus on its way to Birmingham would pick us up. I tried to tell Joan of my recent experiences on top of the bus. It sounded like a script for Woody Allen. 'Would you like a sandwich now?' she asked.

1989

Wednesday morning's post brought me, among other letters, one from an old friend addressed to Dr. Dr. D. Abse. I had been double doctored because my friend had read that the University of Wales intended to confer the degree of D.Litt. upon yours truly. I cannot pretend not to be pleased about this — I am not one who spurns honours, they don't usually come my way. My parents, were they alive, would have been even more pleased. True, my father, in his teasing way, would probably have reacted little differently from when, forty years ago, I telephoned home to Cardiff informing him that his wayward, poetry-writing son had passed his final medical examinations. Then, my father had barked over the phone, 'About bloody time, too.' My mother, on the other hand, I'm sure, would have boasted to anyone sweet enough to listen, 'My son, the doctor, the doctor...'.

Some people are very respectful of titles. I remember having to speak on the telephone to Philip Larkin. He had been honoured, doctored, by hundreds of universities and his secretary was evidently proud of this. You would receive a withering response if you asked for Philip Larkin or Mr Larkin.

'This is Dannie Abse. Is Philip Larkin there, please?'

'You want to speak to *Dr* Larkin?'

'Yes, Philip Larkin.'

'*Dr* Larkin?'

'Yes, Dr Larkin.'
'Whom did you say was calling?'
'*Dr* Abse.'
'Just a minute, please.'
Alas Philip Larkin is no longer with us. I cannot phone his secretary to say 'Doctor...Doctor Abse is here.'
Anyway, she would not have blinked. She would have assumed I had a Philip Larkin stammer.

The only time I practise as a doctor these days is when a member of the family complains of symptoms. 'Dad,' one of my daughters recently groaned, 'I have a pain here, ever since I had a cold. Do you think it's muscular?' In the old days I would have prescribed for her a bottle of evil-tasting medicine — the more disgusting the taste the more it would have been effective. Assertive reassurance plus a placebo works well in mild affective disorders.

Colour, apart from taste, is important when placebos are prescribed. Some years ago *The Lancet* reported that green tablets work better for anxiety than do red ones. On the other hand those who were depressed responded most favourably to yellow tablets. I recall an experiment in which a class of medical students volunteered to participate. They were given either blue or pink tablets and believed that one or the other colour indicated that it was a sedative or stimulant drug. They were deceived. The capsules were harmless placebos, quite inert. However the blue ones produced symptoms of sedation whereas the pink ones tended to stimulate those who swallowed them.

I once received a sample of vitamins from a drug firm which happened to have the same initials as me. D.A. had been stamped on each tablet. My elderly mother tended to feel train-sick when she travelled back and fore from Cardiff to Paddington. On one occasion she asked me to prescribe something for her. 'These,' I said firmly, 'are powerfully good for travel nausea. I've had them specially made up for you. Look you'll see my initials on them.' She looked. 'Good heavens, son, that's thoughtful of you.' Whenever she travelled thereafter she took a disguised vitamin tablet and never felt sick again. Sometimes I think the means justifies the end. Years later, she remarked, 'Those tablets you had made up for me. Wonderful. You should have had them patented.'

One reason, apart from the evident talent of Seamus Heaney, for particular interest in poetry from Northern Ireland is the lamentable, unending war going on there. It is interesting to note that not one significant English, Welsh, or Scots poet has referred in his or her work to the 'Irish troubles'. Yet, as I know from being a judge in poetry competitions, British weekend poets often focus on calamitous events in Ireland — as indeed do, of course, the professional Ulster poets, Catholic and Protestant. They feel forced to comment directly or obliquely, as if silence about the war would be itself a crime.

In some ways, poems of protest can be like screams uttered in physical tranquillity. Seamus Heaney has commented directly and indirectly on the murderous events in Northern Ireland; but the lines which stay in my mind, and which I think of sometimes when I view on television yet another instalment of the Irish tragedy are these that conclude a poem called 'Wounds' by Michael Longley:

> He collapsed beside his carpet slippers
> Without a murmur, shot through the head
> By a shivering boy who wandered in
> Before they could turn the television down
> Or tidy away the supper dishes.
> To the children, to a bewildered wife,
> I think, 'Sorry, Missus' was what he said.

*

Here's an exotic title for a poetry anthology: *The Orange Dove of Fiji*. It has been published by Hutchinson in aid of the World Wide Fund for Nature and is edited by Simon Rae. A note from Buckingham Palace follows the Contents List. The Duke of Edinburgh, a patron of the Fund for the Conservation of Nature, writes, 'Poetry can reach parts of the mind that simple facts and statistics cannot reach.' The Duke did not come to the launch party for the book at the Groucho Club. In his stead Prince Edward mingled with scores of contributing poets (of whom I was one) and media people. The decibel-loud Babel sound in the crowded room rose higher as the party proceeded. I was content to sip wine and converse with colleagues in the art when, suddenly, I felt my elbow gripped by Bridget Sledden.

Bridget works in the publicity department of Hutchinson and obviously had been detailed to look after Prince Edward. Now, though, she seemed to be in a small panic. She approached me because I was a Hutchinson author and so we had known each other for some years. 'Dannie,' she said, 'please come quickly and speak to Prince Edward. He's with Simon Rae. Simon's having a hard time. Not much is being said.'

When I did dutifully converse with the Prince not much was said then either. I asked him, for rather obvious openers, if he enjoyed poetry while Simon Rae, unsmiling, and Bridget, smiling, stood by.

'No,' he said, after a hesitation that Prince Hamlet would have been proud of.

Bowled middle-wicket, first ball, I prattled on. 'Perhaps you were put off poetry when you were at school?' He did not respond. So I continued desperately. 'When I was at school at first I, too, did not like it. I was more interested in playing rugby and chasing girls. But later...'. I observed Simon Rae still unsmiling, Bridget fixedly smiling and Prince Edward blank-faced. Another person with heavy eyebrows had now moved closer to our group. I wondered if he were a Secret Service man. Then, inspiration! — I said, 'Ah, of course, you're interested in the drama.' Again a significant hesitation before the Prince replied, 'Not really.'

'Dannie's President of the Poetry Society,' Bridget offered helpfully and I added how useful it would be if the Society had royal patronage, for poetry was a neglected art, before Bridget led the Prince and docile Simon Rae to conversational pastures new. The heavy-browed Secret Serviceman, however, remained behind. He was not a Secret Service man. He was a reporter from the *Evening Standard*. 'Did you say poetry is a neglected art?' he asked.

Next day the Evening Standard's 'Londoner's Diary' ran the headline: PRINCE TURNS DOWN POETRY SOCIETY. But what astonished me was the far from benign, fictional report of our minimal dialogue. The reporter had written, 'Prince Edward's reputation as an aesthete was in question last night after the President of the Poetry Society, Dannie Abse, sharply rebuked him for preferring 'soccer and rugby and chasing girls' to poetry.... The

Prince was taken aback by Abse's challenge at what should have been an uncontroversial affair... In front of an audience of poets which included James Fenton, Wendy Cope and Fiona Pitt-Keth-ley, Abse scolded the Prince. 'When you lose interest in playing rugby and soccer and chasing girls, you too will come to poetry, sir.'

It was late when I left the ruins of Ewenny Priory to go back three miles to 'Green Hollows', our house in Ogmore. They had come this way centuries ago. Who? Did rain-noise sulk in the leaves, be a palimpsest for their voices? At Ewenny, monks in white, on their knees, and perhaps Maurice de Londres watching the clouds clear. At sunset, who went ahead on horseback before the rest would follow? It was my turn now. I passed the companiability of the Pelican pub, overlooking the ruins of Ogmore Castle and continued towards 'Green Hollows'. Soon, there, across the silent river, in the fragrance of the thyme and marram grass of the sand dunes, it was already night. I had no appointment. I heard my breath, not theirs. I waited alone in the dark. I was roofed with stars.

1990

I arranged to meet my cousin, Richard Shepherd, a sports journalist who works for BBC Wales, outside Reading Football Club. 'Be there by 1.30 p.m.,' he had told me, 'and I'll fix a seat for you in the Press Box.' Reading, needless to say, were playing Cardiff City. Richard was to broadcast a commentary on the game and he would be accompanying the Cardiff team in their private coach.

Saturday had turned grey with rain clouds threatening when I set off from home and it was still a grey day with even more rain clouds when I arrived in Reading at 1.20. Soon I was standing on the pavement at the shabby back of the stand near the Players' Entrance alongside some mean-looking Cardiff City fanatics, a number of whom had shaved their heads and looked as if they would enjoy shaving a few other people too. They were also awaiting the arrival of the Bluebirds' coach so that they could give their heroes a rousing welcome. They and I waited and waited. By 2 p.m. the coach, presumably held up on the M4, had not appeared and the fanatics were becoming audibly impatient so that I was beginning to learn a few new Splott swear words.

'At least it's not raining,' I said ingratiatingly to the blue and white-scarfed, centre-half-tall, burly yob standing next to me.

'Yeh,' he said, examining me now with slow-mounting suspicion, perhaps wondering whether I was a Reading espionage agent and supporter.

'Pike might get a goal or two today,' I said swiftly, in order to display where my sympathies lay.

'Yeh,' he said.

When the coach finally came into sight it was almost an hour late. The fans surged forward as the coach slowed to a stop. As they did so the skies, with far from exquisite timing, opened up and torrents of rain descended — not just ordinary rain but hundredweights of of it, soaking us all to the bone. My friend, the blue and white-scarfed yob next to me, tilted his face upward, stared fiercely up at the swirling, emptying sky and screeched in frightening decibels, 'You fuckin' Jewish bastard!'

That odd, throaty, obscene cry left me somewhat bemused. Even as I saw Richard leaving the coach with the City team, I was trying to work out, soaked as I was, whether I should accept this hurling and despairing cry as pro- or anti-Semitic!

As I drove from Ogmore that May morning to attend the memorial service for John Ormond at Llandaff Cathedral, I kept thinking of his sudden efflorescent generosity. For instance, sometimes when I visited my aged eighty-something mother in her Cathedral Road flat in Cardiff I would find a vase of splendid fresh flowers on her sideboard. 'That's very nice,' I'd say. 'Who gave you these, mother?' It was nearly always John, of course, who lived nearby and who had, on a whim, knocked at the front door and standing in the porch had offered them, probably with a gallant apology. 'Your friend, John Osmond, gave them to me, son. He's a very nice man.' 'Not John Osmond, Mother. John Ormond.'

I remembered other characteristic Ormond acts of unpremeditated kindness and then recalled ridiculously the first time he and his wife, Glenys, came to a dinner party at our house. The other guests were Huw and Jay Wheldon. We placed John next to Jay but were shortly surprised by the change in their posture. Though side by side at the table they somehow, comically, had swivelled around to face each other like contortionists even while they sipped their soup. I assumed that they must be much attracted to each other. I did not know then that John was secretly deaf in his left ear and Jay, on his immediate left, happened to be secretly deaf in her right ear!

John died three weeks ago. I, like many others, lost a friend, and Wales lost one of its best post-war poets, one whose poetry owned, as Leslie Norris has accurately remarked, 'a curious glitter, a kind of brilliant sobriety, a careful eloquence.' His poetry is too little known, especially east of Chepstow; but Welsh colleagues in the art know his work as do a number of English poets including John Heath-Stubbs, John Wain, Jon Stallworthy, Ted Walker and Vernon Scannell. Indeed, as I parked my car, I saw ahead of me, walking towards the Cathedral, John Heath-Stubbs and his helpful friend, Eddie Linden. Obviously they had travelled from London in order to signal their admiration for our dead friend and his living poetry.

Inside the Cathedral I recognised a Welsh contingent of writers along with pub acquaintances, friends and old B.B.C. colleagues of John's. Present, of course, were all his lamenting near and dear. Seeing Glenys, I thought of John's gentle love poem addressed to her; it seemed, now, suddenly more poignant:

> Be bread upon my table still
> And red wine in my glass; be fire
> Upon my hearth. Continue,
> My true storm door, continue
> To be sweet lock to my key;
> Be wife to me, remain
> The soft silk on my bed.
>
> Be morning to my pillow,
> Multiply my joy. Be my rare coin
> For counting, my luck, my

Granary, my promising fair
Sky, my star, the meaning
Of my journey. Be, this year too,
My twelve months long desire.

I first met John Ormond twenty years ago when he presented himself as a B.B.C. producer. He came to our house in London with a TV crew to make a programme. On his return to Cardiff he sent me his book of poems, *Requiem and Celebration* which had been published by a small Welsh press. I soon discovered his poems were often elegiac and sometimes wonderfully witty. He had a marked historical imagination and his speculation about the past led him to be refreshingly affirmative of human achievement. His work reflected the man for he himself was vibrantly affirmative, quick to laugh, witty in his story-telling and generous of spirit.

In his TV films, in his conversation, in prose and in poetry he would often be revealed as a vivid portraitist. Once he described how Tom Richards — father of the painter Ceri Richards — occupied a corner in the Big Seat in Dunvant's Ebenezer. (John was born in Dunvant.) 'The preacher,' John observed, 'would open the Welsh Bible to his text: *Yn y dechreuad yr oedd*. "Oh," Tom Richards would say, clearly surprised. Then with a clatter of bindings falling off and a whispering of rice paper — for there were two bibles in the pulpit and both were used: *In the beginning was the word*. "Oh... I *see*," Tom Richards would add, as though the whole meaning of everything that ever was now struck him.... He would draw his left hand (half his thumb, half his index finger and the top joint of his middle finger missing from an accident in the works) slowly across his brow, clearing his mind for the next revelation.'

This perceptive and economical kind of humorous observation of Welsh character is evident in a number of his poems, and always John Ormond communicated a rare warmth of feeling for those he portrayed — unlike, say, R S Thomas in his Welsh portraits.

What John revered most in men and women was their creative spirit, irrespective whether that spirit resided in poet, painter, musician, cathedral builder or the neighbour that visited his local pub, The Conway. He relished odd behaviour, Welsh eccentricities, Welsh exaggerations, providing they were not phoney. His amusing portrayals became almost a kind of love poetry. In an open, vulnerable, unashamed manner he said to his dusty kinsfolk, 'I love you':

> Early and lately dead, each one
> Of you haunts me. Continue
> To tenant the air where I walk in the sun
> Beyond the shadow of yew.
> I speak these words to you, my kin
> And friends, in requiem and celebration.

And now here we were, kin and friends, in Llandaff Cathedral, none of us too far from the shadow of the yew, in requiem and celebration, hearing Purcell's 'Dido's Lament' being throbbingly sung before the touching and considered addresses from Alun Richards and Dai Smith.

Strange to think I'll not hear John, eyes almost closed, blowing a raspberry laugh again. 'Sleep, well-remembered.'

The phone was ringing in the hall. I picked up the receiver to hear a male voice say, 'Is this Dannie Abse?'

'Yes,' I said.

'This is Dannie Abse.'

'No, no. *This* is Dannie Abse.'

Puzzled, I hesitated and the voice began again:

'Is this Dannie Abse?'

'Yes, this is Dannie Abse.'

'And this is Dannie Abse,' insisted the cipher voice.

I was losing my bearings. I felt a strange sense of someone trying to delete my personality by claiming to be me, someone, as it were, leaping into my existence by inhabiting my name.

'I'm Dannie Abse,' the voice again claimed.

Who was this imposter? I was becoming irritated by what seemed like an existentialist joke. The voice sounded American. I suddenly imagined that the ghost of Henry James had descended, or perhaps ascended, and had decided to act out a supernatural story and this was but the prolegomenon to it.

'Hello, hello, are you there?' the voice said.

We all live, as has been said, next door to terror, perdition, annihilation; but the explanation of the phone call soon became clear and was mundane enough, in no way threatening. The voice, I learnt, belonged to a schoolboy who was on an educational trip to London with his school from Philadelphia. In truth, his name was the same as mine and because of that he had read my books.

I arranged to meet him — I was curious. I drove over to Notting Hill Gate where, in a café, we had coffee together. I asked him about his origins. 'We came from Wales,' he said, 'way back — but I'm vague about details.' He would be leaving school shortly, he told me, to study law at Temple University in Philadelphia; and he was most anxious that I shouldn't write any books that would disgrace his name.

When Maxim Gorky was taken ill, Lenin is reported to have advised him to consult a non-communist doctor. A communist doctor, he suggested, may be well versed in historical and dialectical materialism but might be shaky about recent advances in medical knowledge.

I do not know the provenance of this anecdote. True or not, it makes the point that doctors with an obsessional interest in disciplines other than medicine — politics, literature, whatever — may be less informed than they should be about their own speciality. Certainly, if I happened to be seriously ill I would not wish to consult a Dr David Owen, a Dr Jonathan Miller, or be complacent about being on the National Health list of a dreamy Dr Keats or a preoccupied Dr Chekhov, living in the alternative world of a story or play.

I read recently a well-researched book, *This Idle Trade* , by the now retired eminent radio-therapist, Sir David Waldron Smithers, about British and Irish doctor-writers, among them Tobias Smollett, Oliver Goldsmith, John Keats, Oliver St John Gogarty, Conan Doyle and Somerset Maugham. Most of these would not inspire patients with great confidence.

Smollett, for instance, was no great shakes as a physician. After thirteen years he gave up the practice of medicine for literature. 'To his advantage and ours,' Sir David pithily remarks. Samuel Johnson's friend, Topham Beauclerc — Topham is a splendid name for a surgeon — advised Oliver Goldsmith 'to give up medicine on the grounds that if he were resolved to kill, he should concentrate on his enemies.' And sensitive, honest John Keats concluded his medical career by confessing, 'My last operation was the opening of a man's temporal artery. I did it with the utmost nicety, but reflecting what had passed through my mind at the time, my dexterity seemed a miracle and I never took up the lancet again.'

I had agreed to talk about and read my own poetry at a local library in Uxbridge. Apparently they had not organised a poetry reading there before. I was taken aback by my 'welcome'. At the door a woman sat behind a wooden table.

'One pound fifty,' she demanded.

'I'm...er...Dannie Abse,' I explained, noting behind her head my name printed large above an announcement of the meeting.

'I don't care who you are,' she said. 'One pound fifty if you want to come to this poetry reading.'

'But I'm giving the reading,' I said, smiling.

'What?'

'I'm Dannie Abse,' I repeated.

'You're not the poet,' she said authoritatively.

'Yes', I said.

She peered at me. I was being very closely examined. Worse, a queue was forming behind me.

'Go on,' she jeered. 'You look ordinary.'

'Look — ?'

'You look ordinary', she announced. 'I could cuddle you.'

This was very different from the welcome I had received at the Cambridge International Festival. Then, as I arrived, I heard people say excitedly, 'Dannie Abse's here, Dannie Abse's here.' And I was surprised and warmed by their apparent delight at my arrival. As I moved through the corridor to the reception centre, again the murmuring, 'He's here, he's here.' This is the best welcome I've ever had, I thought. When I finally arrived at the reception one of the organisers sprang to her feet as if I was the messiah at last manifest. 'Oh, Dannie Abse, I'm so pleased you're here,' she said. 'Thank God. We're desperate. Could you please write a prescription for one of the Greek poets who has a terrible, painful gum infection and is due to read tomorrow!'

The Uxbridge reading, if only for one reason, did prove memorable. At one point there was a disturbance at the back. Some time later I became aware of someone in the street outside looking through the window and, the window being slightly ajar, listening to me read. He remained there, so after some five minutes I moved towards the window and invited him to come inside and take a seat.

'Can't,' he shouted. 'They threw me out. I'm pissed.'

Though I have trained and practised as a doctor there are many articles that appear in *The Lancet* and other medical journals that I cannot understand. Specialisation has brought with it a jargon-language of its own so that these days it is not simply a question of artist and scientist belonging to different cultures. Doctor cannot fully understand doctor, scientist cannot speak to scientist. It was said that when Freud and Einstein met they got on famously with each other. Freud asserted that this was so because he did not talk about psychoanalysis and Einstein refrained from discussing physics. 'He is cheerful, sure of himself and agreeable,' Freud said of Einstein. 'He understands as much about psychology as I do about physics so we had a very pleasant talk.'

The case-history of a man found sprawled semi-conscious on the pavement outside the Heart Hospital in Queens Square, London, serves as a parable. It seems that he was carried into the Heart Hospital where medical attendants felt helpless to deal with him and suggested he be taken across the Square to the nearby General Hospital. There, in the Casualty Department, the Registrar was soon on the phone to the Registrar at the Heart Hospital asking, 'What do you want us to do with the patient who fell out of one of your windows?'

I was asked, 'Are you religious?'

When I was so high I echoed the early Kabbalists by asking, 'What is the essence of creation? From whence have we come?' Actually I asked, 'Mama, who made the world?' 'God,' she answered. Then, being an unremarkable child, I asked, 'Mama, who made God?' My mother's grey eyes stared into the distance.

Later, when an adolescent, I declared myself to be an atheist, though when one of my school friends egged me on, dared me, to swear out loud at God, *really loud*, I hesitated to utter reversed deuteronomical curses. I was far from sure that God knew that I did not believe He existed. Soon after, I happened on Llewellyn Powys's *The Pathetic Fallacy*. 'Some compensating explanation has to be sought for the swift passing of the generations,' Powys magisterially argued. 'Not even a Pharoah, a Caesar or a Tamburlaine can reconcile himself to an existence inconsequent and empty of meaning. The egoism of the species is involved. Let the lives of pismires, of pygargs, be without significance, but not those of cardinal man ... Some of us today are content to find the secret of life in poetry and acknowledge thereby that wonder remains still the homage that our nature pays to the unknown.' I liked that. I quite like that still.

As an adult what I dislike, what I loathe, is the way toxic fanatics claim God as their own, how in doing so they would excommunicate or jail or murder those others who would also possess Him/Her like property — a piece of Him, His right hand, Her left hand, His right auricle, Her left ventricle, His right testicle, Her left ovary. And so God is dissected daily, painfully, in Northern Ireland, in Lebanon, in Jerusalem, in India, and at and in all the other 70 religious outposts of the world.

'Are you religious?' I was asked. 'I'm a secular Welsh Jew,' I replied.

I did not admit how, after certain solitary occasions, when I have, as it were, fallen through a hole in the air into wonder, I could be temporarily persuaded that, as Thomas Aquinas said 'The truths of revelation are not the same as the truths of reason.' Nor did I tell how I have used these rare, pure experiences of hearing a theurgic aleph not in the moral realm but in the irresponsible attempt to write the next poem or the one after while sitting, comfortably of course, under a sinless apple tree in our own back garden, far from the deserts of religion and the thistle-eating donkey.

1993

January

Nine. A record. One each for the Muses! I've been turning over the pages of my 1992 workbook. I wrote nine poems last year — at least nine that I am satisfied with at present. Since I ceased to practise medicine I have had more time to write. Shareholders in Abse Inc. should be pleased. Production has gone up. Now it takes me four years to gather together a book of poems rather than five.

But is the writing of verse a fit occupation for a man of my age? I'm cheered by the thought of grey-haired Hardy, in 1912, fiddling with recalcitrant words in order to hear the sound of their meaning, and of Yeats, at his desk, in his later magnificence.

There are, of course, temporary moments of uneasy vacancy in one's life when a voice very much like one's own whispers with enmity and heartache, 'What's the point of an ambition to write the next poem, then the one after? Would it be more valuable to conjure toy sailing boats into glass bottles?' Questions as cold as that must be particularly pressing and depressing for those poets who have reached middle age or beyond and who still remain largely unpublished, entirely neglected, as once was Manley Hopkins or Edward Thomas. They were not youths who could persuade themselves, 'Well, few people read me now, ah, but one day, you wait, you'll see.' To write poetry in later life and still not to have readers, must make a poet wonder not only about the authenticity of his gift but also whether the writing of poetry itself is a private, neurotic activity; and yet it may be that a poet needs only one devoted reader, a Robert Bridges for a Manley Hopkins, a Robert Frost for an Edward Thomas, an assenting, sympathetic wife for many others:

> Love, read this, though it has little meaning,
> for by reading this you give me meaning.

*

We visited the National Gallery to view the Edvard Munch exhibition. So many disturbing pictures — 'Evening on Karl Johan Street', for instance. As we approach the painting we meet a haunted procession coming towards us whose mask-like faces have seen what no man should ever have witnessed. We, the viewers, look beyond them to where they have come from and, for the time being, know that we do not know yet the terrible and forbidden secret. Then there is the intolerable and famous painting, 'The Scream'. From reproductions, I had always thought the open-mouthed woman with her hands on her ears was the one screaming. But it is a chorus of screams. She is but one in a choir: the whole of nature is screaming also, the very paint is screaming. The woman on the bridge, finding it all unbearable, places her hands over her ears. We, in the gallery, listen and hear the scream that is beyond the range of general human hearing — the scream only the alert mad can hear. We do not place our hands over our ears; rather we soon must close our eyes or turn away from the picture.

Not all the paintings in this Munch exhibition are strident. A wonderful tenderness is depicted in some of the portraits of men with women. What a shame that the painting called 'Vampire' should be known as such. Simply, a woman, superior, strong, gentle, kisses tenderly the back of the neck of a desolate man, defeated, who hides his face as her long hair cascades over him. Mother and child? She is not sucking blood as the title suggests; rather she offers comforting succour to a man who has visited, of an evening, Karl Johan Street and seen what he should not have seen, and hears the Scream of Eternity, Ennui and Forgetfulness.

My granddaughter, Larne aged 7, listening in the car to a song about the human race, demanded to know the meaning of 'race'. Susanna, driving, inexpertly endeavoured to tell her how human beings were categorised as Celts, Aryans, Semites, Mongolians and so on. Max, Larne's 4 year old brother, attentive to the list, suddenly piped up. 'Mum, mum, don't forget the egg-and-spoon race, mum.'

It is a year now since I resigned as President of the Poetry Society. Tired of the conspiratorial quarrelling of opposing factions led by Sebastian Barker, the Chairman, on one side, and Alan Brownjohn, the ex-Chairman on the other, two agreeable people who, however, were frequently disagreeable to each other; dismayed by the political duplicity of one thought to be a friend; dubious about some of the Events promoted by the Society, especially the cabaret Pop-Poetry gigs; I felt it was time, after 13 years, for the Council to appoint a more approving President.

I read in today's newspaper that they have offered the crown to the blind poet John Heath-Stubbs. He is a good choice — because of his considerable gifts as a poet, his remarkable erudition, his tact, his courage and his humour. As I write this I recall how on one occasion we read in tandem at the House of Commons. Eddie Linden, a close friend of Heath-Stubbs, had persuaded an M.P. to organise a Poetry Reading there — the first, apparently, since the days of Chaucer when, as Heath-Stubbs told me, John Gower held forth in Norman-French, Latin and Middle English. That must have been an odd occasion; but so was our contemporary Reading. All the 1950s denizens of Soho, uncharacteristically wearing ties, suits refused by Oxfam, and mostly sober, turned up — John's supporters to a man, including ex-poet Sir John Waller.

In the corridor beforehand (one of the corridors of power?) as the Heath-Stubbs claque milled this way and that, John Waller loudly announced to John Heath-Stubbs — perhaps forgetting that Heath-Stubbs was blind not deaf — that he was going to make a speech. 'Poetry is being honoured this day,' Waller insisted in a megaphone voice. 'It is a unique occasion so I think I had better say a few words.' Before John Heath-Stubbs could respond Waller sped away and John being sightless, unaware that his friend had vamooshed, began to chastise empty air. 'You must not,' said John to nobody. 'Not a word.' He then launched a lengthy dissertation on why Waller should keep his mouth shut.

I tried to join John Heath-Stubbs who was now being regarded by non-Sohoites with curiosity as he continued his peroration; but I was buttonholed by an American who said, 'Gee, this is sumpthin! This *is* sumpthin. Can't imagine anything like this at the White House. You've got sumpthin to sell here, boy.'

When the reading eventually began I observed Charles Wrey Gardiner, looking so much older than I had remembered him, sitting between Joan Lestor M.P. and John Waller. Wrey Gardiner had edited *Poetry Quarterly* in the late 1940s and he had published some of my earliest poems. I thought it would be appropriate if I commenced my reading with one of them, 'Letter to Alex Comfort' and acknowledged Wrey Gardiner's kindness to me and his valuable encouragement. But as I rose to my feet I realised that though the reading had not yet begun, Wrey Gardiner had already fallen asleep. Indeed, as I read 'Letter to Alex Comfort' John Waller ostentatiously attempted to arouse him.

During John Heath-Stubbs's reading Wrey Gardiner slumbered on and nearly fell off his chair, while at the back a hairy member of the Soho audience raised high a banner on which was written no anti-government slogan but LONG LIVE DADA.

Afterwards I drove John Heath-Stubbs home. Though blind he authoritatively gave me directions. 'We've passed The Swan? Ah then, turn left here. No left turn? Then we must have reached ... yes, turn right now.' I drove straight on. It was not the first time I had driven John home.

On this occasion, because of road-works, I took an unfamiliar divagation so that we approached John's house from the south rather than the north. I halted his car finally on the opposite side of the road from his home. John, talking about Pre-Raphaelitism and the Aesthetic Withdrawal, or some such subject, levered himself out of the car. He had begun to feel his way to the nearest gate, still talking like Coleridge, twelve to the dozen, before I managed to stop him.

'What?' he cried out under a lit lamp-post, 'the wrong side of the road? What number is on the gate I'm going through? What? WHAT? Oh my God, you fool, I nearly went into the brothel.'

February

I was nine years of age when I went to Ninian Park for the first time on my own. I watched a game between Cardiff City and Torquay United. Cardiff were floundering near the bottom of Division 3 (South) and it seemed increasingly likely that they would have to bid for re-election at the end of the season. No matter; the spruce military band, with infinite sadness, played the

Bluebirds' inappropriate signature, 'Happy Days Are Here Again' as the City team ran from the dark tunnel.

Yesterday Torquay were again visiting Ninian Park and I followed the crowd that converged with sanguine expectation towards the City ground — men and blue-jeaned youths mainly, some wearing blue and white Cardiff City scarves. All walked purposefully in the same direction, past an unhygienic-looking van whose owner purveyed sizzling sausages and onions, past the Ninian pub and the stern, distrustful police, then under the deteriorating railway bridge into Sloper Road with its cloth-capped programme-sellers near the looming Stands and the high unlit floodlights of Ninian Park itself.

In 1933 I, a small boy, had been handed down above a mass of friendly faces from the darkness at the back of the now demolished Grangetown Stand right to the front, behind the goal posts. There, breathing in neighbouring pipe and Woodbine or Craven A cigarette smoke I could observe, at acrid eye-level, my blue-shirted heroes display their rare skills and their common blunders.

Yesterday, though, I, a Season Ticket holder, sat among the aspiring middle-class Taffy toffs in Block D of the Grandstand, not too far from the Directors' Box. Once more I watched the teams that now represent the Bluebirds and Torquay United stampede like recidivists out from the tunnel. The game is speedier now than in 1933 so there are greater skills to admire and greater blunders to groan about as this or that player stumbles, staggers, totters, dithers, tumbles to crowd cries of 'You cart'orse, you.' The shouts of my neighbours sometimes surprise me. For instance, the respectable man, a few seats away, stood up enraged and shouted, 'Fuckin' ungentlemanly behaviour!'

Some things don't change. The Referee still remains a wonderfully defenceless scapegoat. How often have I heard a foaming spectator complain, as his father and grandfather once did, 'They never do 'ave Welsh referees down 'ere. We always play English teams see, and the bloody referee's always English. Well, fair do's, they're prejudiced as 'ell so we always 'ave an uphill battle.'

Oddly, the referee for yesterday's Torquay match had the Asian name of G. Singh (from Wolverhampton). Some of his decisions seemed to be idiosyncratic and soon he had to endure the verbal wrath of 7771 people whose faces were suffused with cartoon anger. (As Delmore Schwartz, the American poet, once remarked, 'Even the the paranoiac has real enemies.') Happily, no racial prejudice laced their chants. As in previous weeks they merely yelled THE REFEREE IS A WANKER. Masturbation certainly has a very poor reputation amongst the crowds attending Ninian Park. And when City began to score goals the referee was quickly ignored. The chanting changed into a rhythmic, melancholy, concussed:

Card-iff City
Card-iff City
Card-iff City
— — — F.C.

The Bluebirds finally won 4-0. It might have been 5-0 if the referee hadn't been such a wanker.

I felt like that doctor in Chekhov's *Ivanov* who, just before the last curtain falls, totters alone on stage, picks up a stethoscope and listens to his own chest with solemn concentration as the lights dim. My temperature had reached 101 degrees Fahrenheit. I felt as hot as Port Talbot Steelworks. Nauseous too. For a moment, as I reclined in the bed, I wondered whether I should consult a doctor. 'I *am* a doctor,' I reminded myself. 'Maybe a second opinion,' my wife tentatively suggested as she offered me tomato soup and sympathy. 'It's flu, just flu. You don't have to read the 87 treatises of the Hippocratic Corpus to diagnose what's wrong with me,' I protested. Hippocrates's contemporary, Plato, believed that the best doctors should experience diseases themselves. What an idiot!

My Florence Nightingale wife, for the next week or so, ascended and descended the stairs to our bedroom offering orange juice, hot drinks and revived hot water bottles. I tried not to enjoy the 'monarchal prerogatives' of a sick patient. I tried to be good. I tried to remind myself what terrible sufferings there were in the world. 'Count your blessings,' my mother used to say with regular and terrible predictability. But one fit of a hacking cough and my thoughts once more became utterly self-directed. Bosnia, for instance, momentarily did not exist.

*

An odd dream last night. I know not whom I was visiting nor whom I was with nor why I was explaining to him or to her the identity of the other guests. In the armchair on my left, utterly silent and motionless sprawled Bertolt Brecht; opposite me sat Elias Canetti. I whispered to my companion that Canetti had once told me how he, when a young man, had met Brecht in Berlin and had thought him to be an awful fellow.

Even as I, busy busy, whispered this evidently secret information, Canetti stood up. Suddenly he had recognised Brecht and now he walked over to him. Much to my surprise he tried to embrace him but after bending over him he, at once, sprang startled backwards — a kind of reverse loop — so that Canetti landed back almost where he had been. It was as if Brecht had doused himself with an abominably vile, repugnant, malign, obnoxious scent.

'Typical of Canetti to exaggerate and make a melodrama of their encounter,' I sighed confidentially to my companion. I woke up. And, immediately, revelation! I realised that I had been unjust to Canetti. He hadn't overdramatised anything. Brecht had been dead. That was it. It was Brecht's cadaver that had sprawled in the armchair. That's why that life-size dummy had been so silent and so motionless; that's why he had smelt so obnoxiously. Canetti had almost embraced a corpse.

Happy with my dream interpretation, clever as Daniel of Babylon, brilliant interpreter of dreams, I fell asleep again. Now, one hundred per cent awake, I wonder why I felt so pleased with myself for recognising that Brecht was dead. Perhaps Daniel of Babylon would know why. I close my eyes, trying to summon him. Here he is, clothed in scarlet with a chain of fine gold from Uphaz about his neck, master of magicians, of excellent wisdom, but dead, terribly dead, and unable to consult the scripture of truth.

The future of the *New Statesman* is in danger because of litigation set in motion by the Prime Minister. I am told the journal has already incurred costs of £150,000. Like many another I received a letter from the *New Statesman's* editor, Steve Platt, in which he wrote, 'Would you be willing to append your name to an appeal statement in support of our Defence Fund? We are launching the appeal publicly next week, so an early response would be appreciated?'

Some days later I replied, 'I used to be a regular reader of the journal and still gain reward and pleasure from it when, these days, I read it occasionally, despite its boring typography. I hesitate to sign the statement because I suspect that the article in which the Prime Minister figures should not have been published. From newspaper reports the article sounded like a ventilation of so much tittle-tattle. However, not having read the article I felt I ought to be less judgemental until I had done so. Accordingly, I traipsed around to Golders Green library to read the relevant back issue. "Yes," I was told, "we have it here but we are not allowed to show it to you." It seems that the Controller of Libraries and Arts, Barnet, gave instructions to withdraw the journal from display and that censoring command is still in operation ...'

I have received a further letter from Steve Platt in which he expresses indignation and alarm at the Golders Green censorship. He enclosed a photostat of the article. Alas, it proved to be as I had suspected. It was hardly worth the frontal wrath of a Prime Minister surely but the article was accompanied by a fabricated picture of John Major enjoying, with fork and knife, his repast while a grinning woman observed him in the background. A political cartoon may legitimately be as aggressive as a scalpel but this was simply a snide dramatisation of nudge-nudge. I hope nobody's going to sue me for expressing my fallible, self-important opinion. Listen, you potential litigators, I'm broke. Indeed I'm going into the red for I'm shelling out a year's subscription to the *New Statesman* for my eldest daughter, Keren. I don't want the journal to go under because of one dubious article. Who knows, one sub. may save it.

Is your doctor a slow reader? He is probably as slow as I am. I attribute the hesitant, tortoise-speed of my reading to my early education. I had to memorise, in detail, pages of medical text books. Moreover, scientific hypotheses and concepts are frequently couched in abstract terms and peppered with jargon. The truth is few scientists write clearly. I have long believed that if Adam had been trained as a scientist he might not have named the creatures and plants in the Garden of Eden but given them numbers. The obstacle course of a textbook written by a scientist slows up the reader and leaves its mark for life.

The scientist-author of the second-hand book I picked up in Charing Cross Road had not heard the secrets of lucidity. I agreed with a previous reader who had made precise comments in the margins. 'Misquote,' he or she had thundered and 'Unreadable.' Best of all, the one word, 'Questionable,' opposite, 'The desire to repeat actions reminds one of the pleasures of defecation.'

In Golders Hill Park I walked past the breeze-swayed daffodils praying like orthodox Jews, on past the house where Pavlova used to live, past the Bull and Bush pub (humming to myself 'Come come come and make eyes at me down at the old Bull an' Bush'), up further, past Jack Straw's Castle to Hampstead proper. It was too nice to stroll back. I walked on until I bordered Hampstead Heath. I was retracing steps I had taken when, as a 19 years old medical student, I had first arrived in London.

Then I had threaded my way for the best part of a mile through strange surroundings, not knowing where I was, not knowing where I was going. I had arrived at a large pond overlooked by a row of tall houses. Absurdly I had crouched down to write my name in the water with one of the many fallen twigs beneath the trees at the pond's edge. Afterwards, somewhat lonely, certainly lost, I had stumbled on Keats' Grove and, soon after, had come to Keats's house. So this was where Keats had lived! I knew that Keats had lived in Hampstead but had no knowledge of the exact location. Then Keats's epitaph, the one he himself had suggested, came to mind: 'Here lies one whose name was writ in water.' I was startled. Gosh. Unthinkingly I had written my name in the water, maybe in the very pond he had literally autographed — for was it not a striking image that he might have conjured from a real experience?

Now, in this morning's returning sunlight, I came to the same pond where, beyond, the same tall houses asserted themselves. I stood in my old footprints remembering it all. I observed the liquid sparkle of light on the pond, the scores of inland seagulls soaring above the water and there, surely there, under that tree, twenty yards away, stood Keats's ghost, invisible, five feet high.

Next month I travel to the U.S.A. I have a book of poems being published there and I am to give readings, mostly at Universities. Through the post I am receiving letters from the different organisers suggesting last minute details. These American letters are warm and welcoming — all first names.

Despite the song, 'We'll keep a welcome in the hillsides, we'll keep a welcome in the vales,' a Welsh welcome can be barbed. Some years back I received a letter from a Mr E. Howard Harries, (now no longer in this world, may his soul rest in peace). It read, 'Our chairman, Mr Vernon Watkins has arranged for you to visit us in Swansea. As Secretary of our Poetry Society, I need to tell you that we expect an audience of about eighty people. I trust you will not read too long as really the audience would much prefer to hear my poems about the Gower coast. Yours truly, E. Howard Harries, esquire.'

April

The British Airways plane to New York is full. Surely my legs have grown longer since I last travelled across the Atlantic? We are all stacked together, breathing in together — hold it — exhaling together. We are a respiratory team. The air hostess in front of us should be holding a conductor's baton. My shoulders are too wide. Why aren't I sitting next to an arm-amputated anorexic? Seven and a half hours of this. 'In ... out.'

I am travelling to the U.S.A. for several reasons. Because Daniel Hoffman has kindly, unsolicited, arranged a number of readings for me; because I have a book of poems being published in New York by Persea Books this week; because I shall have the opportunity to meet several American friends, including such poets as Dan Hoffman, Ted Weiss, M.L. Rosenthal, Stanley Moss and Louis Simpson; because I like the quality of American sunlight; because

I like hamburgers and hot dogs.

I open the book I've brought with me: Andrew Motion's biography of Philip Larkin. Four hours later I have only read half a dozen pages. My reading rate is slowed down by Undo your seat-belts. What do you want to drink? Fasten your seat-belts. Here's your lunch. Undo your seatbelts. Do you want any Duty Free? Fasten your seat-belts. Pull down your blinds for the movie you don't want to watch. Undo your seat-belts. What would you like to drink? I think of the old *Punch* cartoon: 'If what you gave me last was coffee I'll have tea. If it happened to be tea I'll have coffee.'

The inconsiderate swine sitting in front of me now levers his seat back into the reclining position. I hold Motion's book at right angles as it touches my chest. It weighs a ton. I should have brought a paperback. I put Motion's book down. I was about to say something about Philip Larkin but I can't remember what it was. Themistocles could call out the names of more than 20,000 citizens of Athens without faltering; Ben Jonson could recite blindfold whole books that he had read; but I can't recall what passed through my mind a few minutes ago about Philip Larkin. We have not landed at Kennedy airport yet but already I'm suffering from jet-lag.

In the November-December 1985 entry of these *Journals* I speculated amongst other cheerless matters that, 'Sooner or later someone will write a biography of Philip Larkin. My guess is that the biographer will not have to be a crude Jake Balokowsky to discover that Sidney Larkin (Larkin's father) was an unambiguous, fervent Nazi sympathiser.' Soon after the publication of the first edition of these journals in 1986 I received an imperious, how-dare-you, 'upstairs' letter from Larkin's future biographer, Andrew Motion.

But just over a year ago, at a pre-election Neil Kinnock rally, Andrew Motion approached me and apologised for his earlier letter. 'You were damn near right,' he said quietly. It was generous of him to tell me so. We were at a political rally. Politicians never apologise. Poets do.

I have now read further into Andrew Motion's biography, *Philip Larkin, A Writer's Life*. He does not flinch from recounting how

Larkin's father 'had been an ardent follower of the Nazis and attended several Nuremberg rallies during the 1930s; he even had a statue of Hitler on the mantelpiece (at home) which, at a touch of a button, leapt into a Nazi salute.' Sidney Larkin decorated his office in Coventry's City Hall with Nazi regalia until war broke out. Then the Town Clerk ordered him to remove it. Nor does Motion hesitate to dwell on Philip Larkin's own repugnant racialism and right-wing, Blimpish prejudices.

Admirer though I was and still am of Philip Larkin's memorable poetry — his poems have given me much perdurable pleasure — they are so sharp-eyed, appropriate with arresting detail and do not eschew sentiment, feeling — I am reminded of my 1950s quarrel with him, or rather with the Movement thesis. Howard Sergeant and I at that time edited *Mavericks*, an anthology intended to rival Robert Conquest's forthcoming Movement anthology, *New Lines* (1957). On the surface, our publicised arguments were about poetic style, about different linguistic strategies in the making of poems, about romantic or anti-romantic allegiances; but underpinning these postures opposing socio-political attitudes occasionally peeped through.

I disliked their insular gestures, their parochialism. One of the Movement's most influential propagandists, J.D. Scott, the literary editor of the *Spectator*, was revealing when he reviewed William Golding's *Lord of the Flies* in the *Sunday Times*: 'This is a strikingly un-English novel. In abandoning the parochiality which so often irritates foreign students of the contemporary English novel, and in seeking universal experience, Mr Golding may have walked with kings but he has lost the common touch which is particularly appreciated by English readers...perhaps it will be his fate to become one of those English writers more deeply appreciated abroad than at home.'

Similarly, in a Fabian tract, *Socialism and the Intellectuals*, Larkin's friend and fellow Movement writer, Kingsley Amis, sounded off: 'Romanticism in a political context I would define as an irrational capacity to become influenced by interests and causes that are not one's own, that are outside self.' The only social consequences, Amis felt, with which we should be concerned were those that might have a direct, immediate impact on an English way of life. It would not be caricaturing Amis's attitude (which Larkin shared) to summarise it thus: foreigners don't matter and we should only be moved to moral indignation when a particular injustice or pressure threatens English vested interests.

Once, when asked how he enjoyed holidaying in Portugal, Kingsley Amis replied without irony, 'It's a bore. It's just that the place is located abroad and the people are foreigners.' Larkin, with Amis, relished a consciously contrived philistinism. One or two other Movement poets, though not so crassly nationalistic, exhibited right-wing, proto-Thatcherite views. 'The Movement is anti-wet,' announced Conquest before 'wet' had become a political curse.

So prior to reading Andrew Motion's book I had inklings of Philip Larkin's views and prejudices. I did not know, though, about his stinginess, his almost comical 'Jack Benny' focus on money. Motion's references to it made me recall a telephone conversation I had with Philip Larkin in 1973. That winter I happened to be Writer-in-Residence at Princeton University. Though abroad, I co-judged with Larkin the current Poetry Book Society choices and recommendations. Every now and again a batch of poetry books would be sent by the Arts Council to our temporary trans-Atlantic home in Pine Street, Princeton, New Jersey. But there was a gap in the post. When I received a letter from Philip Larkin in which he outlined his preferences for the quarter I realised that some books must have gone astray. Several of those he cared for had not arrived. Because of an Arts Council deadline a swift response from me was required. So I telephoned Philip Larkin to explain what had happened. It was not as customary in 1973, nor as cheap, to make telephone calls to or from the U.S.A. as it is nowadays. Thus, when he heard my voice, Philip Larkin seemed puzzled.

'Where...where are you speaking from?' he asked.

'From Princeton.'

'Princeton?'

'Yes, Princeton.'

'But that's where I've been writing to,' Larkin said.

'Well, I'm still there.'

'At the University?'

'Yes.'

'The University?'

'Yes. Look, those books...'

'You're phoning from the U.S.A.?'

'Yes.'

'The U.S.A.!'

'I want to talk to you about the books.'

'Are you phoning from the University?'

'I'm phoning from home actually but listen, the books never...'

'Are you paying for this call then?'

'Yes, I am. I haven't received the books from the Arts Council so I can't comment on...'

'Can you reclaim the money, do you think?'

'How do you mean?'

'From the Arts Council.'

'I don't think so. Look, in your letter...'

'I've never had a phone call from the U.S.A. before!'

'About the choice and the recommendation ...'

'It must be costing you a packet.'

There is a story I like about Jack Benny. A masked highwayman, gun in hand, says to Jack Benny, 'Your money or your life.' Benny pauses, 'Let me think.'

After the Friday Poetry Reading at the University of Pennsylvania (where Ezra Pound and William Carlos Williams had once been students), an unusual-for-me weekend. For on Saturday Dan Hoffman drove us westwards of Philadelphia into the Amish country. We had a rendezvous with the past. After an hour or so in the car, Liz Hoffman said, 'Look! An Amish farm. An Amish home. You can tell. See, a windmill for their power. They shun contemporary technology. No electricity, no gas. No tap-water or modern sewage. No T.V. No radio. No motor cars.'

The Amish Folk, who speak Pennsylvania Dutch, settled in this part of the country in the early 1700s. They continue to live and farm as they did then. In this self-imposed ghetto world they are schooled — they have their own schools — to inhabit the strait-jackets of their 18th century ancestors. Naturally their anachronistic way of life draws tourists and we were not alone on the Pennsylvania roads on the look-out for Amish folk who would be wearing wide-brimmed hats and special sombre clothing.

'We'll come across them soon,' Dan said.

Sure enough we did. We passed their horse-drawn buggies at regular intervals and I fear I stared at each bearded driver as if I were at a zoo! The men, I learnt later, only start to grow beards on the day of their marriage — continuing, though, to keep their upper lip naked. The Amish are pacifists. Moustaches are associated with 18th century soldiery.

I suppose most tourists find the Amish people quaint. But I could not help wondering how many of the youngsters yearn to be emancipated, wishing to enjoy the best things of this world. Not the trash of American T.V. but the best movies, the best theatre, not to mention our Western heritage: the treasures in our museums, and Bach, and Haydn, and Mozart, and Beethoven. 'God has given us voices to sing His praise,' the Amish insist, 'so why should we bother with musical instruments?' The Bible also directs the Amish folk 'to till the soil by the sweat of the brow and to bring forth fruitful harvests.' So before we headed back towards Philadelphia, to Dan Hoffman's home in Swarthmore, we stopped to eat of those harvests at an Amish *haimishe* restaurant.

Next morning my 'religious' education continued for Dan, who is a Quaker, took us past the magnolia trees dressed in their Sabbath best, to a Friends Meeting. Not having been to one such before I was startled by the silence of the hour, by individuals occasionally rising from the wooden benches to interrupt the silence by personal testimonies. Mostly it was silence. And I listened to Silence, to inaudible music. I did not feel the secular hair rise on my head; rather I felt myself to be, as I do in a synagogue, in a mosque, in a chapel, in a vast cathedral, the man from somewhere else.

Despite the excitements of a new Government in the U.S.A. — the temporary death of a cliché — political comment, if made at all by my American friends, was brief. 'If Clinton really tries to change things here, something serious, he'll be bumped off.' If I was asked about the incompetence and moral exhaustion of our own government it was out of politenesss rather than curiosity. Rather, I was invited to talk about literary or personal matters. Sometimes my interlocutor had hesitant medical concerns: at Rutgers, about a friend with Parkinson's disease; at Princeton about a friend's wife with myasthenia gravis; at Delaware about a friend's friend with haemoglobinuria; at Tampa, about the new selective cerebral vasoconstrictor used for severe migraine. 'I know you're not a doctor any more but...' Such medical preoccupations simply signify my friends are getting older, as I am.

Nothing has happened of great moment to me during these last three pleasurable weeks in the U.S.A. Some images will surely linger: the endless magnolia trees of Swarthmore in their different whites and pinks — to an astigmatic, angels transmogrified; that Degas in the Philadelphia Museum; the stern Amish in their horse buggies; the patient heron on the beach standing two yards away from a patient man fishing the sea of Siesta Key; the silence in the woods of Suffern; the cross of a plane's shadow on the sea coming in to land at La Guardia that this time did not quite crucify the Statue of Liberty.

My book has been published. I have given half a dozen readings and have gladly met those whom I only knew through correspondence along with those I know well and feel affection for. Tomorrow I shall be returning to my real life, across the other side of the Atlantic, in London and in Wales, three weeks older and no doubt, since the relentless katabolic wheels invisibly turn, many brain cells less.

May

May is my favourite month even though the weather is so changeable. As my mother used to say, as millions of mothers have said, continue to say, 'Cast not a clout'. I listen with my ear to the future, to the 21st century, to the 22nd century, and I hear a woman's stern voice still shouting, 'Keep your vest on, son.'

It was a May morning, a sunny ten o'clock of the morning in our Ogmore garden with bird-whistle insane with pleasure in the trees' blossom while below white butterflies staggered over the bluebells. And between our garden and the blue sky, tons of unpolluted sunlit air vibrated where a small bi-plane from R.A.F. St Athan sounded like a far away mowing machine. Every now and then the joker in the propellor plane would abruptly cut off his engine and the sheep chewing at our front hedge outside our wooden gate would jerk up their yellow-eyed heads for a moment before that dread, suspended interval of sky-silence terminated and the mad pilot of St Athan reassuringly headed for base.

Who would have thought that within the hour the weather would turn around? I intended to walk a virtuous mile on the shore towards Southerndown and pass those small monuments of myth-like fishermen who perpetually stand mute on the sea-wet rocks. I did not notice the sea-mist advancing and that the coast of Somerset had ceased to be. I was thinking great thoughts. Cardiff City had been promoted while I was in the U.S.A. and here I was preparing the team for the Second Division, transferring this player, buying that. Would Waddle come to Cardiff? Preoccupied with such important considerations I did not hear how quiet and muffled everything had become. Then I looked out to sea and saw the sea-mist wading towards the shore. It progressed over Hardee's Bay with a sullen, indeed sinister, deliberation deleting all animate and inanimate things. Surely some evil spirit, some psychopomp in a small boat, not wishing to be observed, was about to land on the coast of Glamorgan, at Ogmore-by-Sea, at Hardee's Bay to be precise, where I was standing? No one was about, nobody at all. Already the hooting, doleful foghorns from Nash Point warned and wailed. No. They were a monster's orisons. Courageously, I walked through what seemed like frozen cannon-smoke, over the rocks, to the pebbles, to the sound of almost obliterated sea, to its obsessional ministrations. And in the sleep-walking densities of sea-mist I uttered those lines of Whitman to myself, misquoting them probably:

> Whereto answering, the sea
> Delaying not, hurrying not,
> Whisper'd me the delicious word death
> And again death, death,death, death,
> Hissing melodious, neither like the bird nor like my arous'd
>   child's heart
> But edging near as privately for me rustling at my feet,
> Creeping thence steadily up to my ears and laving me softly all
>   over,
> Death, death, death, death, death.

*

Returned to London, in my study I took down a large art book from
the highest shelf. It was one I had not looked at for years: *One
Hundred Details from Pictures in the National Gallery* with Notes by
Kenneth Clark. On the flyleaf I had possessively written my name
and after it, the date — 1946. I had owned this large book with
green covers since I had been a youthful medical student. Some of
the black and white reproductions I had torn out (a dubious
practice) and had tintacked them to the wall of the first floor room
in the boarding house at Swiss Cottage which I occupied during
the immediate post-war years. Now, in nostalgic mood, I turned
over the pages of the book and examined the plates, so many of
them details from Italian paintings of the 15th and 16th centuries.
I saw once more how the angels depicted seemed unsmiling,
discontented. But suddenly I felt it was time to peer at the real
thing, not merely at substitutes, black and white reproductions. So
I closed the book and off I went on a Number 13 bus to Trafalgar
Square. My mission — to meet angels.

Less than an hour later I was climbing the twenty-one stone steps
and walking through the Gallery's revolving doors to climb again
to the picture rooms. Why does one often have to ascend to view
important paintings whether in the galleries of Europe or the
U.S.A.? Anyway, soon enough I was breathing religious ozone in
rooms rich with early Italian paintings. Here there were angels
galore but no Fallen Ones.

An old legend tells us that some angels came to earth and beheld
the beautiful women of our world. They could not restrain their
passion. Did not Naamah, the lovely, graceful sister of Tubal-cain,
lead some of these defecting angels astray? But the angels in the
National Gallery were spotless. They had not been tempted by any
women, young, old, pretty or not. Though overdressed, one could
be sure they owned neither genitals nor pubic hair. Those angels
in Piero della Francesca's marvellous 'Baptism' were merely
statues, dressed in human garments, but without hormonal desire.
They stand there virtuously, cloakroom attendants, waiting patiently to look after Christ's robes. Even the stern archangel in
Piero's 'Saint Michael' — though carrying a blood-stained sword
in one hand and the decapitated head of the serpent in the other,
resembled a eunuch.

213

I walked into another room in the Gallery thinking how William Blake believed sincerely — he was certain — that angels descended literally for the great painters to paint their portraits. Soon, before me, was the canvas of Fra Lippi's 'Annunciation'. Had this school-boy angel, this Gabriel, descended from invisible heaven to be a model for Lippi? It had obviously been a special day out for young Gabriel. He had dressed himself up to the nines. There he was kneeling, meek and mild, on a carpet of flowers. I felt that if I clapped my hands loudly, sternly, this timid angel would vanish. Instead, I gazed closely at his wings. I had seen those feathers somewhere before. Yes, they were, without doubt, peacock's wings — beautiful, to be sure, but they didn't look as if they could lift Gabriel higher than a tree top.

In front of Leonardo da Vinci's 'Virgin of the Rocks' I stared at the heavy-lidded angel whose face belongs to one almost too beautiful to be desired. As I did so two men approached. They spoke in loud voices, one English, one American.

'Ever met with the Marquis of Bath?' the American boomed.

'No.'

'Didja know he's got the biggest collection of Hitler paintings in the world? I know a guy who bought Goering's wedding sword for 69,000 dollars.'

'I bet it's a bit rusted by now.'

'Mmm. Uh, huh.'

These two men then decided to give the 'Virgin of the Rocks' the eye. They stood in front of me bulkily. How irritating it is when others take up your viewing space — like people close by, continually coughing at a concert. Worse, these two men continued to talk about the value of Nazi memorabilia. Suddenly — revelation! These two were in disguise. They were, surely, wicked progeny of ancient Fallen Angels who had come in from Trafalgar Square, interested in their far-off genealogy, in the visages of their virtuous cousins in this 15th and 16th century Family Album.

A recent survey of some 2000 doctors in the London area reveals that 1 in 12 have been assaulted by patients on some occasion during the last two years. I find these statistics astonishing. Have patients changed so much lately? Or have doctors altered, become less caring?

Perhaps this ubiquitous aggression is related to the present ethos of medical truth-telling. The general public deems the patient's 'right to know' to be a good thing; but this openness has come about not as a resolution of an argument about ethics. Rather it is because doctors are increasingly concerned about litigation. In the U.S.A. this truth-telling is called Defensive Medicine. If the patient is given all possible information, irrespective of the need to do so, the doctor is less likely to be involved in a malpractice suit.

In Britain, too, doctors are enjoined to tell the truth even though there are fewer chances of being sued. Alas, some doctors forget that without hope the heart may break. Moreover, some doctors are particularly blunt and maybe a number of patients have become violent because they have apprehended that these blunt truth-tellers were gaining some sadistic pleasure in imparting bad news. There are patients, certainly, who would behead the messenger however tentative he or she may be. Especially if that messenger is transparently full of gusto and brimming with health! Perhaps that is why Plato believed that doctors should 'not be robust in health and should have had all manner of disease in their own persons'! While I practised Medicine no-one physically attacked me when I had to suggest, adagio, a possibly unhappy diagnosis. Most patients proved to be quietly defensive, soft-eyed, even unnecessarily apologetic for being unwell. I remember one patient, though, who was particularly bellicose. I had told him that he needed further special investigations and he responded by shouting at me, 'I'm all right. You're wasting my time. I don't need to be messed around by an incompetent doctor.' I tried again without success and all I shall say here is that none of us lives up to our highest ideals. Later we both calmed down and I did persuade him, at least, to seek a second opinion. As someone else has said: to be a good doctor one should have the heart of a lion, the eye of an eagle and the hand of a lady.

As for bad patients, there is, according to Sir Adolph Abrahams, no such thing: *all* patients are the doctor's best textbook. Years ago I was on a ward round with Sir Adolph at Westminster Hospital and when we retired from the bed of a certain Mr Jennings the following short conversation ensued:

1st student: Mr Jennings is a bad patient, sir.

Sir Adolph: No such thing, boy, as a bad patient.
2nd student: Dr Lloyd said there are two kinds of patients.
Sir Adolph: What are they, boy?
2nd student: Rich patients and poor patients, sir.

On the Northern Line the stupor of the journey's boring routine was interrupted: two youths loudly argued with each other and seemed to be centimetres away from blows. They happened to be black. As their fevered voices rose I observed the wary passengers opposite me observing the electric fracas or studiously ignoring it. Then I realised that I owned the only white face in the carriage.

What bothered me, when I thought about it later — at Euston the agitated youths quit the train — was that, though I live in a multi-racial society I cannot claim any black friends. I know a few black writers. When I attend some literary party I may well meet James Berry or some young black poets such as Fred D'Aguiar and Jackie Kay. I'm on pleasant nodding terms with them; but they don't visit my house and I don't visit them. I may be invited occasionally to a friend's dinner party but I never see a black face at the table. The truth is, like many of my class and interests, I do not really live in a multi-racial society. I may make occasional excursions into it but, whether in London or Wales, I inhabit essentially the fortunate, white, middle-class centre and I cruise, for the most part, along the white middle-class roads and flatlands.

Last month, while I was in the U.S.A., I had dinner with Jacqueline and Clarence Brown at Princeton. Clarence confessed, 'I am a racist. You don't grow up in South Carolina in the thirties and forties and come out of the experience with the soul of an extraterrestrial. Attach those electrodes to my head and I assure you that my brain will faithfully execute the programme loaded into it in the South by people whom, as a child, I trusted. *But I choose not to be a racist.* I override the behaviour built into my brain... There is no way I can prove that I am not racist. My worshipping at a black church is inadmissible evidence.'

How many of us, I wonder, can choose to override stencilled-in prejudices. How many of those who meet me, for instance, begin a relationship with me, have to stifle an early imprinted anti-semitic bias, or, indeed, are even aware of one. And am I unblemished, without early acquired prejudice? As a small boy, was I not told authoritatively by other small boys that when walking on the pavement I must take great care to avoid stepping on the black lines else, when I grew up, I would marry a black lady!

I do not believe I am a racist in any way at all. Yet I am uneasy when I recall a certain day in 1949 when I was a medical student living in digs in Swiss Cottage, London. I was walking towards the roundabout near the Britannia pub during the lunch hour when I saw ahead of me quite a large crowd. When I reached this gathering I understood why they had all hesitated there. A cat, some minutes earlier, had been struck by a passing car. It could not move but it was still alive. 'Somebody put it out of its misery,' a woman cried. A girl in the crowd knew me slightly. 'He's a medical student, he'll do it.' 'No, no,' I automatically responded. I pointed to a stranger some yards away from me. 'You do it,' I said. He was black. Why did I, reflexly, choose that black man out of the dozen and more people there to be the executioner, the one who could kill a living, though suffering, creature? There are moments such as those when one meets oneself, a stranger. A glimpse, a hint, something deciphered momentarily, then, more often than not, lost again.

June-July

We went to a dinner party given by Alan Sillitoe and his wife, Ruth Fainlight. Both are good friends of ours so that when Ruth told us she had written a libretto for an opera that was presently being performed at the Riverside Studios in Hammersmith, we thought we should go along and shout our hurrahs. Only one snag — or rather two — as far as I was concerned. First, I am not an opera fan. Second, I prefer the intermittent cacophony of a building-site to most modern music. I am reminded of a saying of Lou Costello. 'Two things I can't bear — mustard and bridges. So if you really want to drive me totally insane just put me in the middle of a bridge with a pot of mustard.'

I wish I felt about opera as does another friend — the American poet, William Meredith. William once wrote:

It's not the tunes, although as I get older
Arias are what I hum and whistle.
It's not the plots — they continue to bewilder
In the tongue I speak and in several that I wrestle.

An image of articulateness is what it is:
Isn't this how we've always longed to talk?
Words as they fall are monotone and bloodless
But they yearn to take the risks these noises take.

What dancing is to the slightly spastic way
Most of us teeter through our bodily life
Are these measured cries to the clumsy things we say,
In the heart's duresses, on the heart's behalf.

Alas, my view of opera is closer to that of Mark Twain who, after a visit to the opera — *Tristan and Isolde* — at the Metropolitan in New York, admitted that he felt unmoved, unlike the rest of the audience: 'Tristan and Isolde last night broke the hearts of all witnesses who were of the faith, and I know of some who have heard of many who could not sleep after it, but cried the night away. I feel strongly out of place here. Sometimes I feel like the sane person in a community of the mad; sometimes I feel like the one blind man where all others see; the one groping savage in the college of the learned, and always, during service, I feel like a heretic in heaven.'

At the Riverside Studios, an equally rapt audience — there was hardly an empty seat — listened to farts in different keys with evident appreciation. I looked about me and felt like Mark Twain, a groping savage in the college of the learned. The opera, I'm delighted to say, was a great success and Ruth certainly did not need our additional hurrahs. I understand she has a new book of poems coming out next year. I look forward to that genuinely and without reservation.

*

At present, when we stay in Wales, William and Patricia Oxley occupy our house in London and look after our sixteen year old cat, Caitlin. She likes the Oxleys. She understands that they understand her. They realise that at 8 a.m. precisely they must turn on the cold water tap in the bathroom basin so that she can spring up and revolve her head under the gushing tap as if it were a forthcoming, nourishing nipple. The Oxleys know, too, that when she, somewhat arthritically, walks into our front room at 10.30 p.m. she would be discountenanced if they did not switch on the TV set to B.B.C.2 so that she could watch *Newsnight*. Caitlin seems to be very interested in the News.

Sometimes we receive fitful messages from the Oxleys. 'X called, would you telephone him? By the way, Caitlin is fine, in very good fettle.' Or, 'Could Dannie meet Giles Gordon for a pizza, usual place, usual time on the 22nd? Caitlin ate a tremendous amount of crunchies today.' Or, 'Y telephoned to say she could cut Joan's hair on the 15th. Caitlin tested the water in the bath before Patricia could get in.' This evening William signed off with, 'Someone knocked at the front door with one of Dannie's books. He wanted it signed. No problem with Caitlin, Joan.'

I was surprised that somebody so hemlock-deranged should come to our front door for a book-signing session. Could not have been an Englishman. A man's house is his castle, etc. I asked Joan, 'Did William say the signature-seeker was an American?' Joan absent-mindedly replied, 'He said Caitlin was O.K.'

A couple of months ago when I was in New York I visited my American publisher, Michael Braziller, hetman of Persea Books. He introduced me to his agreeable assistant, Sean, offered me a coffee, remarked promptly that he never, never, went out at night but hoped that my 8 p.m. poetry reading at the Academy of American Poets would be attended by many enthusiastic, bookbuying poetry lovers for the Persea books would certainly be on sale there. Then, looking wildly round the room, he added, 'You've got royalties coming in June. You seem to have some American readers.' He seemed somewhat astonished that this should be so and, for my part, I wanted to ask him if he knew their names. That evening, amazingly, Michael Braziller did courteously come to my reading and some books were sold; and not all sought my signature. Maybe the man importuning our front door in London was one such, one who at first decided he did not want any graffito on the title page but later had changed his mind.

The last time I visited a second-hand bookshop in Hay-on-Wye I plucked from the shelf a soiled copy of one of my out-of-print books, *Way Out in the Centre*. Having only a single copy of it at home I decided to buy it. When I carried the book to the goitrous cashier he confided conspiratorially, 'It's signed, you know.' Silence. I blinked, looked quickly round the shop to make sure nobody recognised me. 'Really?' I said and flicked over the pages. Yes, there was my signature bold and clear on the title page. The cashier watched me closely as if I might bolt without paying. Someone behind the bookcases was coughing. 'We don't charge much extra,' the cashier continued to reassure me, 'because Abse signs quite easily.' I nodded nonchalantly, though I did not feel nonchalant. He gave me the book in a paper bag and, furtive, I slunk out of that second-hand bookshop utterly defeated. Still, come to think of it now — it's a good job I sign easily — otherwise I might have had to pay a packet for that second-hand copy of *Way Out in the Centre*.

We were driving through the narrow roads in the Vale of Glamorgan, intent on visiting the ruins of Beaupre — in Welsh, Bewpyr — a once magnificent, late-Tudor mansion. We had taken a wrong turning and were passing through the village of Llantrithyd. Next to a very small church with a tall Norman tower we spotted an interesting-looking ruin. We parked the car and the other side of a wall we were confronted by a group of black and white cows who stood in front of the charcoal-grey ruins of an imposing, almost roofless mansion. 'It's Tudor, judging by the windows,' Joan said, 'like Beaupre.' We wondered who had lived there and what and when. As we returned to the car we met one of the old men of the village. He had just quit the village telephone box. No-one else was about. 'Can you tell me anything about that ruin?' I asked.

He looked at me, baffled. 'Been there some time,' he said. 'I'm sure that's so,' I agreed. 'Oh aye,' he said pensively, 'I've lived by 'ere all my life and do you know that buildin' was a ruin when I was a boy.'

We thanked him, smiled, and went back to the car to find our way to Beaupre. I wanted to visit Beaupre because there, after Xmas in 1603, a party took place during which a local bard, Meurig Dafydd, (possibly from nearby Pentre Meurig?) eulogised the Squire. Afterwards Meurig Dafydd was asked if he had another copy of the praise-poem. 'No, by my fayth,' sayd the rhymer, 'but I hope to take a copie of that which I delivered to you.' Alas, the poem was then promptly, insultingly, thrown on to the blazing fire.

The castellated Elizabethan ruin of Beaupre is beautifully situated. From the road we walked through meadows beside the narrow River Thaw to reach its higher, secluded position. Much of the original mansion is still standing. We approached the house through an outer gatehouse and there, in front of us, was a beautiful, decorated porch which beckoned us to pass through. Did I then find the room I was looking for, that long room with its gallery — roofless now, of course? Here, certainly, was a great fireplace; and it was easy to imagine the harpists and lute players above us in the gallery, and the assembly below where we were standing. Surely the fire once blazed in that large grate and the blackened, charred bits of Meurig Dafydd's poem swirled up the chimney while John Stradling, one of the Squire's English guests, a man of letters himself, laughed out loud at Meurig Dafydd's discomfort.

Emyr Humphreys, in his book *The Taliesin Tradition*, is justifiably angry that Meurig Dafydd was so insulted by the Squire and his guests. Humphreys writes, 'The old squire's action was more than a calculated insult. A great deal more than a few lines of alliterative poetry was being thrown away. His gesture was a symbol. An entire class was relinquishing responsibilities that in former times had held the Welsh culture and social fabric together. An aristocratic tradition of more than a thousand years duration was being tossed "into the fire".'

For my part, I imagined Meurig Dafydd telling his mistress later what had happened at the party in Bewpyr, he, full of Welsh endearments for her, and spilling over with curses for the Squire and his guests, especially that rival poet, John Stradling:

> No word I huffed when Stradling urged the squire
> to throw my eulogy on the fire.
> The fiddlers laughed. I, snow-silent, proud,
> did not melt. But I'm spitless now,
> my pearl, my buttercup, my bread-fruit.
> I rattle their silver in my pocket.
> I have other stanzas for harp and lute,
> other gullible lords to flatter.

What do I care for that big-bellied Englishman
that bugle, that small-beer, that puff-ball,
that dung-odoured sonneteer, John Stradling?

Does he sing perfect metre like Taliesin?
Not that gout-toed, goat-faced manikin.
What does he know of Welsh necks crayoned
by the axe, blood on our feet, our history?
Has he stood pensive at the tomb
of Morian, or Morial, or March?
Wept at any nervous harp, at the gloom
of a dirge for Llywelyn the Last,
or the lament by Lewis Glyn Cothi?
That fungoid, that bunt, that broken-wind,
that bog-bean, can't tell a song from a grunt.

Clean heart, my theology, my sweet-briar,
he'd put our heritage on the fire.
Each night he swigs mead in a safe bed —
never sleeps roofed only by the stars.
At noon, never signs the euphonious nine
sermons of the blackbird. O my lotus,
his lexicon is small compared to mine.
His verses are like standing urine — tepid.
My Welsh stanzas have more heat in them
than the tumbling flames in the fire-place
of the Minstrel Hall of Bewpyr.

*

There is a Welsh doctor, a Dr Julian Tudor Hart, who suggests that
the relationship of physician and patient is all wrong. His is a
significant voice much respected in the profession. He urges that
the patient should be treated as a colleague, not as a supplicant,
and so they should collaborate, make decisions together. In short,
doctors should step down from their pedestals.

I think, in this, he is wrong. The doctor needs to be, for the
patient's sake, above the patient, a charismatic healer. However
sceptical or sophisticated patients may be when they are healthy,
a vestigial awe of the doctor-figure is precipitated when they are
ill and should not be dissolved. Something primitive in us, deep
down, leads us all to half-fancy that there are secrets in this world
about healing that some doctors are privy to — secrets antecedent
to all recorded history, and, in more recent times, translated into

Latin and Greek from the hieroglyphs of a lost language. These secrets some doctors have in their possession — and if we know that this is not so when we are healthy, we may well think otherwise when we are stressfully ill. Then, longing for a wizard, we send for his surrogate, the doctor, who bears no wand but a stethoscope and a prescription.

Oliver Sachs is surely right when he declares, 'There is, of course, an ordinary medicine, an everyday medicine, humdrum, prosaic, a medicine for stubbed toes, quinsies, bunions and boils; but all of us entertain the idea of *another* sort of medicine of a wholly different kind: something deeper, older, extraordinary, almost sacred, which will restore to us our lost health and wholeness.' That other medicine is one of the secrets.

One of my heroes knew that secret: Franz Anton Mesmer, Viennese physician and showman who carried a wand and wore a purple cloak. I can imagine him now in his Paris clinic, two hundred years ago, darting this way and that, to stop and catch hold of a patient's hands, to hold them in his while he gazed deeply into wild eyes. Then the purple-cloaked figure would touch the sick person with his wand and a cure would sometimes result. Mesmer claimed his healing power to be the result of 'animal magnetism' which emanated from the stars and which he believed he had the gift to transmit. Mesmer had been trained as a doctor and was sincere in his beliefs; but he had the fringe-healer's intuitive understanding that showmanship and the awe inspired by a reputation could heighten suggestibility and aid the healing process.

Mesmer has been dead these many years and his purple cloak in rags. Those who would agree with Dr Tudor Hart would simply see Mesmer as a gesticulating charlatan, a man in a purple cloak who set himself up on a pedestal.

Between London and Oxford on the M40 there are still no Service stations. Some travellers will hardly be reassured by a new sign that has been erected EMERGENCY W.C. 20 MILES. No wonder that soon after I had passed this sign, a car in the outer lane whooshed past me at 120 m.p.h.

August

In 1951, *The Ham and High* reported the marriage on the 4th of August of Dannie Abse, 50 Belsize Square, London NW3 to Joan Mercer, 50 Belsize Square, London NW3. Oh the raising of some bourgeois eyebrows. For living in sin then was...well, living in sin. No matter, happy and hippy, Joan and I left the Registry Office in Haverstock Hill to lunch with a few friends at The Blue Danube Club where Lotte Lenya used to sing. That lunch reduced our meagre finances so we left England for a hitchhiking honeymoon via France to Spain. Cash short, we stayed in some crumby, mice-odoured places including, surely, the original Hotel Insomnia.

August 4th was soon to come round again this year and Joan remarked that she would like to visit Lacock Abbey. 'It's not too far from Bath,' she said. 'After the dissolution of the monasteries Henry VIII sold the Abbey and it was converted into a house. But the cloister court and lots of medieval features still exist. John Piper lived there during the war and painted the Abbey.'

I booked into a highly recommended country hotel fifteen miles from Lacock to make up for those long ago hitchhiking abodes.

'A really good hotel for our anniversary,' I told Joan smugly.

'It only took you 42 years,' she said.

Lacock Abbey, with its different architectural styles, medieval, renaissance, 18th century Gothic, intrigued both of us as did the ancient National Trust village of Lacock. During the Middle Ages, a score of nuns lived in the Abbey, aristocratic women who had sworn to remain celibate. Why, I wondered, had Joan suggested we visit a nunnery on our wedding anniversary?

The thought of nuns made me narrow my eyes. All who lived in Britain during the war know that spies dress themselves up as nuns. They seemed a suspicious lot then, especially if they had big feet. No wonder John Piper's wartime painting of the Abbey proved to be so sinister.

Twenty minutes after leaving Lacock we turned our car into the long drive of Homewood Park hotel which is situated in its own private ten acres. We had passed the tennis court when Joan shouted, 'Look, a unicorn.' Behind railings a beast with one horn stared at us. I knew it could not be a unicorn. Unicorns don't exist because — as someone has pointed out — they have better things to do. Besides, behind the one-horned beast several two-horned beasts appeared. 'Jacob's sheep,' I said, knowingly. Beyond a white summer house and an immaculate croquet lawn lay the hotel itself, unassumingly gracious and welcoming, quiet as its own pastel shades and oriental carpets. Not a bit like Hotel Insomnia.

No sooner had we settled in than we learnt something that opened our eyes wide. At Lacock we had learnt that Ela, the Countess of Salisbury who was the founder of the 13th century Abbey for women, had also founded another religious house for men in the district. Now, on reading the Homewood Park brochure, we discovered that its foundations had once belonged to the Abbot's house of Ela's 13th century Hinton Charterhouse Priory. It was one of those coincidences that novelists have to eschew but which happen so often in life.

That night, during our five star — no, six-star dinner, Joan raised a glass to the monks of Hinton Charterhouse, I to the nuns of Lacock Abbey, and we were both of us so glad, as were our children, that we had a horror of celibacy.

I was walking down Old Compton Street in Soho when I was approached by a sorry-looking middle-aged man. 'I'm hungry,' he said simply. Reflexly I put my hand in my pocket, searching for change. Round the corner, across the road, I could see the French pub and I remembered how, at this same geographical location, Paul Potts, inveterate Soho sponger, had once accosted me saying, 'Dannie, I haven't eaten for days. I'm starvin', starvin'.'

Paul was always genuinely short of money though it was rumoured that George Orwell had left him a small legacy. Perhaps Orwell had admired Paul's occasional aphoristic remarks — 'Poems are old before they are made and young after a hundred years' or 'Surely anything worth saying twice is worth listening to once.' The trouble was Paul recited his aphorisms over and over, especially, 'A slave is only a free man in chains.'

Anyway, I had no sooner handed Paul Potts a ten shilling note so that he could end his fast when a red-suited commissionaire, one who regularly stood outside a rather grand Indian restaurant nearby, accosted us and demanded that Paul should pay for the meal he had just consumed! Paul muttered haughtily and strode off like an insulted General. The commissionaire, frustrated, grabbed *my* arm. 'Here's the bill for his lunch, sir,' he said threateningly as a small crowd gathered.

This lunch-time no such embarrassing scene unravelled in Old Compton Street. Ungripped, I decided to visit the French pub where I had first met Paul Potts. A minute after I had been introduced to him by my friend, Tony Cronin, Paul confessed to me, 'I'm a poet who cannot write a poem. I'm a failure. I've loved two women in my life. One rejected me, the other killed herself. I've no sex appeal. Lack of sex-appeal is as fatal to a man as the absence of a rifle is to a soldier.' And when Tony Cronin moved out of earshot Paul whispered, 'Don't trust Tony. He's too much like me.'

Now I crossed the road and entered the French pub. I recognised nobody. No Dom Moraes, the Indian poet, no George Melly. But ghosts presided: the ex-convict and dramatist, Frank Norman; Vogue photographer, John Deakin; painters Francis Bacon and the two Roberts — Colquhoun the groom, and MacBryde the bride. And most of all, Paul Potts.

As I sipped a liver-denying drink I heard his voice expostulating, 'The greatest thing in life is to witness the triumph of the insulted over the bully. That's more beautiful than the sculpture of Brancusi. Speaking of triumphs, did you see the review of my book, *Invitation to a Sacrament* in *The Observer* last Sunday? You didn't? You sure you didn't?' Then his voice, angry, loud, 'You're not worth talking to.'

Last night we viewed a video: 'Husbands and Wives' written, directed by and featuring Woody Allen. It was unashamedly autobiographical. As a boy, of course, Woody Allen knew the sorrows of a boy. Probably, like most boys, would weep only when unobserved, behind the privacy of a shut door, with curtains drawn perhaps or lights out. Now, as a man, he knows the sorrows of a man but performs on a public stage, sits on a spotlit chair and weeps and weeps till the curtains close and the audience applauds.

'We murder to dissect,' Wordsworth said.

*

Scene: Golders Hill Park. Time: 7.10 p.m. I am on my way home. The park is almost deserted except for a tall man ahead of me who halts to look at the Canada geese camped on the grassy verge of the duck pond. He begins to spit over and over at the geese. Strange. Absurdly I remember from my childhood a sign in trams and buses. *Penalty for Spitting £5.* As I draw close I see he is Japanese — oriental anyway. A tall Japanese who continues to aim his prolific sputum at the indifferent geese. I ask him, 'Why are you spitting at them?' He smiles benignly. 'They like water,' he says. What can I do? I walk on leaving him spitting like bill-yo at the geese.

September

A lunchtime invitation for the launch of Giles Gordon's recent Chatto book, *Aren't We Due for a Royalty Statement?* brought me to Soho's Groucho Club yesterday. I had already read Giles's stern account of literary, publishing and theatrical folk. After all, since he is my literary agent, he has had, perforce, to read so much of my work it was time that I, voluntarily, read his. Having shared countless lunchtime pizzas, red wine and gossiping dialogue with Giles over the last quarter of a century, I knew that his book would be rich with indiscreet, amusing anecdotes. Even so, I was startled by his patent, unflagging, stage-struck interest in and innocence of Celebrities.

Few of us are utterly immune to the synthetic charisma of Fame, even though we may agree with Boris Pasternak who asserted, 'It is not seemly to be famous. Celebrity does not exalt.' Indeed, it must be disadvantageous, if not destructive, to be truly famous, never to go anywhere without being intrusively recognised. Once, I had been working with Spike Milligan in a Birmingham TV studio — 'Muses with Milligan' — and on the way back to London, both of us exhausted and hungry, we stopped at a service station for a late meal. We had hardly sat down before the hum of voices, like wind in the telegraph wires, started up and paper napkins were being sent to our table from all over the restaurant for Spike to sign. Then came the gush of the waitress — and Spike, though adrenalin-drained, felt obliged to be witty. 'I saw you come through the door,' the waitress said. 'Ah,' said Spike, 'I hope the door was open.' And so on, and on.

I expected to see many of the celebrities named in Giles's book at the Groucho. The media were there in force; from the highest, e.g. the editor of *The Ham and High*, to the lowest, the editor of *The Times*, but as Giles Gordon himself sadly remarked, those authors who made real money for his firm — the Prince of Wales, Lord Tonypandy, Fay Weldon, Vikram Seth, Robert Nye, etc. had not turned up, whereas others had. At this point, I felt he was looking accusingly at me as I swigged my free glass of champagne.

Another book about to be published and likely to receive much attention is the authorised biography of Harold Wilson. It was originally commissioned by Lord Weidenfeld. Hardly surprising that Weidenfeld should be the Onlie Begetter of this biography for he remains a great fan of the one time Prime Minister.

Some years ago, at one of Weidenfeld's notorious Chelsea literary gatherings, I was asked to step into my host's bedroom. A fellow guest, a poet, had collapsed and evidently needed medical scrutiny. Lying on the bed, supine, I discovered the American poet, Robert Lowell; his wife stood by anxiously. Simply, Lowell had fainted — a combination of alcohol and the heat of a crowded room had surely been the cause. He soon revived and indeed the three of us spent the rest of the evening in Lord W's bedroom discussing the merits and demerits of English and American poetry. But overlooking us all stood a framed and signed photograph next to the bed. Weidenfeld, lying down and turning his head, would see not Marilyn Monroe, not a beloved relative, but the touched-up image of pipe-smoking Harold Wilson himself. Is this, sir, what they mean by the secrets of the bedroom?

I wonder if a photograph of our present Prime Minister, John Major, overlooks some stranger's bed? Unlikely. True, fellow politicians, even those with opposing views, tend to chorus, 'Oh,

John's a nice man.' Then, to be sure, come the 'buts'. But not up to the job. But no strong leadership. But no charisma.

Charismatics have some strangeness about them, something that does not permit too much familiarity, something akin to distance, something that reminds of fearful mountains unclimbed. 'When your nearness is far,' wrote Rilke, 'then your distance is like the very stars.' When we sleep our pagan ancestor sleeps too. Sometimes, though, the pagan dreamer awakens and misworships and misbelieves as, temporarily blinded, he or she looks towards some charismatic leader or medicaster. Consider those men around Mrs Thatcher, the optic nerve of their souls severed, their rationality reduced as they renounced responsibility for self and were overcome by Thatcher theopathy. But no dreamer within us lifts John Major on to some divine pedestal. On the contrary, Major himself unwittingly disallows it. He presents himself as the man next door. See him on TV and note the way he shakes hands, how he holds the right hand of some foreign potentate in both of his, how he touches the waist or back of some VIP welcomed at number 10 or Chequers. There is nothing in him of distance. Instead he has an anxiety to draw closer to whomever he is, at that moment, dealing with. By touching to be in touch.

The man next door may be a nice chap but come on, do you want a photograph of him next to your bed? Come to think of it, who would have thought Wilson would have been somebody's pin-up?

Amongst this morning's post a letter from an American woman, a stranger to me, someone who appears to be interested in the romantic sixth century Bedouin robber-prince poet, Antara al-Abse. She has translated one of Antara's boasts: 'My sword, in the battle, was a doctor dispensing medicine to those complaining of headaches.' I did not know that. I like that. As I have said before, the more I learn of Antara's swanking, the more I wish to claim him as my ancestor!

But what engages me most about the letter is her odd autobiographical confession. For, after telling me that she is a Jew and Welsh, she adds, 'I am a convert — to Judaism, of course, as few would choose to be Welsh.' I am reminded of the interview with Leonard Cohen, the singer, on Canadian TV. The interviewer seemed highly conscious of Cohen's Jewishness but somehow found it difficult to approach the matter directly.

'Does your name ever worry you?' she eventually blurted out.

'How do you mean?' asked Leonard Cohen.

'Your name, Leonard Cohen.'

'Oh yes, yes. I've often thought of changing it.'

'To what?'

Leonard Cohen hesitated. 'To September,' he said.

'Oh,'said the interviewer happily. 'Oh, September, that's a very interesting name. I can see it in lights — Leonard September.'

'Oh no no no,' said the singer, 'September Cohen.'

The first time I visited Israel was long before the six day war. As I travelled to the then peaceful border with Lebanon I was struck by how small the country was — barely the size of Wales. But the register, had it been called, would not have been answered by a Davies, an Evans, a Jones, a Thomas, a Williams but sombrely with, 'I am Auschwitz, I am Dachau, I am Treblinka.' A country then of survivors and one intent on surviving.

I went to Israel again in February 1971. The British Council sponsored a poetry-reading tour of Tel Aviv, Haifa and Jerusalem by five British poets. I was accompanied by D.J. Enright, Peter Porter, Jeremy Robson and Ted Hughes. Ted brought his new wife with him, Carol. It was really their honeymoon.

The six day war was over, Jerusalem no longer a divided city. The country seemed tranquil enough. We received generous Israeli hospitality, met their poets, saw their sights, drank their drinks. D.J. Enright descended to breakfast each morning more pale, more whacked. Soon he resembled, as he put it himself, 'the six-day whore'. We swam in the February waters of the Sea of Galilee. It was very cold. No wonder Jesus merely walked on the water.

We visited the Basilica of the Annunciation, peered at the Virgin on the wall of the church while the Christian Arab guide began his peroration. Suddenly, mid-sentence, he stopped. It seemed he had observed Ted Hughes putting his arm affectionately around Carol's waist. 'This is no place for love,' he boomed out, intending no irony. But in Jerusalem, for a small averted moment when I happened to be walking nowhere with Jeremy Robson, some Arab boys began to follow us and soon, their faces utterly hostile, sent our way a useless rage of stones. There was no love here. They were sons of the Defeated and we were allies of the Victorious. Despite the then prevailing euphoria following the six day war Israel was still embattled, still threatened. Those small boys with stones in their right hands were an omen of things to come.

With the present welcome news from the Middle East has the threat substantially diminished? I watched the TV screen fascinated when Rabin and Arafat shook hands. I half expected each of them, immediately afterwards, to take a handkerchief from their pockets and wipe their hands clean. Rabin, in civilian clothes, stood straight and stiff like the soldier he was; Arafat, in uniform, shrunken, like a murderous civilian dressed up in fancy clothes and bent down with the graves he carried. I turned the TV off feeling an effervescent sense of hope mixed with a nameless foreboding.

October

I've been judging the 1993 City of Cardiff International Poetry Competition. Over 3000 poems have been entered and, along with my co-judge, Jo Shapcott, I am dazed by their word-noise. I'm reminded of Segovia who once cried out forlornly, 'There are 2,000,000 guitar students in Japan alone.'

Of course, some of the poems can be dispatched swiftly. I read 'myriad', I read 'tis', I read 'o'er' and with one flick of the wrist they flutter downwards into the waiting waste-paper basket. Yet not always. Something catches my eye and I retrieve it, feeling guilty that I cast it away in the first place. Besides, so many of these 'amateur' outpourings are like confessions. They whisper, to someone they cannot see — me! — my husband has died, or my wife has Alzheimer's, or my son has been killed in a motor-bike accident. Others send signals, short long, short short long, a kind of morse, S.O.S. messages calling, Help, I'm unloved, I'm lonely, I'm sexually frustrated, I'm angry with God.

Reading such poems I feel like a voyeur. It is a relief to turn to poems about public horrors — even those about Bosnia. And there are rewards. There are a score of real poems among the three thousand that give me pleasure and make me feel the whole enterprise has been worthwhile.

In paintings of the Crucifixion before 1630 wounds are depicted on the right side of the body of Christ. Later painters generally moved the wound to the left side. Why? Surely it was because William Harvey had published his revolutionary *The Circulation of the Blood*. Harvey had dissected eighty different species of animals and had discovered that earlier medical doctrine was wrong, that the heart was on the left and the circulation of the blood circular. Harvey's discovery left its mark on the representation of the Crucifixion in art.

Inevitably, medical knowledge also penetrated literature. Yet, powerful as medical facts may be the personal experience of them regularly is even more sovereign. Therefore we would expect the dramatic clinical experiences of doctor-writers to colour their novels, their plays, their poetry. This is not always the case. We could read say, the poetry of John Keats or Robert Bridges without realising they were once, as doctors, buffeted by unforgettable, often brutal, medical experiences.

Other doctor-writers, though, have captured these real life, bloody scenarios and transformed them. Even Somerset Maugham, who gave up medicine soon after qualifying, recognised how much he, as a writer, was indebted to his doctor- experiences. 'Even now forty years have passed,' Maugham confessed, 'I can remember certain people so exactly that I could draw a picture of them. Phrases that I heard still linger in my ears. I saw how men died. I saw how they bore pain. I saw what hope looked like, fear and relief.'

Many things are common to the practice of authorship and medicine, not least an inordinate interest in people and a keen, observing eye. Both professions, too, recognise the ubiquity of cause. Writers know they must eschew the arbitrary, that their plots, for instance, must have an inevitability about them, that their characters' actions should not be without causal motive. Similarly, medical students are taught that all symptoms have causes. I sometimes think that Chekhov's law — fire a gun in the last act only if it is loaded in the first — was one he learnt in medical school.

Doctors, as a profession, have a poor reputation as communicators. In the past, deliberate obfuscation seemed the order of the day when it came to conversing with patients — their prescriptions written in Latin, their handwriting notoriously difficult to read, bombast their best vocal language, their whole demeanour open to the joyous satire of a Molière, a Bernard Shaw or, most recently, our own lavatorial Alan Bennett. Today, while trying not to be recondite, too many doctors fail to supply the patient with simple explanations. Besides, sometimes the truth is harder to tell than a lie. Yet, here's a conundrum. The one characteristic general enough to doctor-writers of note is their stylistic accessibility. 'Only connect.' And they do.

It would seem, in their case, that their medical education, their experience of regularly decoding mysterious signs and symptoms, and their physicians' sense of community, have made them impatient of those who, as Nietzsche put it 'muddy their own waters so as to appear more deep.' Oliver St John Gogarty was being very much a subversive doctor-poet when he objected to Robert Browning's opacities. 'When I read his translation of Aeschylus,' he remarked, 'I find it very useful to have the Greek beside me so that I may find out what the English means.'

Certainly 20th century doctor-poets such as William Carlos Williams in the U.S.A., Miroslav Holub in Czechoslovakia, Gottfried Benn in Germany, Rutger Kopland in Holland, Edward Lowbury in England, are not among those difficult to read — unlike say, the German writer Paul Celan or the American, John Ashbery. No, doctor-poets have clarified their own poetry for us without losing depth. Nor have they avoided portraying emotion any more than earlier doctor-writers such as Chekhov. After all, emotion articulated is something all doctors have listened to who are not deaf — and those doctor-writers who have contributed to the genuine pages of literature have, like William Harvey, dissected in order to bare the heart.

Surprise: a phone-call from 'Charlie' Westbury. 'Would you and

Joan join Hazel and me over dinner? We've asked Russell Barton also. He's here in London on a short visit.' Once upon a Doctor-in-the House time, Russell, Charlie and I were medical students at Westminster Hospital. Charlie, brilliant, caring student became a famous surgeon, recognised as among the best in Britain. Russell, unpredictable as ever, trained as a psychiatrist at the Maudsley and soon after emigrated to the U.S.A.

I have met Charlie intermittently over the years. He has hardly changed. His humorous one-liners continue to be as sharp and precise as his scalpel; but Russell was now a stranger to me. How much had he altered? Once, in the formaldehyde-odorous Dissecting Room I had shared a cadaver with him. Later, in the wards, in those immediate post-war years, he always compulsively wowed the nurses, provoking them with laughingly-pitched erotic verbal harassment, innuendo-charm and audacious flattery. He was a good-looking fellow with intense blue eyes and women, more intrigued than offended, generally took to him. In those days, the nurses at Westminster Hospital were often virgins from upper middle class families. They became watchful as Russell, who liked to shock them, walked by swinging a stethoscope. For nobody could utter the then taboo word 'fuck' in refined feminine company with such piquant innocence as Russell Barton. You would think, on such occasions, that he had just that minute stepped out with still intact rectitude from the Garden of Eden. Though Russell was a teller of multiple salacious jokes he would also in a fit of spontaneous combustion recite lines of pure poetry. Ezra Pound's early poems, I recall, were favourites of his:

> For a moment she rested against me
> Like a swallow half blown to the wall,
> And they talk of Swinburne's women
> And the shepherdess meeting with Guido,
> And the harlots of Baudelaire.

In the whispering intimacy of a St John's Wood restaurant, through the large window facing me, I stared at the dazzle on the branches of a tree in the anterior courtyard. They were alight with small electric bulbs. Around and about us heads leaned towards each other over candle-lit tables. Across the table from me, next to Joan, sat a man with Father Xmas white hair who answered to the name of Russell and whose once intense blue eyes seemed to have been washed many times, washed lighter behind the spectacles he now wore.

'And your hair is grey,' Russell reminded me.

Charlie, who had become somewhat balder, remarked, 'I'm quicker now when I'm out of doors to notice when it begins to rain.'

'We're old,' Russell remarked — not with a quiet desperation but with characteristic laughter.

I thought of my own recent birthday. There is something aging about birthdays! Vanishings...the years gone like change. Over dinner, though, our conversation regressed to another time. The years O! The years. We hardly spoke of the matters of the day; not, for instance, of the destruction of the Health Service, not about the mismanagement of the British economy, not about how leading Tory ministers had given the nod to arms-making machines illicitly bound for Iraq — not, in short, about how our Government is criminally inefficient and inefficiently criminal, but instead we encamped in the easy nostalgia of reminiscence.

I reminded Russell how once Dr Taylor had rebuked us both for not wearing ties and had earnestly insisted that the next day we should wear them else he would not teach us. We obeyed. We both wore ties round our waists. 'Those waists were of smaller dimension then,' Joan said quietly.

Russell then offered us blue suggestive jokes as if he were sweet and twenty again while Charlie, blinking, punctuated the chatter with youthful one-liners. We were happily silly and Hazel and Joan, for the next hour or two, knew they were still married to mere boys. Our grey hair and lined, aged faces were but a master-disguise.

I have been trying to re-read the poems of Paul Celan, in English translation since I have no German, and for the most part — his 'Death Fugue' is an extraordinary exception — I put up my hands, defeated. I think the reputation *in English* of a number of eminent foreign poets, some of them hermetic in their own language, is a 'con' insofar as they have to be taken in blind trust by monoglots such as myself. Celan, Mandelstam, Paz, Elytis and others, Nobel Prize winners among them, may in their own language be wonderful to behold, but little leaks through in translation. Reading them in English — to echo Thomas Peacock — I discover that I have not been charmed by harmony, moved by sentiment, excited by passion, affected by pathos, nor exalted by sublimity.

I said as much to the American poet, Paul Zimmer and his wife Sue, when they visited us in London. Paul told me how one of his slim volumes had been translated into Japanese. 'That book was dedicated *To Sue with love,*' he continued, smiling at his wife. 'But when the book arrived I showed it to a Japanese friend. He happened to open it up at the dedication page which read, when re-translated into English, *To press a law-suit with love.*'

'Poetry is that which is lost in translation,' Sue nodded, quoting Robert Frost.

I was reminded of my visit a few years ago, along with Seamus Heaney, to the International Poetry Festival at Struga in Macedonia. One of my poems, 'Hunt the Thimble', had been translated into Macedonian and, with other translations from different countries, it was read not only at Struga but also at other nearby towns. This version which spread over two pages was declaimed by a native actor. After a few readings he evidently mislaid the second page. Thus 'Hunt the Thimble' ended abruptly. The first time we heard this abbreviated poem, as the actor stepped down from the platform, Seamus whispered Irishly to me, 'Sure, Robert Frost was right. Poetry is that which is lost in translation!'

Too many poems, it seems to me, published at present in books or periodicals, read with their arbitrarily cut-up lines like failed translations from a foreign language. Indeed, quite a number *are* failed translations! It would seem many young poets have taken renowned 20th century poets, in translation, as their models.

It is a mystery why poems — in their original language so dependent on aural subtleties, on linguistic associations, on national inferences, on internal logomachy — ever survive their English metamorphosis. Yet a scattering do so magnificently. Some of those from the German of Rilke and Brecht come to mind or those from the Greek of Cavafy and Seferis or the Polish of Zbigniew Herbert and Wislawa Szymborska. One could name 20th century poets from other languages also: Lorca (Spanish), Prevert (French), Primo Levi (Italian), Marina Tsvetayeva (Russian).

So Robert Frost's definition is not invariably true — not even for Celan, as Clement Greenberg's translation of 'Death Fugue' proves:

Black milk of the dawn we drink it evenings
we drink it noon and morning we drink it nights
we drink and drink
we dig a grave in the wind you won't lie cramped there
A man lives in the house who plays with the snakes who
        writes
who writes at dusk to Germany your golden hair Margarete
he writes it and comes out of the house and the stars
        twinkle he whistles his hounds out
he whistles forth his Jews has a grave dug in the ground
he orders us strike up now for the dance

Black milk of the dawn we drink you nights
we drink you morning and noon we drink you evenings
we drink and drink
A man lives in the house who plays with the snakes who
        writes
who writes at dusk to Germany your golden hair Margarete
 Your ashen hair Sulamith we dig a grave in the wind you
        won't lie cramped there

He cries dig deeper in the ground you ones you others sing
        and play
he reaches for the iron in his belt he swings it his eyes are
        blue
dig your spades deeper you ones you others keep playing
        for the dance

Black milk of the dawn we drink you nights
we drink you noon and morning we drink you evenings
we drink and drink
a man lives in the house your golden hair Margarete
your ashen hair Sulamith he plays with the snakes

He cries play death sweeter death is a master from
        Germany
he cries fiddle lower then you'll rise in the air as smoke
then you'll have a grave in the clouds you won't lie
        cramped there

Black milk of the dawn we drink you nights
we drink you noon death is a master from Germany

we drink you evenings and mornings we drink and drink
death is a master from Germany his eye is blue
he strikes you with leaden balls his aim is true
a man lives in the house your golden hair Margarete
he sicks his hounds on us he gives us the gift of a grave in
        the air
he plays with the snakes death is a master from Germany
your golden hair Margarete
your ashen hair Sulamith

Paul Celan survived the Holocaust but both his parents died in the Nazi Death Camps. His dramatic, bitter, paradoxically musical poem, 'Death Fugue' remains memorable in English and is one of the most arresting poems written over the last fifty years. How disappointing it is, therefore, to discover that the other poems of Celan do not work in English.

A week or so ago I gave a lecture at the Cheltenham Literary Festival on Keats in which I focussed on Dr Keats's desperate need to fly away on the wings of Poesy from the screaming wards of 19th century Guy's Hospital: 'O for a beaker of the warm South... That I might drink and leave the world unseen.'

Afterwards, with Waterstone's bookshop in conspicuous attendance, it was book-signing time. A number of books thrust towards me for signature proved to be by Keats. I hesitated to sign *The Poems of John Keats* — but pressed to do so I wrote down p.p. J. KEATS or *Signed in his absence*.

This morning, October 31st, Keats's birthday, after reading the Sunday newspapers with their shrill headlines about the most recent Ulster psychopathic murders, Joan and I drove over to Keats' Grove in Hampstead. For here, at Wentworth House, where Keats once lived with his friend, Charles Brown, a gentle ceremony was about to take place: a replanting, in the front garden, of a plum tree. Soon we joined an invited group of Keats's admirers as Gerald Isaaman shovelled earth on to the sapling. Among the observing crowd of faces I spotted Michael Foot, Glenda Jackson, Alan Brownjohn, Lee and Ruth Montague.

In the Spring of 1819 Charles Brown wrote, 'A nightingale had built her nest in my house. Keats felt a continual and tranquil joy in her song; and one morning he took a chair from the breakfast table to the grass-plot under a plum tree where he sat for two or three hours...' Here, under that long-gone plum tree, Keats had composed his 'Ode to a Nightingale'. And now, here on the same grass-plot, next to the living plum sapling, Gabriel Woolf, the actor, declaimed Keats's impassioned meditation.

Joan and I stood on the lawn with Alan Brownjohn. Across from us, the gathered, upturned faces listened under a grey orbicular sky. 'Forlorn! the very word is like a bell,' Gabriel Woolf intoned. The out-of-doors ceremony over, the guests trooped into the house for a glass of wine. Soon the lawn was empty; only the reduplicating litter of yellowing leaves, the colour of banana skin, remained on the green grass, and an elegiac hole in the earth, half-filled, for the baby plum tree.

November

The newspaper headline: RECORD TOLL OF GRADUATES WITHOUT JOBS. Hence the unkind joke:

Question: Do you know what to say to a succesful graduate, one with a first class degree?

Answer: I'll have a Big Mac, please.

Rummaging through papers I came across a record of the notes I made when interviewing that notorious post-war spirit-healer, Harry Edwards. In the spring of 1964, I interviewed for a Sunday newspaper half a dozen notable medicasters, among them Professor Niehans in Switzerland and Harry Edwards, here, in Britain.

Niehans, through his ridiculous 'cellular therapy' — he injected fresh foetal liver cells (from an unborn lamb) to rejuvenate diseased livers; fresh foetal heart cells to revitalise a failing heart; fresh brain cells in brain conditions and so forth and so on — claimed to rejuvenate such aged politicians as the German Chancellor, Adenauer, actresses such as Gloria Swanson, writers such as the wrinkled Somerset Maugham. Harry Edwards, too, had his famous patients including, it was said, some of the Royal family. He was the foremost spiritualist medium in Britain and his spirit guides, he told his patients, were no other than the ghosts of Louis Pasteur and Lord Lister.

I confess that before I interviewed such fringe-healers I had believed them to be charlatans. After meeting them I realised it was more complicated than that. Nietzsche once wrote, 'In all great deceivers a remarkable process is at work to which they owe their power... In the very act of deception, with all its preparation, the dreadful voice, expression and gesture, amid their effective scenario they are overcome by *their belief in themselves*; it is this belief which speaks so persuasively, so miracle-like to the audience.' Surely, though, fringe-healer or politician, needs to be a borderline psychotic to believe that he owns such a God-given power. I do think this is so. The most successful fringe-healers are dangerously encamped near the night-borders of insanity.

When I interviewed Professor Niehans on March 14th 1964 in his spacious home in Switzerland, overlooking the lake at Burier-Vevey, he sounded like a paranoid with grandiose illusions. He spoke of himself, often, in the third person as certain inmates of mental hospitals tend to do. 'Niehans is a revolutionary,' he said. 'And revolutionaries in medicine have much opposition. That's why I kept my discoveries secret for twenty years, why I had to give 3000 injections before I released information about what I was doing. Niehans had to be absolutely sure. Lately I've been working on diabetes. Ha! When I publish my results what a storm there'll be. The drug firms. How they'll cry out against me once more. There are many people against Niehans. They tried to take my clinic away from me. They have succeeded now in barring me from the abattoir at Clarens where I obtain the fresh cells from the embryos of ewes.'

I recall how, while he ranted, I glanced out of the window at the quivering reflections of mountains in the lake, at clouds on mountains, and mountains on clouds, everything in a dream and beautiful, sheer opera, sheer fake.

My conversation with Harry Edwards had been equally bizarre. It took place not in a mental ward but at his mansion in Shere, Surrey. Here is an extract from the notes that I made at the time:

Edwards: I had 8750 letters this week. Most of 'em tell me they're incurable. As a result of my meditations 80 per cent record a measure of improvement. 30 per cent of these — a complete recovery.

Me: When do you meditate?

Edwards: In the early hours of the morning.

Me: To tune into your spirit guides?

Edwards: Yes.

Me: Louis Pasteur and Lord Lister?

Edwards: Yes. It's a matter of love an' compassion.

Me: You told me you treat people who suffer illnesses like leukaemia, cancer, multiple sclerosis. Don't you feel worried about raising false hopes?

Edwards: The gift of healing is a divine gift, one given to me as it has been to others. We never limit the power of spirit-healing however apparently intractable the illness. As a result, people who've been deaf are deaf no more, hunchbacks no longer hunchbacks, cripples can now walk unaided, their crutches discarded.

Me: What of the power of suggestion?

Edwards: Can you suggest things to animals? Why, only this week an Alsatian was brought here for spirit-healing. The dog was unable to walk. It was paralysed. But it left this sanctuary cured.

The years have vanished and Niehans is dead; so is Harry Edwards. Nowadays, others with similar claims and similar methods would gull the gullible. It seems to me that these so-called charismatic healers, like the somewhat presidential Professor Niehans and the more grubby Harry Edwards, need their patients not only for financial gain but to save themselves from a total break with reality. Their relationship with patients is a symbiotic one. By trying to cure them and by occasionally relieving them of symptoms, if not the underlying disease, they not only gratify their own powerful inner needs but reinforce their own delusions of grandeur.

I suppose everybody experiences some time, if only for one elongated moment, that almost indescribable feeling of dread — a premonition that seems to signal a fall into a hollow blackness past precipitous chasms between azoic rock-masses, on and on — that feeling without evidence of a beginning and no apparent prospect of an end. When I was a boy, if I inarticulately complained of such a feeling my superstitious mother would say, 'Someone has walked over your grave, son.'

Fortunately, most of us know occasional 'highs' too, those other moments too rare, almost out of time, when, intemperate, we could take off all our clothes and youthfully dance while far away, *inaudibly*, the sweet psalmist of Israel, hearing the note G in the natural scale of C major, sings of 200 loaves of bread and of 100 bunches of raisins.

Over an Indian meal last night, Jeremy Robson, the publisher, told Joan and me an amusing story about Mohammed Ali. Jeremy had published a biography of the ex-champion and when Ali visited England he agreed to promote the book. On one occasion, after a signing session in the bookshops of Birmingham, Jeremy, accompanied by his wife Carole, drove the boxer and his American minder back to London. Carole sat in the front seat next to Jeremy as they sped down the night-dark M1. Halfway to London a silence pervaded the car. Mohammed Ali had apparently fallen asleep and his minder, too, as Jeremy observed through the mirror, was yawning.

Soon, though, Jeremy and Carole heard the boxer moaning and groaning. 'Don't worry,' said the minder. 'Sometimes when he's dreaming he relives his fight with Joe Frazier.' Sure enough, Mohammed Ali started mumbling and growling, 'I'll getcher, I'll getcher.' And almost simultaneously Jeremy felt Mohammed Ali's formidable right fist hit the back of his driving seat. 'Yeh, yeh,' muttered Ali as Jeremy slowed down. Again Ali smashed the driving seat, two fists this time. 'Don't worry,' the minder repeated. Jeremy edged the car into the slow lane when he felt another wham to his back. 'I'll kill you, I'll kill you,' shouted Ali, his eyes closed.

'It'll be O.K.,' the minder insisted somewhat shrilly. Wham! Wham! 'Joe Frazier, wham. Wham wham, Joe Frazier,' groaned Ali, again two-fisted.

Jeremy admitted that he and Carole were not only utterly silent but somewhat white-faced until they heard both their passengers in the back seat roaring and rocking with laughter. Jeremy put his foot on the accelerator and moved out to the fast lane.

December

Caitlin likes to hunk down on my desk while I am working. This morning, as is her custom, she attempted to spring up on to my papers. She did not make it. I had to lift her up. She is getting old. She has been lodging here almost seventeen years now, ever since she was a ginger kitten no bigger than my hand.

She may not have the muscular power she once had, she may be somewhat deaf, but she could, I swear, still pass her cat 'O' levels. I am continually surprised by evidence of her cat intelligence. My naive surprise derives, I think, from my early medical training in the Physiology Department at King's College, London, where eminent Professor MacDowell maintained that animals were only motivated by three instincts, by the three Fs — Fear, Food and Reproduction. We witnessed experiments on cats and were taught to despise them. 'Reflex creatures,' our professor would insist, 'slaves of the three Fs and without intelligence.' We did not challenge his authority and perhaps a number of medical students felt more comfortable, less squeamish, having to observe these dissected, nerves-exposed, living cats, believing them to be devoid of worthy intelligence.

Years later, when I learned in some detail about the happenings within the Nazi Death Camps — how, for instance, those torturers needed to assert the worthlessness of their so-called sub-human victims, I recalled how Profesor MacDowell had to stress the lack of intelligence of the cats experimented on, their pathetic inferiority.

Given Auschwitz, Belsen, Buchenwald, given the bloody wars enacted right now in the world, given the inaudible human screams provoked by other human beings in the different, secretive dungeons all over the world — in 90 countries according to Amnesty International — how odd it is that we consider ourselves to be the most superior in the hierarchy of the animal kingdom.

Post-Darwin era it may be, but we still distance ourselves from the other creatures. We do it in many ways, not least verbally. We give the animals, by and large, such a bad press. Why, for instance, should swine and other animals be so deprecated? 'That swine,' my father used to say of Hitler. 'That dog,' my mother used to expostulate about Oswald Mosley.

In conversation we abuse a whole Noah's ark of animals. He's as clumsy as an elephant. She's as stubborn as a mule. He's a shark, she's a vixen. He's a rat, she's a cow. That lawyer's a snake, that official's a worm. He's a skunk, she speaks weasel-words. Here they come out of the ark — adagio, the lounge-lizard; allegro, the road-hog. Man's a wolf to man.

Even the extinct animals are arraigned. His wife is a dragon of a woman. Her husband is a political dinosaur. As for curses, Shakespeare says it all — what a zoo of abuse. One man has a goatish disposition, another is a fawning greyhound. One is pigeon-livered, another is as tedious as a tired horse. Would one not wince to be called, 'Thou deboshed fish thou'? Or 'Thou whoreson little tidy Bartholomew boar-pig'? Or to be referred to as 'That roasted Manningtree ox with the pudding in his belly'?

We did not always demean the animals. On the contrary, we worshipped them. Did not the very gods assume animal disguises in myths and in the pre-historic representation of them? As Freud remarked, 'In the course of his development towards culture man acquired a dominating position over his fellow-creatures in the animal kingdom. Not content with this supremacy, however, he began to place a gulf between his nature and theirs. He denied the possession of reason to them, and to himself he attributed an immortal soul.'

As I write, Caitlin now lies full stretch on my desk, a mere foot away from me. She purrs. She does not know that, unlike her, I have a soul. Silly goose!

Over breakfast I read letters. The first Xmas card has arrived already. One letter proves to be from Gavin McCarthy of B.B.C. Wales. He invites me to participate in a radio programme which involves an interview interspersed with six or seven pieces of music that hold a significant place in my life. Soon, upstairs in the bathroom, I find myself sub-vocally thinking nostalgic tunes — so much so that I cut my lip shaving. I bleed. Damn.

Oh the ineffable potency of old melodies! Like a faded photograph or a whiff of a strong scent they remind us of gone days, gone nights. Even as they pleasure us they induce feelings of small regret and greater loss. Søren Kierkegaard once confessed, 'In Stralsund I almost went mad hearing a young girl playing the pianoforte, among other things Weber's last waltz over and over again. The last time I was in Berlin it was the first piece I heard in the Thiergarten, played by a blind man on the harp. It seems as though everything was intended to remind me of the past.' Yes indeed. Those old remembered tunes can make a man bleed!

It is some twenty years now since I chose eight Desert Island Discs for Roy Plomley. Half a dozen of them were classical pieces; but these I shall not repetitively choose for Radio Wales. One classical composition that has entranced me over the last two years, ever since my daughter, Keren, gave it to me on a cassette, is Mozart's Divertimento K563. We play it sometimes in the car, journeying from London to Ogmore-by-Sea. It is a spiritual unguent, one conducive to calming driver and passengers in the tensions of the M4. It is, as Rilke would put it, 'The breathing of statues.' I think it is a musical medicine. Iamblichus, writing in the fourth century A.D., in his *Life of Pythagoras*, relates how a raving, lovesick youth, insane with jealousy and about to burn down his rival's house, heard a flute player sound a Phrygian melody and was, as a result, restored in time to quietude and sanity.

I am glad Mr McCarthy has asked me to contribute to his 'Music of My Life' programme. I have an excuse not only to listen to musical medicine but to wallow wonderfully in obstinate nostalgia. I can indulge myself with musical calories. I can put on old records and pretend I am slaving away, working like billy-o, preparing myself in a melodic sweat for a radio programme.

I sit at this desk half in a trance. I am transferred more than half a century back to a house in Cardiff, to a room with too much furniture in it. My eldest brother, Wilfred, is playing his favourite 'Georgia' on the gramophone as growled out by Nat Gonella and I remember each nuance of the trumpet solo. I go back even further to hear Leo singing that politically-sound bitter lyric, 'Once I built a railroad...they called me Al', and my sister, more romantically, crooning, half to the mirror and with such a drastic look on her face, 'Some Day He'll Come Along' or 'Mad About the Boy'.

When my parents focussed on popular music it would be that, of course, which was fashionable for an even earlier generation.

Those jaunty tunes of the Music Hall! And could anybody, in the whole wide world, whistle so skilfully as my father 'Daisy, Daisy, Give me your answer do', and 'The Lily of Laguna'? My parents took me sometimes to the ornamented — all crimson and brass — New Theatre for a Saturday night Variety Show. Two Ton Tessie, Vic Oliver or The Mills Brothers topped the Bill. And suddenly, now, as I write, The Mills Brothers are heavy-breathing in my ear: 'Where's that Tiger? Where's that Tiger?' I wait for silence but all I hear is my father laughing inexplicably at someone dressed up, surely for Budget Day, someone called Max Miller. Was it he who sang with innocent vulgarity: 'I never knew what a little girl could do... She did her dancing in the East, she did her dancing in the West, but she did the dancing where the dancing was best'?

Those occasional Saturday nights my father would buy a rustling box of Black Magic chocolates for my mother and, of course, they would let me dip into it. Marzipan, Turkish Delight, Coffee Cream, Nougat, Cherry Liqueur, I cannot bite now into the dark hearts of such chocolate without experiencing a Proustian evocation of a time and a place and a circumstance. So it is with the lovely malice of music that can take a man back and further back down the indigo roads.

At an animated dinner party, our host told us how a certain doctor, investigating the verbal composition of articles published in *The British Medical Journal*, had discovered that, on average, 42 per cent of the words in each issue were adjectives. After some further discussion I asked, 'Is it worth travelling around the world to count the cats of Zanzibar?' Satisfied that I had triumphantly put all opposing discourse to an end with that propitious quotation from Thoreau, I sat back, smugly, waiting for the pudding to be served.

Then, unexpectedly, one of the guests, John Heath-Stubbs, emphatically replied, 'Yes!' He provoked laughter because of his intervention, and urgently he repeated, 'Yes, yes, it is worth going around the world to count the cats of Zanzibar.'

John Heath-Stubbs, besides being a poet, is a considerable scholar; and at the time I thought it was as a scholar that he had answered Thoreau's rhetorical question in the affirmative. After all, scholars should not prejudge the value of any harmless investigation before it is embarked upon. Now, though, I have come to believe that John Heath-Stubbs replied 'Yes' because he was a poet also. Most people, after all, have as little regard for the activity of writing poems as they have for the kind of scholarship that involves the counting of adjectives in succesive issues of *The British Medical Journal*. They are somewhat baffled by those who are engaged in such apparently useless activity, unless that activity brings monetary reward or is simply an expression of a hobby. Writing poetry as a central concern, not as a marginal pastime, year in year out, putting the right words in the right order for no evident reason, neither wishing to persuade anybody nor to legislate, must seem to many a very odd occupation indeed. No wonder I'm asked, as no doubt other poets are, 'Do you really consider writing poetry important?' They are politely asking, 'Why is a grown man like you playing with words?'

In attempting to justify one's trade as a poet it is no longer possible to resort to arguing the moral nature of poetry. Those nineteenth century claims that 'Poetry strengthens the faculty which is the organ of the moral nature of man in the same manner as exercise strengthens a limb', seem hollow now. Even T.S. Eliot's 'poetry refines the dialect of the tribe' appears in all its ambiguities to be a grandiose assertion, if not a dubious one. The very multiplicity of definitions about the Function of Poetry proves, does it not, that most people are suspicious that poetry has no function? I know of no long essays in Defence of Carpentry or in Defence of Surgery. Everyone is convinced that such technicians are necessary. Even so, if by chance professional poets somehow commanded, in the future, regular salaries I suspect there would be fewer essays in Defence of Poetry; and if that salary was considerable, no longer would poets be thought to be playing childish word-games, a sort of Radio 3 Scrabble. In judgement of activities it is the motive, the motive that is all, however wrongly interpreted. A man who murders another for no evident reason is thought to be a criminal madman; if he happens to rob the man he murders he will be judged a sane criminal.

But just as certain existentialist novelists have written in praise of the pure 'pale criminal', so poets perhaps ought to praise those who satisfy their own needs, in a less anti-social way, *without rationalisation*. Certainly I would like to raise two cheers for those who are engaged in such apparently useless activities as assessing the percentage of adjectives in medical articles. In so doing, I praise all scholars, all pure scientists, and all those poets who do not pattern words to convert readers to a point of view. I'm half way, I think, to Zanzibar.

The wind has gone mad. An hour ago, as I bent forward into the blinding wind to the village Post Office store, the sun, indifferent, keeping its own obsessional time, sank lower towards the small quivering shore-hills of Somerset. Some minutes later, carrying the *South Wales Echo* and a bottle of refrigerator-cold milk, I walked back, my fingers freezing, my eyes still watering, in this lunatic gale. The telegraph wires howled like B.B.C. radio sound-effects for a play about a havoc storm at sea.

Looking out towards Somerset, I thought how I would dread being out there on a bucking ship in that fairground, switch-back, elephant-grey Bristol Channel. Not that one single boat was visible. Indeed, nobody appeared to inhabit the numb, land-locked afternoon either. Ogmore seemed nerveless, deserted. Some sheep huddled behind a stone-armoured wall, a few separate silhouettes of seagulls were flung off course, lifted giddily wide and high against the sky, and an idiot tin can, animated by the relentless wind, scraped the macadam as it bucketed past me, its sound diminishing with each step I took.

Though it was still afternoon, the lamp-posts began to glow. Soon it will be the shortest day of the year. Tomorrow we return to London. This will be our last sojourn in Ogmore this 1993. And, somehow, when I opened our wooden gate, I had that old familiar sense of something ending, 1993 going out as I was coming in. Perhaps it was something to do with the impending early darkness and the fury of the wind — something like a regretful au revoir, a smileless valediction, an end of a book also which, however, possesses a few blank pages after the print has run out. The coalhouse door was flapping and I bolted it tight. Inside the safe house the wind was defeated despite the rattling windows.

It is night now outside. The river, unseen, drifts into the glutted sea, the scarce ghost-stars wheel about the dark poles of the sky.

Appendices

1. Authors Take Sides

The pure, pale criminal is one who admits to killing his victim solely because he enjoys the dramatic act of murder. For no other reason. Does he exist outside the pages of fiction? A real nice human-type murderer wishes to be thought of as sane, if not by others, then by himself. So in a gloomy cell he whispers to the Father Confessor or to the psychiatrist what he thinks to be the true cause of why he dismembered so bloodily his victim. The reason given may be momentous or apparently trivial: because, Father, the swine was possessed by the devil; because, doctor, the swine stole my wife; because, Father, the swine had treasure under the floorboards; because, doctor, each night the swine came into my garden and ate my gooseberries.

We who go to war, to patriotic murder, need for sanity's sake, a cause. The Greeks besieged Troy because beautilul Helen, they sincerely believed, had been abducted, forced into a coloured ship, that sailed for Troy. Yet there is another legend, another report, less sensational: Helen never went to Troy. She left home, yes, but not for Troy and she was not forced. She was elsewhere, Egypt perhaps, Cyprus perhaps, and those Trojans, those Greeks, slaughtered each other for ten long years because of a fairy story, a lying headline, a cloud, a ghost, an empty garment. I am one who believes this other story, that Helen was spotted by travellers on the banks of a delta:

> Deep girdled, the sun in her hair, with that way
> of standing...
> The lively skin, the eyes and great eyelids,
> 'She was there, on the banks of a Delta',
> 'And at Troy?
> Nothing. At Troy a phantom.
> So the gods willed it.
> And Paris lay with a shadow as though it were solid flesh;
> And we were slaughtered for Helen ten long years.'
> (G. Seferis)

We British are an aggressive nation. We seem to have become more violent this last decade: look how we drive fast and furious, with fists clenched; listen, at the stadiums, how the crowds shout,

'Kick his fuckin' head in', or to the sirens of police cars and ambulance in the shoddy streets of Brixton or Liverpool. Listen to the usual thud of an explosion in Belfast. Most of the time, though, we turn our aggression inwards, we punish ourselves: we elect a leader who believes in Capital Punishment, who can punish us with conviction and with style, who with her male, public-school educated legions can sanguinely dismantle our Health Service, ruin our cities, pollute our air with lead or radioactivity, and make us unemployed.

Once we were told, 'You've never had it so good', and indeed we had never had it so good. It seems we felt we did not deserve it; our left hand was guilty; and our right hand was so guilty that we needed relief, we needed to be punished. But mother and Margaret, six of the best was not enough, is still not enough. We still have aggression to spare. We boil over. Ulster is getting boring; besides, there the issues are not black and white, they're complicated, confused. What we need is a clear issue. If we are going to murder anybody, God, we must have a clear issue, we must be *virtuous*. So what about a faraway island, one most of us had never heard of before — oh, don't tell us about treasure offshore — if we murder it must be for a pure principle.

No question, the Argentinian government are thugs in uniform. Yes, Argentinian thugs, who can deny that? It is true, it is documented. What a cause! What a Helen! So pass the drum, the gun and the blood-drip. Ta ra ra. Ta ra ra. Ta ra ra. (9 July 1982)

2. The Chairman

Those who pronounce your name wrongly: 'We are pleased to welcome you 'ere tonight, Mr Abs.' Those whose welcome seems over-profuse, flatulent. Those whose introductions are long and tedious, or just untrue: 'Mr Abse is not only a poet but also a Member of Parliament.' Those who alienate the neutral audience with killing overpraise — that time in Kent when the chairman's eulogy concluded with — 'And, in addition, Dr Abse's the greatest British comic poet since Chaucer!' I felt then I should be funny, render the now melancholy-eyed audience (they resembled mourners at a funeral) 'seismic with laughter' by emulating, perhaps, Spike Milligan: 'I thought I'd start, as a matter of fact, by reading you some of Chaucer; but then I decided, the hell with that, why should I? He never reads any of mine.'

Less rare are those chairmen who prove to be not merely inept but plainly malignant. Mr Norman Moore, for instance, who officiated— that is the correct word — at a reading I gave in the Lake District, one summer's evening in 1981. Not long before that occasion I had, perhaps foolishly, contributed to a series of articles in *Punch* called 'Success'. When Alan Coren commissioned me to write that piece perhaps I should have quoted Chekhov: 'Success? Write about my success? What's the criterion for success? You need to be God to distinguish success from failure unerringly. I'm off to a dance.' But how was I to know that Mr Norman Moore was later to pick up that copy of *Punch* in his dentist's waiting room?

When I was called for at the hotel and taken to the poetry-reading venue the nice blonde driver said, 'I'm worried about the chairman for tonight. You see Bill who wrote to you had to go into hospital to have his appendix out. It was an emergency — and they've asked Norman Moore to substitute.'

'Norman Moore?'

'He knows nothing about poetry. But he's the local panjandrum, a Tory councillor, and used to acting as chairman. I suppose it will be alright.'

In the hall I was introduced to Mr Moore, a tall man, tall as a publisher. He was talking to some of the audience and my blonde friend interrupted him in mid-flow. He was not *homey*. He did not even offer me a glacial hand. He hardly nodded before turning back to his admirers. Five minutes later, before we went together on to the slightly raised platform, he did deign to address me briefly. 'I take it you'll be through in an hour. I have a later appointment.' Someone once said that there is no one so pompous as a local celebrity. Norman Moore was obviously one helluva local celebrity and I felt no antagonism nor did I expect him, of course, to harbour any ill-feelings towards me.

Soon he rose to address the audience. About eighty men and women draped the wooden chairs, having come to this focal point from different parts of the Lake District. 'I have never read a book by Dr Abse,' Mr Moore commenced, 'but recently I came across a piece he wrote in *Punch*, a magazine I might add that does not usually come my way. In *Punch* it says, ha ha ha, that he's a success.'

I glanced towards him surprised by the acidulous tone of his voice. 'A success!' he jeered loudly. 'Moreover it appears he has two elder brothers, one called Wilfred, a psychoanalyst, an *eminent* psychoanalyst, it says in *Punch*. Ha!'

The audience, I sensed, had become nervously alert. This was not going to be a conventional introduction.

'We've had a *psy-cho-analyst* living around here,' Mr Moore boomed as loud as nitro-glycerine, 'and now he's gone to New Mexico for good. Ha! And...are...we...all...*glad*.'

The audience, unsmiling, silent on their wooden chairs, looked shifty as Norman Moore continued, assuming the role of prosecuting counsel in a murder case. 'Moreover in *Punch* — hmmm! — it says he has a second brother, one Leo Abse, an MP., a *Labour* MP. Why, we've heard of his activities. I tell you if he came here and put up for election he'd come *last*. After the Communist!'

At this point I felt obliged to interrupt mildly with, 'Thank you for your kind introduction.' I looked towards the jury, I mean the audience, for support and somebody in the back did titter. But our homomorph of a chairman thundered on. 'To be frank I have read one of Dr Abse's poems and I tell you it is *blasphemous*.'

As he continued with his bizarre invective I thought what the hell am I doing here, a sitting target. I thought I may as well go home, but home was hundreds of miles away; besides, many of the audience, too, had travelled some distance. Mr Moore was now gently pointing out that I was a *medical* doctor and how *medical* doctors these days were responsible for so many iatrogenic diseases. He was not trying to be funny and by the time he sat down I felt too full of arrows, too bruised to be witty about his lengthy, abusive introduction.

Instead, I found myself on my feet remarking seriously that, yes, I did have two elder brothers and yes I was fond of them both, both valuable citizens and yes as a matter of fact I was proud of them etc. Then I began my poetry reading.

I have never encountered an audience so sympathetic. Thanks to Mr Norman Moore's rousing introduction they laughed at all my tired jokes, applauded poems loudly, and listened to my every word as if I were, if not the messiah come, at least poor old St Sebastian, bloody and heroic.